JA4281

574 SCI

BIOLOGY

HUMAN BIOLOGY

ECOLOGY

 etc.

SCIENCE VISUAL RESOURCES

BIOLOGY

An Illustrated Guide to Science

The Diagram Group

CHELSEA HOUSE
PUBLISHERS
An imprint of Infobase Publishing

Biology: An Illustrated Guide to Science

Copyright © 2006 The Diagram Group

Author: Gareth Price

Editorial: Jamie Stokes

Consultant: Helen Fortin

Design: Anthony Atherton, Richard Hummerstone,
                     Tim Noel-Johnson, Lee Lawrence, Phil Richardson

Illustration: Peter Wilkinson

Picture research: Neil McKenna

Indexer: Martin Hargreaves

Chelsea House
An imprint of Infobase Publishing
132 West 31st Street
New York NY 10001

For Library of Congress Cataloging-in-Publication data,
please contact the publisher.

ISBN 0-8160-6162-9

Chelsea House books are available at special discounts when purchased in bulk quantities for businesses, associations, institutions, or sales promotions. Please call our Special Sales Department in New York at 212/967-8800 or 800/322-8755.

You can find Chelsea House on the World Wide Web at
http://www.chelseahouse.com

Printed in China

CP Diagram 10 9 8 7 6 5 4 3 2 1

This book is printed on acid-free paper.

Introduction

Biology is one of eight volumes of **The Science Visual Resources Set**. It contains six principle sections, a comprehensive glossary, a web site guide, and an index.

Biology is a learning tool for students and teachers. Full-color diagrams, graphs, charts, and maps on every page illustrate the essential elements of the subject, while bulleted text provides key definitions and step-by-step explanations.

Unity looks at the basic chemistry of all biological systems such as carbohydrates, fats, and proteins and describes the essential instruments and techniques of biology. The section also illustrates the most vital life processes, from photosynthesis to respiration.

Continuity considers the ways in which biological systems reproduce. The section covers the basics of all forms of biological reproduction, from those of unicellular organisms to flowering plants and mammals. It also details the genetic mechanisms of inheritance.

Diversity provides an overview of the vast range of living organisms that inhabit Earth. It describes the major categories that biologists use to classify these organisms and provides examples of each.

Maintenance examines the ways in which various living organisms carry out everyday life processes such as breathing, eating, movement, and excretion.

Human biology takes a closer look at the essential biological structures and functions of the human body. It describes how the raw materials required are taken in, digested, and transported to where they are needed; how waste products are removed; and how the body is able to sense and interact with its environment.

Ecology provides a brief look at how living organisms influence and are influenced by the planet on which they live. It traces the broadest of all biological processes: the complex webs of survival that link the simplest bacteria to the most sophisticated carnivores. Finally, the section outlines the elemental relations by which chemical and geological processes form the conditions for life.

Contents

3 DIVERSITY

4 MAINTENANCE

5 HUMAN BIOLOGY

© Diagram Visual Information Ltd.

Key words

condensation
  reaction
glycosidic bond
starch
sugar

Types of carbohydrate

- Carbohydrates are chemical compounds that contain carbon and the elements of water: hydrogen and oxygen. A few also contain nitrogen or sulfur.
- There are two main groups of carbohydrates: *sugars* and *starches*.
- Sugars are small, water soluble molecules that taste sweet. Starches are very large, insoluble molecules.
- Carbohydrates may be monosaccharides, disaccharides, or polysaccharides.

Monosaccharides

- Simple sugars all have the same general formula $C_n(H_2O)_n$. The simplest common sugar found in animals is glucose ($C_6H_{12}O_6$). Glucose has two molecular forms: a straight chain and a ring. About 98 percent of the sugar molecules in a solution are in ring form.

Disaccharides

- Disaccharides (see page 9) are sugars made by linking together two monosaccharide rings by a *condensation reaction*. An **OH** group from each monosaccharide unit reacts together to make water (H_2O) and form an oxygen bridge between the sugar rings.
- Maltose ($C_{12}H_{22}O_{11}$) is a disaccharide that is a product of starch digestion and is also found in some germinating seeds. It is formed by two glucose molecules joined together by a *glycosidic* (**C-O-C**) *bond*.
- **OH** groups at the end of a disaccharide molecule can link with more rings to make longer chains. However, most sugars have three rings or fewer.

Simple carbohydrates

Types of carbohydrate

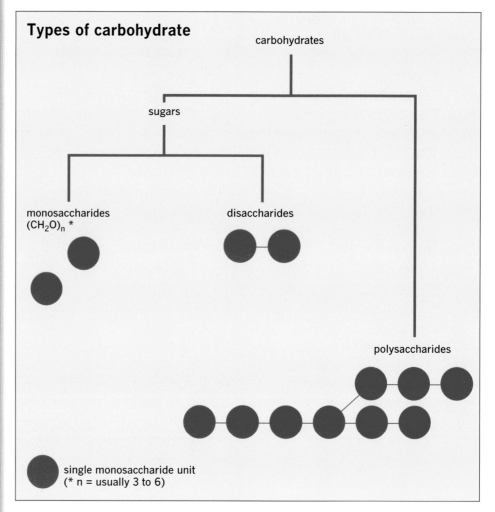

single monosaccharide unit
(* n = usually 3 to 6)

Molecular structure of glucose

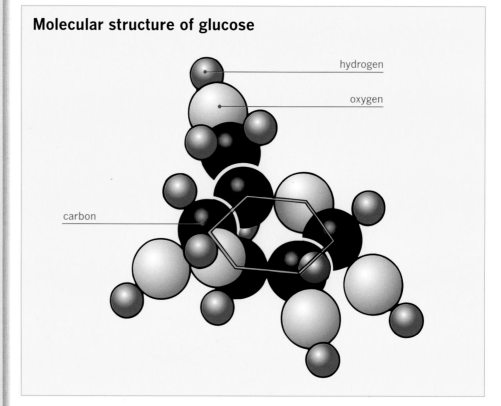

hydrogen

oxygen

carbon

Complex carbohydrates

Complex carbohydrates

Two glucose molecules

+

condensation reaction
(synthesis)

hydrolysis
(breakdown)

H_2O H_2O

Disaccharide: Maltose

glycosidic bond

Key words

cellulose	sugar
glycogen	
polysaccharide	
respiration	
starch	

Polysaccharides

- Carbohydrates with large numbers of rings in their molecules are called *polysaccharides*.
- Polysaccharides are used in living things for energy storage and to build structures (see page 10).

Energy storage

- *Starches* are large polysaccharides formed (synthesized) by joining long chains of monosaccharide units (such as glucose) together. Since starches are insoluble, they form granules within a cell and do not upset the water balance of the cell in the way that the same amount of soluble *sugar* would.
- When energy is needed, a reaction, called hydrolysis breaks the starch down into its sugar molecules. These sugar molecules can then be used to provide energy by *respiration*.
- Animals use the polysaccharide *glycogen* as a carbohydrate energy storage molecule.

Building structures

- Cell walls in plants are made of a polysaccharide called *cellulose*. A cellulose molecule may contain thousands of monosaccharide units bonded together.
- The links between the monosaccharide units in cellulose are arranged to produce a flat molecule that is stronger than a steel fiber. These molecules run through the cell walls of plants like the steel rods in reinforced concrete.

Key words

cellulose	polysaccharide
exoskeleton	
glucose	
glycogen	
gut	

Polysaccharides in animals

- In animals *polysaccharides* are mainly used for energy storage. In humans up to 10 percent of the weight of the liver can be *glycogen*—an instant store of energy that is easier to mobilize than fat, which is used for long-term energy storage.
- A typical glycogen molecule may contain 300 to 400 *glucose* units in a branching molecule.
- Glycogen also occurs in yeasts and bacteria.
- Chitin is made of acetylglucosamine, glucose units with an amino group attached. It is common in shellfish (the edible crab can be 70 percent chitin) where it is an important part of the shell.
- Chitin is also found in the *exoskeleton* of insects.
- Chitin is a structural polysaccharide and is not used as an energy store.

Polysaccharides in plants

- Plants store starch as granules inside their cells. Roots such as potatoes and carrots are often rich in starch, which provides the energy needed for the next generation to develop before it can produce its own food by photosynthesis.
- *Cellulose* is a structural polysaccharide and gives the cell wall its strength. Animals cannot digest cellulose, and so it passes through the *gut* largely untouched as roughage.

Important polysaccharides

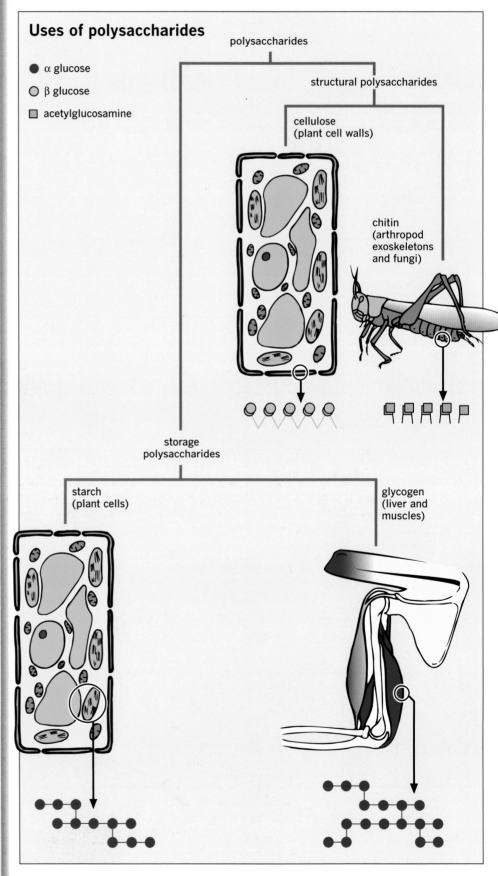

Uses of polysaccharides

- ● α glucose
- ○ β glucose
- ▢ acetylglucosamine

polysaccharides

structural polysaccharides

cellulose (plant cell walls)

chitin (arthropod exoskeletons and fungi)

storage polysaccharides

starch (plant cells)

glycogen (liver and muscles)

Amino acids

Key words

amino acid
peptide bond
polypeptide

Generalized amino acid structure

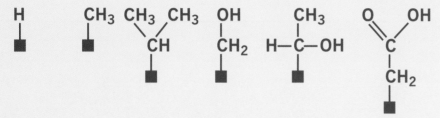

variable group (R)

amino group (basic)

carboxyl group (acidic)

non-variable part

Natural amino acids

Glycine (Gly) Alanine (Ala) Valine (Val) Serine (Ser) Threonine (Thr) Aspartic acid (Asp)

Asparagine (Asn) Cysteine (Cys) Leucine (Leu) Isoleucine (Ile) Methionine (Met)

Glutamic acid (Glu) Glutamine (Gln) Phenylalanine (Phe) Tyrosine (Tyr) Arginine (Arg)

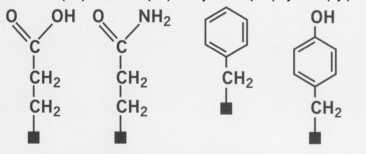

Lysine (Lys) Tryptophan (Trp) Histidine (His) Proline (Pro)

non-variable part of amino acid molecule

Chemical structure

- *Amino acid* molecules are made of four groups bonded with a single carbon atom. Three of these groups are non-variable.
- The amino group NH_2 is a basic group, which means it behaves as an alkali in solution.
- At the other end of the molecule is a carboxyl group (**COOH**), which acts as an organic acid.
- The third group is a hydrogen atom.
- The fourth group is variable. It is often shown in diagrams by the letter **R**. Different amino acids have different **R** groups.

Natural amino acids

- There are about 20 naturally occurring amino acids.
- The simplest amino acid is glycine. The **R** group here is a single hydrogen atom.
- More complicated amino acids, such as proline, have **R** groups containing many atoms, complex rings, and sometimes elements such as sulfur or phosphorus.

Joining amino acids

- Amino acids can join to make chains called *polypeptides* when the acid group from one amino acid reacts with the carboxyl group of another. The reaction releases water and produces a link called a *peptide bond*.
- More amino acids can be added at each end of the new molecule (see page 12).

© Diagram Visual Information Ltd.

Key words

amino acid
hemoglobin
insulin
peptide bond
protein

Small molecules

- All *proteins* are made of small *amino acid* molecules linked by *peptide bonds* in long chains resembling a string of beads.
- The number and order of amino acids in the chain decides how the protein will behave.
- Some proteins have more than one chain of amino acids and some have extra groups of atoms added. For example, *hemoglobin,* which transports oxygen from the lungs to cells throughout the body, is a protein with four amino acid chains wrapped around a central group containing iron.

Protein size

- *Insulin* (right) is a small protein molecule with only 51 amino acids on two chains tethered together by 3 disulfide bridges.
- Some of the large immunity proteins have thousands of amino acids and are bigger than some simple living organisms!

Twisting and turning

- The amino acid chain twists as it grows. The twisted chain then forms a spiral. The spiral shape is held together by links along its length.

Protein structure

Example of protein structure

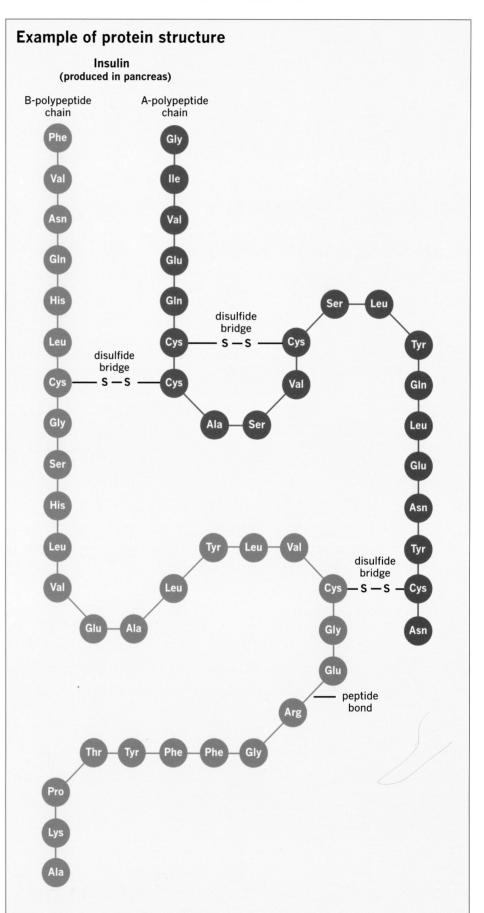

Insulin
(produced in pancreas)

Classification of proteins

Key words
collagen
enzyme
hemoglobin
hormone
peptide bond

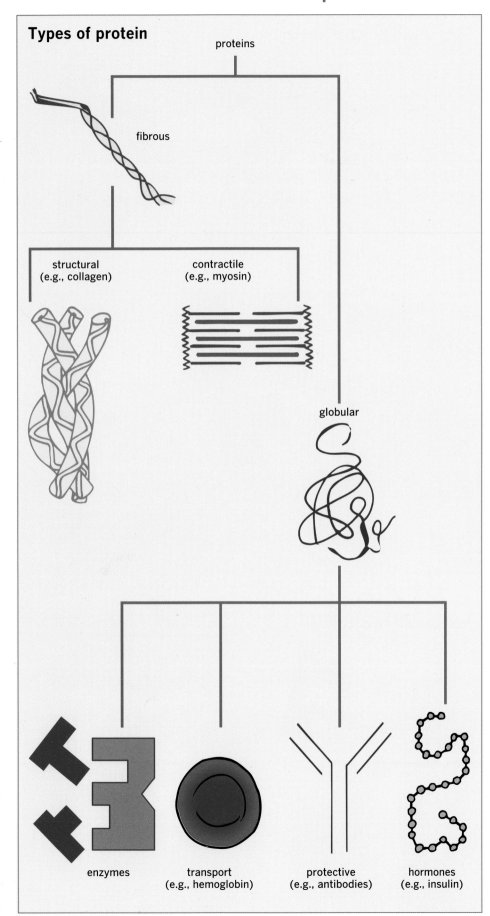

Types of protein

proteins

fibrous

structural
(e.g., collagen)

contractile
(e.g., myosin)

globular

enzymes

transport
(e.g., hemoglobin)

protective
(e.g., antibodies)

hormones
(e.g., insulin)

Types of protein

- There are two main groups of proteins: fibrous and globular.
- Both groups have the same basic structure—they are long chains of amino acids joined by *peptide bonds*.
- The difference between the two groups depends on the way the protein chains are arranged.

Fibrous proteins

- Fibrous proteins have chains twisted into spiral shapes held together by strong bonds to make the molecule look like a spring.
- Fibrous proteins can be divided into structural and contractile proteins. Structural proteins form the structure of an organism. For example, they can be found in skin and hair. *Collagen* fibers in the skin give it elasticity and keep it smooth. Contractile proteins such as myosin help muscles contract.

Globular proteins

- Globular proteins have chains that wind in and out of each other, twisting into complex shapes that look like a ball of wood. Their chains are held together with a mixture of strong and weak bonds.
- Globular proteins often have more than one chain and can contain extra non-protein groups. For example, *hemoglobin* contain iron ions.
- Globular proteins are often delicate and easily damaged by heat or chemicals. If their molecular shape is changed by heat they cannot work properly.
- There are various types of globular proteins. Some transport smaller molecules. Some act as *enzymes*, controlling the rate of chemical reactions. Some have a protective function. Still others are *hormones*, the chemical messengers of the body.

Key words

active site
enzyme
substrate

Enzymes and reactions

- *Enzymes* are proteins that control the rate of reactions in living things. Sugar reacts easily with oxygen to give carbon dioxide and water—but outside organisms it needs to be heated to well above 300°F (150°C) to start the reaction. Inside living organisms, enzymes make the same reaction work at temperatures as low as the freezing point.
- Each reaction has its own enzyme—if the enzyme is missing the reaction does not take place. An enzyme for one reaction will not work on another reaction.
- Most reactions in living things are broken down into many steps—and each step needs its own enzyme.
- There are two hypotheses of enzyme action: lock and key and induced fit.

Lock-and-key hypothesis

- In this hypothesis, when the chemicals involved in a reaction (the *substrates*) get near an enzyme molecule, they "fit" into a part of the molecule called the *active site*, like a key in a lock. The enzyme is shaped so that the important parts of each chemical are close enough to each other to react together.
- When the reaction has occurred, the new chemicals (the products) do not fit in the lock and are released. This leaves the enzyme free to catalyze another reaction.

Induced-fit hypothesis

- This hypothesis suggests that the substrate helps the enzyme to form the correct shape to receive it.

Enzymes: mechanism

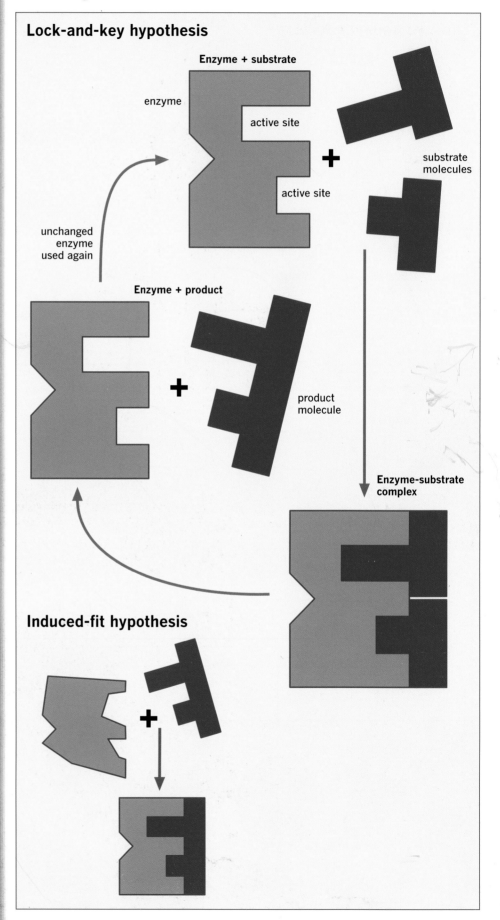

Lock-and-key hypothesis

Enzyme + substrate

enzyme

active site

active site

unchanged enzyme used again

substrate molecules

Enzyme + product

product molecule

Enzyme-substrate complex

Induced-fit hypothesis

Enzymes and coenzymes

Key words

active site	substrate
coenzyme	
enzyme	
enzyme-coenzyme complex	

The coenzyme mechanism

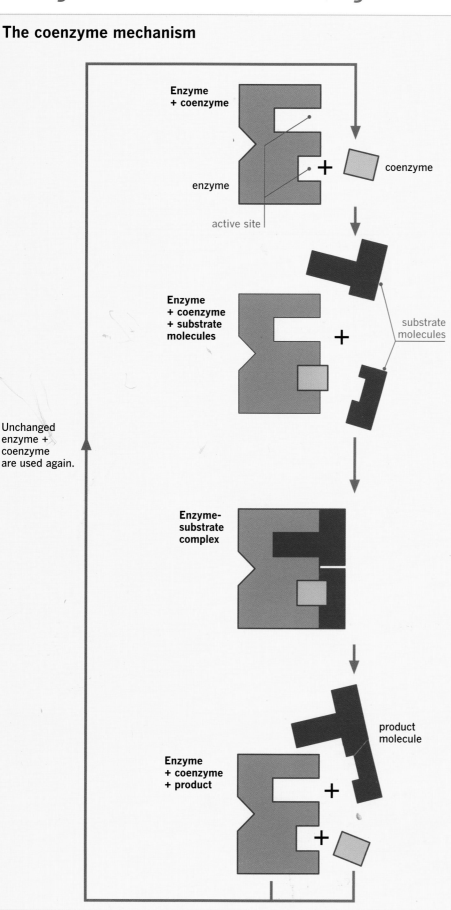

Enzyme + coenzyme

enzyme

coenzyme

active site

Enzyme + coenzyme + substrate molecules

substrate molecules

Unchanged enzyme + coenzyme are used again.

Enzyme-substrate complex

product molecule

Enzyme + coenzyme + product

Coenzymes

- *Coenzymes* are usually small molecules that are needed in some *enzyme* reactions to help the reaction work properly.
- As with enzymes, many coenzymes only work with particular enzyme reactions. If the coenzyme is missing, the reaction will not work properly. The coenzyme from another reaction will not do the job.
- Vitamins and minerals are often involved in reactions as coenzymes.

The coenzyme mechanism

- Most enzymes will not react with any chemical other than their *substrate*. This is known as specificity—the enzyme is specific for a particular substrate.
- Some enzymes can only react in the presence of a coenzyme. The coenzyme binds to the enzyme and changes its shape. The *active site* is now ready to receive its normal substrate.
- The substrate bonds to the enzyme and reacts to produce the required product.

Reusing the coenzyme

- When the enzyme-catalyzed reaction has occurred, the product is released from the *enzyme-coenzyme complex*.
- The coenzyme is also released and becomes available for another reaction.
- Respiration in cells is a good example of a complex enzyme pathway that depends on a collection of coenzymes.

Key words

active site
enzyme
inhibitor
substrate

Inhibitors

- *Inhibitors* reduce or destroy the activity of an *enzyme*—sometimes to dangerous levels.
- There are two types of inhibitors: competitive inhibitors and non-competitive inhibitors.

Competitive inhibitors

- Competitive inhibitors bind with the *active site* of an enzyme. In effect, they "compete" with the normal *substrate* for this site and block it.
- Many competitive inhibitors are released from the active site so the enzyme can be regenerated. The higher the concentration of the "normal" substrate compared with the inhibitor, the less effect the inhibitor has.

Non-competitive inhibitors

- A non-competitive inhibitor does not bind to the active site. It binds with a different part of the enzyme molecule.
- This distorts the shape of the enzyme so it cannot function properly.
- Non-competitive inhibitors are not released from the enzyme molecule so the enzyme cannot be regenerated.
- Even a low concentration of a non-competitive inhibitor can be very dangerous.
- Cyanide is a non-competitive inhibitor that completely blocks an essential enzyme in the respiration pathway. It is therefore a very powerful poison.

Enzymes and inhibitors

Inhibitors

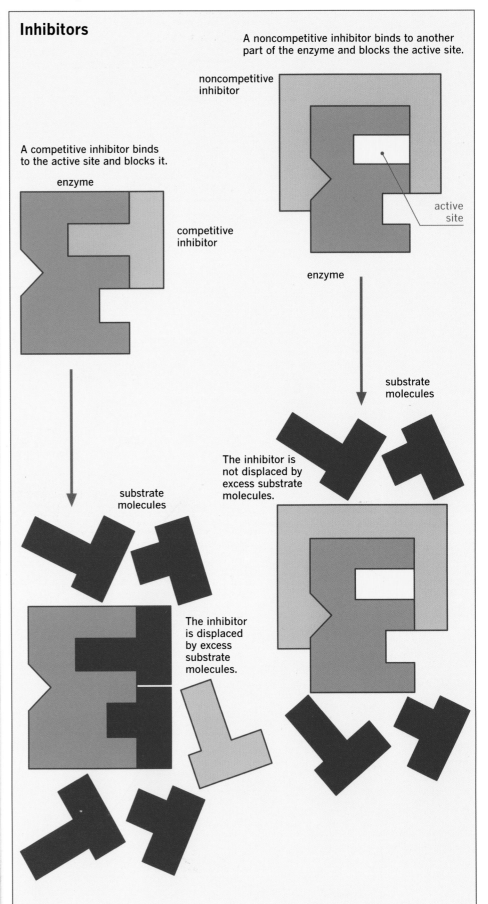

A competitive inhibitor binds to the active site and blocks it.

enzyme

competitive inhibitor

substrate molecules

The inhibitor is displaced by excess substrate molecules.

A noncompetitive inhibitor binds to another part of the enzyme and blocks the active site.

noncompetitive inhibitor

active site

enzyme

substrate molecules

The inhibitor is not displaced by excess substrate molecules.

Fatty acids and glycerol

Key words

fatty acid
glycerol

Glycerol: molecular
structure

Stearic acid (saturated): model

single bond

Oleic acid (unsaturated): model

double bond

Glycerol molecule

H_2O

H_2O

H_2O

Three fatty acid molecules

stearic
acid

stearic
acid

stearic
acid

Tristearin (triglyceride)

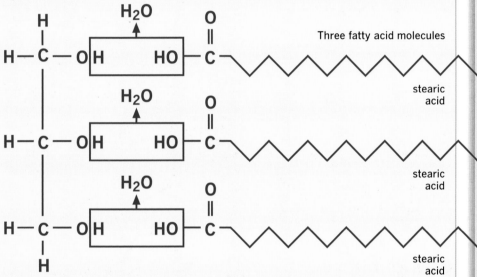

Glycerol
- *Glycerol* is a small molecule with three **OH** groups emerging from a short carbon chain. It is important in the formation of lipids, substances insoluble in water that include fats and oils.

Fatty acids
- *Fatty acids* are long chains of carbon atoms (sometimes up to 30 or 40) with a **COOH** group at one end. The **COOH** group means that they behave as acids in solution.
- Fatty acids may be saturated (having only a single carbon-to-carbon bond [see stearic acid], or unsaturated (one or more double or triple carbon-to-carbon bonds [see oleic acid]). The number and location of double bonds varies.
  - Fatty acids are the building blocks of fat.
  - Fatty acids react with glycerol to bond their long chains to the **OH** group in glycerol. When three fatty acids join on all three of the **OH** groups in glycerol, a triglyceride (fat) is formed.
- Some triglycerides are simple and have only one type of fatty acid joined to the glycerol molecule. Other triglycerides are mixed: they have three different fatty acids joined onto one glycerol molecule.

Triglycerides
- The fat on meats such as bacon consists of a variety of mixed triglycerides.
- Different fats have different mixtures of these triglycerides.

Light microscope

Two lenses

- A light microscope uses two sets of lenses, objective and ocular lenses, to create magnifications of up to 1000X.
- The lens near the specimen is called the *objective lens*. This cannot produce an image by itself.
- The lens in the eyepiece at the end of the viewing tube is called the *ocular lens*. This helps to focus the beams of light to produce the image.
- To calculate the magnification of the microscope, you have to multiply the magnification of the objective lens by the magnification of the ocular lens.

Two focusing devices

- Lenses in microscopes are very delicate. To prevent them from being damaged by scratching them against the sample, the light microscope uses two-stage focusing.
- The coarse adjustment knob moves the low power objective lens through a large distance. When the area you wish to observe is in the center of the field of view and in sharp focus, you may click the high power objective lens into place. The image should already be nearly in focus. If any adjustment is needed, use only the fine adjustment knob.

A clear light

- The diaphragm regulates the amount of light reaching the object.

Light microscope

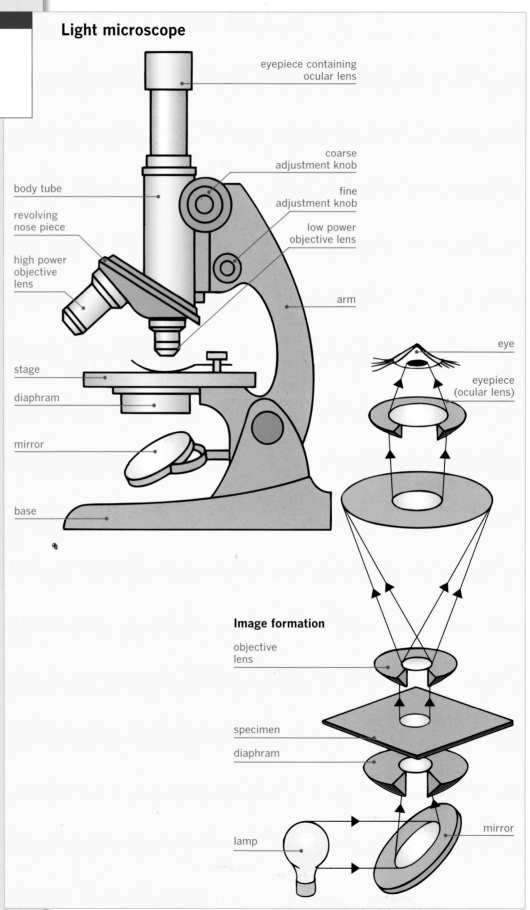

eyepiece containing
ocular lens

coarse
adjustment knob

fine
adjustment knob

low power
objective lens

arm

body tube

revolving
nose piece

high power
objective
lens

stage

diaphram

mirror

base

eye

eyepiece
(ocular lens)

Image formation

objective
lens

specimen

diaphram

mirror

lamp

Cells: light microscope

Generalized animal cell

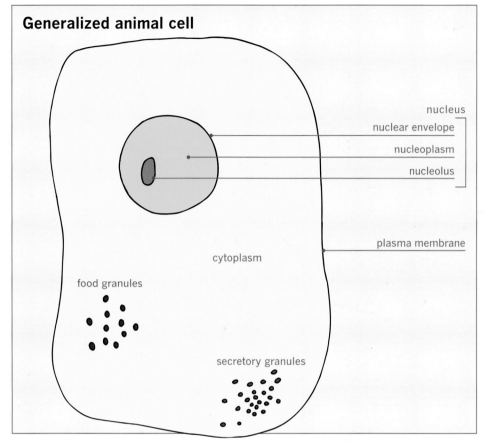

nucleus
nuclear envelope
nucleoplasm
nucleolus

plasma membrane

cytoplasm

food granules

secretory granules

Generalized plant cell

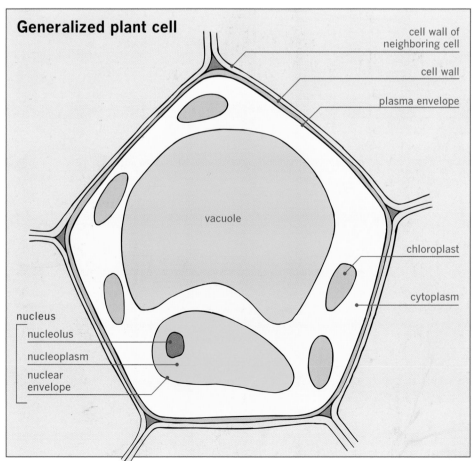

cell wall of
neighboring cell

cell wall

plasma envelope

chloroplast

cytoplasm

vacuole

nucleus
nucleolus
nucleoplasm
nuclear
envelope

Key words

cellulose	plasma
chloroplast	membrane
cytoplasm	vacuole
nucleus	
photosynthesis	

Cell size

- Typical cells are anything between .005 and .025 mm (.0002 and .001 in). This is about ten times smaller than the diameter of a human hair.
- Light microscopes can only see relatively large structures in a cell because they can only magnify up to 1,000X.

Animal cells

- The cell contains a large *nucleus*, which helps to control the cell. The nucleus is separated from the *cytoplasm* by the nuclear envelope (membrane). Inside the nucleus, the nucleoplasm, the liquid matrix of the nucleus, surrounds the nucleolus, where proteins are synthesized.
- The area outside the nucleus but within the outer membrane is called the cytoplasm. It often contains a collection of smaller bodies such as food or secretory granules, and sometimes small *vacuoles* (small sacs enveloped in a membrane). These are often very difficult to see with a light microscope.

Plant cells

- Plant cells are surrounded by a thick cell wall made of *cellulose*.
- Immediately inside the cell wall is the *plasma membrane* of the plant cell. This is identical to the plasma membrane of animal cells.
- Plant cells have a large central vacuole that occupies much of the cell volume. It stores salts, water, water soluble pigments, and potentially toxic molecules in the form of crystals.
- The cytoplasm contains many of the inclusions (globules, granules, etc.) found in animal cells and a large vacuole. Sometimes large green disc-shaped bodies called *chloroplasts* are present: these carry out *photosynthesis*.

© Diagram Visual Information Ltd.

Key words

specimen

Electron microscope

Electrons not light

- An electron microscope (EM) uses electrons rather than beams of light. Magnetic and electric fields are used to focus the electrons instead of glass lenses.
- The use of electrons allows magnifications up to 10,000X and beyond.

Function

- Electron microscopes function just like light microscopes except that they use a beam of electrons instead of light to image the *specimen*. Through a series of magnetic lenses and apertures, the microscope focuses a beam of electrons on a specimen. The beam interacts with the sample, and the microscope records the results of the interaction as an image.

Types of information

- Electron microscopes can examine the tomography (surface features) of an object, the morphology (size and shape of the particles) of an object, the composition of the object, and the arrangement of the atoms in the object.

Disadvantages

- Specimens need very complicated preparation before they can be used in the EM. This treatment can sometimes produce artefacts, objects that have nothing to do with the sample.

Electron microscope
Simplified section through a simple transmission electron microscope

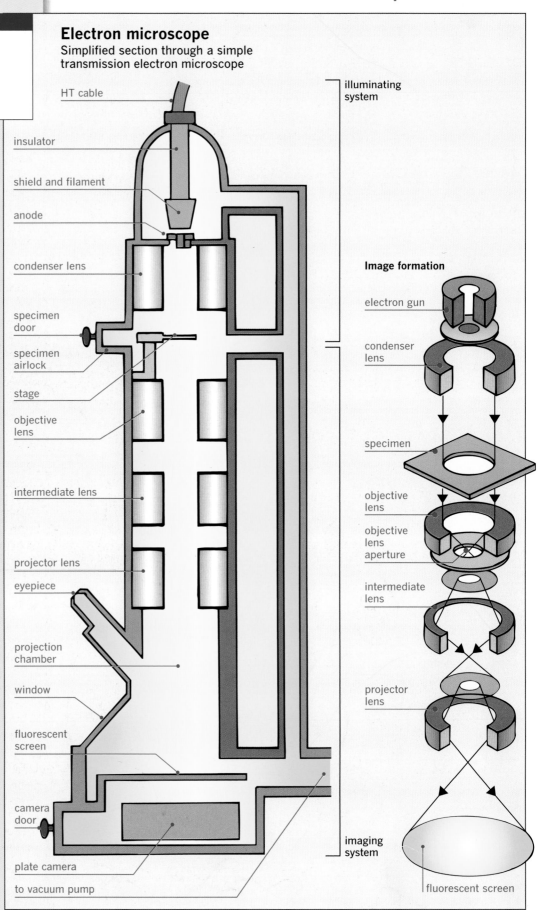

illuminating system

HT cable

insulator

shield and filament

anode

condenser lens

specimen door

specimen airlock

stage

objective lens

intermediate lens

projector lens

eyepiece

projection chamber

window

fluorescent screen

camera door

plate camera

to vacuum pump

imaging system

Image formation

electron gun

condenser lens

specimen

objective lens

objective lens aperture

intermediate lens

projector lens

fluorescent screen

Animal cell: electron microscope

Key words

centriole   mitochondrion
endopasmic   plasma
  reticulum   membrane
Golgi body   ribosome
lysosome

Animal cell

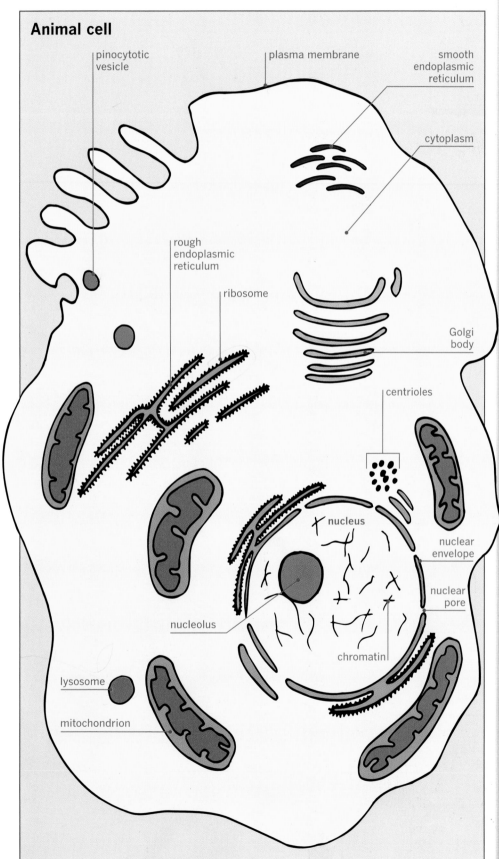

pinocytotic
vesicle

plasma membrane

smooth
endoplasmic
reticulum

cytoplasm

rough
endoplasmic
reticulum

ribosome

Golgi
body

centrioles

nucleus

nuclear
envelope

nuclear
pore

nucleolus

chromatin

lysosome

mitochondrion

Smaller sizes

- The electron microscope can see much smaller objects than the light microscope is able to see.

Membrane structures

- The cell uses a double-layered membrane to build many structures: the *plasma membrane*, *Golgi body*, *lysosomes*, and the *endoplasmic reticulum*.
- The plasma membrane covers the whole of the outside of the cell.
- The endoplasmic reticulum is a meshwork of the same membrane that runs throughout the cell. It is used for intracellular transport. *Ribosomes*, usually found on the rough endoplasmic reticulum, synthesize protein.
- The Gogli body is involved with the creation of the endoplasmic reticulum and in the secretion of some substances from the cell. It is the packaging center of the cell.
- Lysosomes contain digestive enzymes.

Other structures

- The nucleus controls the cell. It is separated from the cytoplasm by the nuclear envelope. The nucleus contains the nucleolus, which contains the DNA templates for ribosomal RNA, and chromatin, the substances from which chromosomes are made. Openings in the cell's nuclear envelope, called nuclear pores, allow the exchange of materials between the nucleus and the cytoplasm.
- *Mitochondria* are the site of aerobic respiration, which gives the cell energy. The mitochondrion is sometimes referred to as the "powerhouse" of the cell.
- Pinocytotic vesicles contain soluble molecules from outside the cell.
- *Centrioles*, found only in animal cells, help the cell to divide.

Key words

chloroplast	lysosome
endoplasmic	mitochondrion
reticulum	plasma
Golgi body	membrane
granum	ribosome

Plant and animal cells

● Many of the structures found in animal cells are also present in plant cells. However, plant cells do not contain centrioles.

Membrane structures

● The plant cell uses a double-layered membrane to build many structures: the *plasma membrane*, *Golgi body*, *lysosomes*, and *endoplasmic reticulum*. These membrane-based structures carry out exactly the same functions in plants and animals (see page 23).

● The plasma membrane in plants has the same double-layered structure as it has in animals but is further supported by a cell wall. The cell wall is a tough cellulose-rich structure that surrounds the plant cell. The plasma membrane is not attached to the cell wall, but when a plant cell is fully filled with water, the membrane is pressed tight against the cell wall.

Other structures

● Plant cells have a large central vacuole enclosed by the tonoplast.
● The nucleus controls the cell.
● *Mitochondria* are the site of aerobic respiration, which gives the cell energy by breaking down glucose.
● *Ribosomes*, usually found on the rough endoplasmic reticulum, make protein.

Chloroplasts

● *Chloroplasts* are only found in green plants. They are green-colored bodies that carry out photosynthesis to make sugar for the plant.
● The *grana* in the chloroplasts contain the photosynthetic pigments.

Plant cell: electron microscope

Plant cell

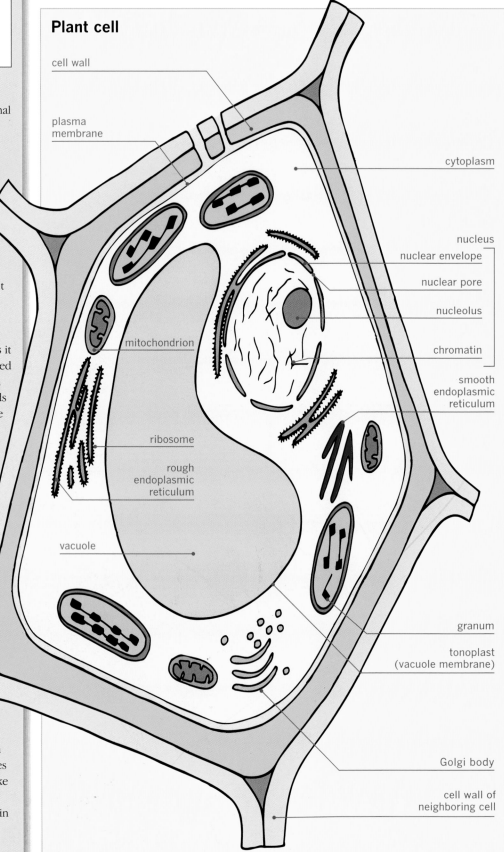

cell wall

plasma membrane

cytoplasm

nucleus

nuclear envelope

nuclear pore

nucleolus

chromatin

smooth endoplasmic reticulum

mitochondrion

ribosome

rough endoplasmic reticulum

vacuole

granum

tonoplast (vacuole membrane)

Golgi body

cell wall of neighboring cell

Cell substructure

Cell contents

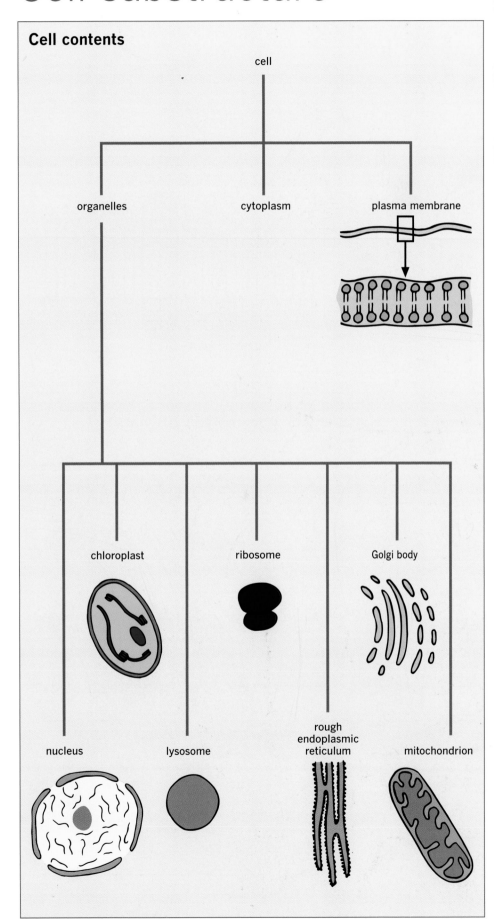

Key words

chlorophyll	*lysosome*
chloroplast	*mitochondrion*
cytoplasm	*organelle*
endoplasmic	*plasma*
reticulum	*membrane*
Golgi body	*ribosome*

Plasma membrane

- All cells are surrounded by a *plasma* (cell) *membrane*, which separates and protects the cell and controls movement in and out of it. The plasma membrane is composed of unit membrane, a two-layered structure with proteins on the outer surfaces and hydrophobic (water insoluble) fat molecules on the inside.

Cytoplasm

- Inside the plasma membrane, *cytoplasm* takes up most of the cell volume. It maintains the shape and consistency of the cell and stores chemical substances needed for life. The cytoplasm is also the site of vital metabolic reactions such as protein synthesis.

Organelles

- Suspended in the cytoplasm are *organelles*, specialized structures that carry out particular functions.
- The nucleus contains the cell's genetic material.
- *Chloroplasts* are concerned with photosynthesis and contain *chlorophyll*.
- *Lysosomes* are membrane-bound vacuoles containing digestive enzymes.
- *Ribosomes* are involved in protein synthesis and are sometimes attached in groups to the *endoplasmic reticulum* (ER) to produce rough ER.
- Many plant cells also contain a large vacuole that stores waste.
- The endoplasmic reticulum is a network of unit membranes running throughout the cell.
- The *Golgi body* is an area of the ER particularly concerned with secretory functions.
- *Mitochondria* carry out respiration and are surrounded by a plasma membrane, as are chloroplasts.

© Diagram Visual Information Ltd.

Key words

lipid
plasma
  membrane
protein

Protein-lipid mix

- All membranes in the cell are made of the same basic structure. This is called the unit membrane and consists of two main chemicals: *proteins* (glycoproteins, etc.) and *lipids* (glycolipids, etc.).
- Lipids are organic molecules that are insoluble in water.
- The main lipid components of *plasma membranes* are phospholipids—molecules composed of glycerol, phosphate, and fatty acid residues—and heads with different chemical properties (see bottom diagram). The tails are hydrophobic (water insoluble) fatty acid residues that face the center of the membrane. The heads, which are hydrophilic (water soluble), form the surface.

Membrane structure

- Phospholipids form wide, thin bilayers. In between these phospholipids are membrane proteins floating like icebergs in a sea of lipid.
- Some proteins reach completely across the lipid molecules. Others protrude above the lipid layer on one side but only get halfway through the fat layer in the middle of the membrane.
- Many of the protein molecules are not fixed—they can drift around in the lipid sea. This fluidity is essential for the proper function of proteins in the membranes.

Double membranes

- A unit membrane consists of one lipid layer with protein found on each side. However, the membranes in cells are made of two unit membranes laid on top of each other.

Plasma membrane: structure

Membrane structure

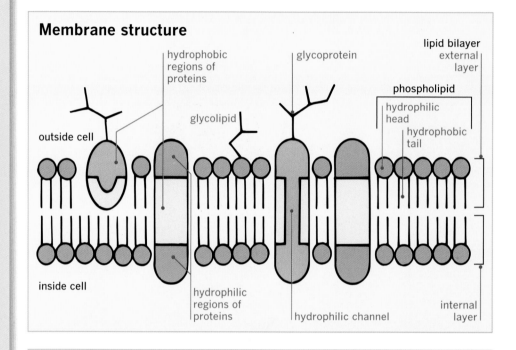

Three-dimensional model of membrane structure

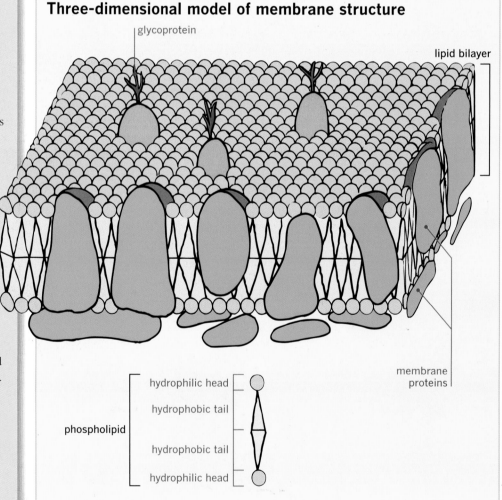

Plasma membrane: osmosis

Key words

concentration	semipermeable
gradient	membrane
osmosis	solute
permeability	
plasma	
membrane	

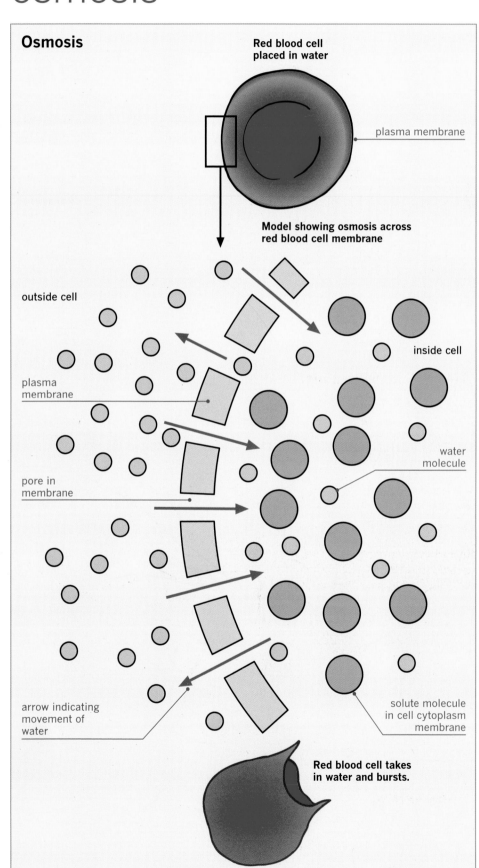

Osmosis

Red blood cell placed in water

plasma membrane

Model showing osmosis across red blood cell membrane

outside cell

inside cell

plasma membrane

pore in membrane

water molecule

arrow indicating movement of water

solute molecule in cell cytoplasm membrane

Red blood cell takes in water and bursts.

Semipermeable membranes

- The *plasma membrane* is semi-permeable. It lets small molecules like water pass very easily but holds back larger *solute* molecules like proteins.
- Water can diffuse through a *semipermeable membrane* almost as if it were not there. Water always moves from areas of high concentration to areas of low concentration.
- If two areas are separated by a semipermeable membrane and there is a higher concentration of water on one side, water moves through to equalize the concentration on both sides. This type of water movement is called *osmosis*.

Concentration gradient

- The difference in concentration of a substance between two areas is called a *concentration gradient*.
- The movement of materials along a concentration gradient depends on the size of the gradient and the *permeability* of the space between them.
- High concentration gradients give faster movements. Lower permeability slows down movement.
- The concentration of water within a cell is lower than the outside when it is placed in de-ionized water. This is because some of the space inside the cell is taken up by other chemicals (sugars, proteins, fats etc.). Water rushes in to equalize the concentrations, which makes the cell swell and burst.

Key words

absorption	concentration
active transport	gradient
adenosine	passive
triphosphate	transport

Active or passive?

- *Passive transport* occurs when particles move down a concentration—from areas of high concentration to areas of low concentration. Passive transport does not require any energy input by the cell. The movements of carbon dioxide and oxygen are good examples of passive transport in living cells.

- *Active transport* can occur either up or down a *concentration gradient*, so active transport can move materials from areas of low concentration to areas of high concentration. Active transport requires an energy input by a cell. *Absorption* of vitamins by the gut in mammals is a good example.

Active transport

- Energy released from *adenosine triphosphate* (ATP)—the main chemical-energy carrier in all organisms—pumps materials across the membrane.

- Carrier proteins in the cell membrane may change shape to take in particles (called passenger molecules) on one side, twist configuration and then release the particle on the other side.

- Low oxygen concentrations or low temperatures will slow down active transport by reducing the energy available for this reaction.

- Some active transport mechanisms are used to create electrical imbalances between the inside and outside of cells.

Plasma membrane: active transport

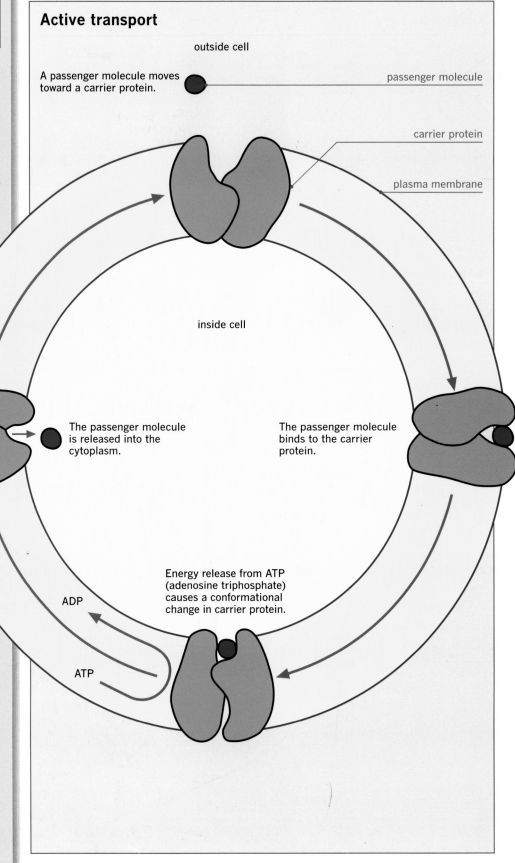

Active transport

outside cell

A passenger molecule moves toward a carrier protein.

passenger molecule

carrier protein

plasma membrane

inside cell

The passenger molecule is released into the cytoplasm.

The passenger molecule binds to the carrier protein.

Energy release from ATP (adenosine triphosphate) causes a conformational change in carrier protein.

ADP

ATP

Plasma membrane: endocytosis

Key words

cytoplasm	phagocytosis
endocytosis	vacuole
enzyme	
exocytosis	
lysosome	

Phagocytosis

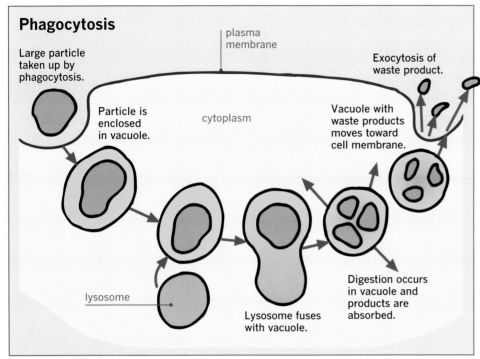

Large particle taken up by phagocytosis.

plasma membrane

Exocytosis of waste product.

Particle is enclosed in vacuole.

cytoplasm

Vacuole with waste products moves toward cell membrane.

lysosome

Digestion occurs in vacuole and products are absorbed.

Lysosome fuses with vacuole.

Pinocytosis

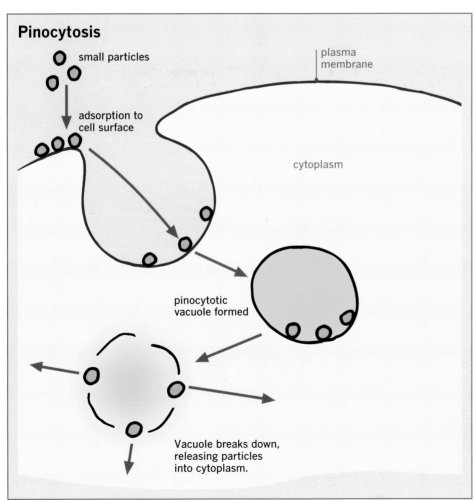

small particles

plasma membrane

adsorption to cell surface

cytoplasm

pinocytotic vacuole formed

Vacuole breaks down, releasing particles into cytoplasm.

Taking materials into the cell

- *Endocytosis* moves materials into the cell. The Greek word *endo* means "inside."
- Endocytosis is further broken down into two forms: phagocytosis, which moves relatively large particles into the cell, and pinocytosis, which moves smaller particles (often in groups) into the cell.

Phagocytosis

- In microorganisms, food particles are often absorbed by *phagocytosis*.
- The *cytoplasm* of the cell flows around small microorganisms and encloses them in a vacuole. *Lysosomes*, which contain digestive enzymes, next fuse with the cell. *Enzymes* then break down the particles into simpler chemicals, which can then be absorbed into the cell.
- Indigestible materials in a phagocytotic *vacuole* are often released back to the outside of the cell through a process called *exocytosis* (see page 28).

Pinocytosis

- Pinocytosis is a slightly simpler procedure than phagocytosis because the contents of the pinocytotic vacuole generally need less processing before they can be absorbed into the cell.

Key words

active process	rough
exocytosis	endoplasmic
Golgi body	reticulum
mytochondrion	
plasma	
membrane	

Moving materials out of the cell

- *Exocytosis* moves materials out of the cell. The Greek word *exo* means "outside." These materials may be secretory, excretory, or may be the undigested remains of materials in food vacuoles.
- Exocytosis is an *active process*—it requires energy input from the cell.
- Exocytosis is common in cells that produce secretions, such as the acinar cells of the pancreas, which furnish pancreatic juice.

Manufacture of chemicals

- In the example at right, the *rough endoplasmic reticulum* deep in the cell uses energy produced by aerobic respiration in the *mitochondrion* to synthesize and transport proteins.
- The proteins are collected in the *Golgi body* and then packaged in small vacuoles made of *plasma membrane*.
- Vacuoles are "pinched off" the Golgi body and move toward the outside of the cell.

Release of materials

- When the vacuoles reach the outer cell membrane, the membrane forming the vacuole merges with the plasma membrane. The vacuole then releases its contents (such as the inactive enzyme zymogen) to the outside world.

Plasma membrane: exocytosis

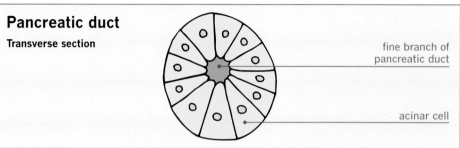

Pancreatic duct

Transverse section

fine branch of pancreatic duct

acinar cell

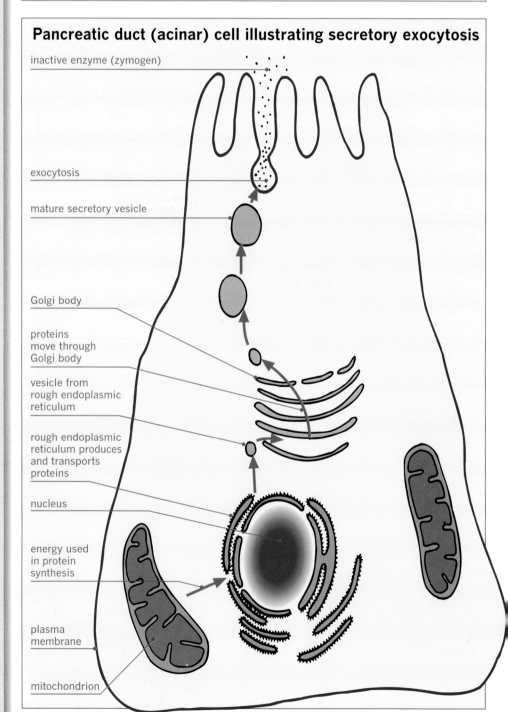

Pancreatic duct (acinar) cell illustrating secretory exocytosis

inactive enzyme (zymogen)

exocytosis

mature secretory vesicle

Golgi body

proteins move through Golgi body

vesicle from rough endoplasmic reticulum

rough endoplasmic reticulum produces and transports proteins

nucleus

energy used in protein synthesis

plasma membrane

mitochondrion

Lysosomes

Lysosomes and phagocytosis

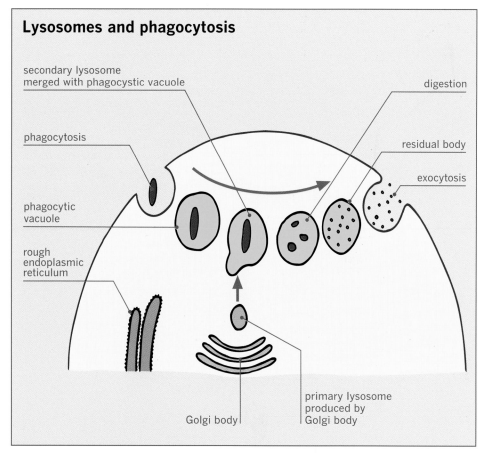

secondary lysosome
merged with phagocystic vacuole

phagocytosis

phagocytic
vacuole

rough
endoplasmic
reticulum

digestion

residual body

exocytosis

Golgi body

primary lysosome
produced by
Golgi body

Lysosomes and autophagy

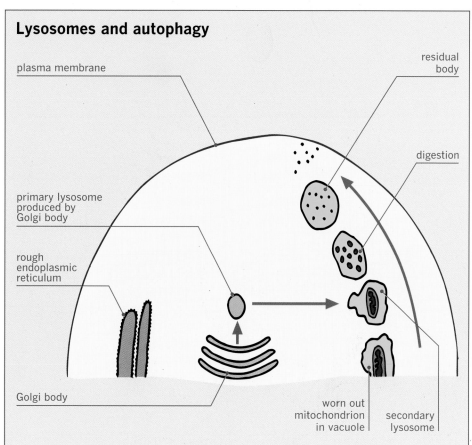

plasma membrane

primary lysosome
produced by
Golgi body

rough
endoplasmic
reticulum

Golgi body

residual
body

digestion

worn out
mitochondrion
in vacuole

secondary
lysosome

Key words

cytoplasm   phagocytosis
enzyme
exocytosis
Golgi body
lysosome

Waste disposal systems

- *Lysosomes* are vacuoles that contain a powerful collection of *enzymes* that can break down a range of compounds into simpler molecules that can be absorbed through a cell membrane.

Lysosomes and phagocytosis

- When a relatively large particle is engulfed by *phagocytosis*, it cannot be absorbed into the cell until it has been broken down.
- Lysosomes, produced by the *Golgi body*, merge with the phagocytotic vacuole so that the enzymes are released into the vacuole and can start to act on the engulfed particle.
- Once the enzymes have broken down the particle, the products can be absorbed. Any indigestible components are released to the outside world through *exocytosis* when the phagocytotic vacuole merges with the plasma membrane of the cell.

Lysosomes and autophagy

- Lysosomes destroy worn out or damaged cell components through a process called autophagy.
- The cell component is surrounded by a membrane, and lysosomes then merge with this vacuole. The enzymes break down the damaged cell structure, and the important components can be reabsorbed into the *cytoplasm* through the membrane.

© Diagram Visual Information Ltd.

Key words

chloroplast	organelle
granum	photosynthesis
light-dependent reaction	thylakoid
light-independent reaction	

Reaction pathways

- *Photosynthesis* is a biochemical process (see top diagram) by which plants harness the energy from light (1) to take carbon dioxide (2) and water (3) and produce glucose (4) and oxygen (5).
- Photosynthesis is a complex series of reactions that fall into two groups: the *light-dependent reaction* and the *light-independent reaction*.
- Both of these reactions occur in *organelles* called *chloroplasts*. Within the chloroplasts are disk-shaped membrane structures called *thylakoids*, which contain the chlorophyll needed for photosynthesis. Chloroplasts are made up of stacks of these disks called *grana* (see middle diagram).

Light-dependent reaction

- The light-dependent reaction (LDR), also called photolysis, captures energy in light (bottom diagram 1) and converts it into chemical energy in the form of adenosine triphosphate (ATP) and nicotinamide adenine dinucleotide phosphate (NADP). The energy is then available for the rest of the photosynthetic reaction.
- The LDR produces oxygen by splitting water molecules (bottom 2, 3).

Light-independent reaction

- The light-independent reaction (LIR), sometimes called carbon fixation, occurs in the light and the dark—provided the LDR has provided enough energy and raw materials to drive it.
- Energy captured by the LDR is used to reduce carbon dioxide in a complex series of reactions to produce glucose (bottom 4, 5).

Summary of photosynthesis

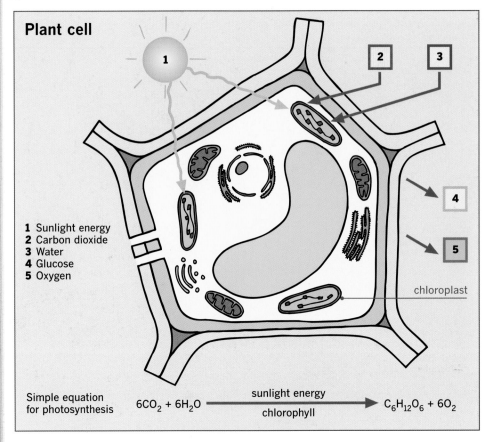

Plant cell

1 Sunlight energy
2 Carbon dioxide
3 Water
4 Glucose
5 Oxygen

chloroplast

Simple equation for photosynthesis

$$6CO_2 + 6H_2O \xrightarrow[\text{chlorophyll}]{\text{sunlight energy}} C_6H_{12}O_6 + 6O_2$$

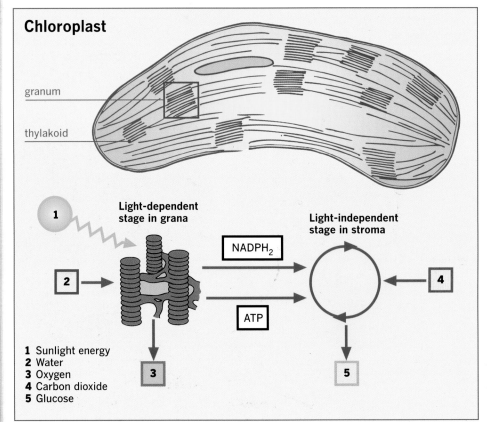

Chloroplast

granum

thylakoid

Light-dependent stage in grana

Light-independent stage in stroma

NADPH$_2$

ATP

1 Sunlight energy
2 Water
3 Oxygen
4 Carbon dioxide
5 Glucose

Chloroplast: structure

Key words

chloroplast	light-independent
cytoplasm	reaction
granum	stroma
light-dependent	thylakoid
reaction	

Plant cell

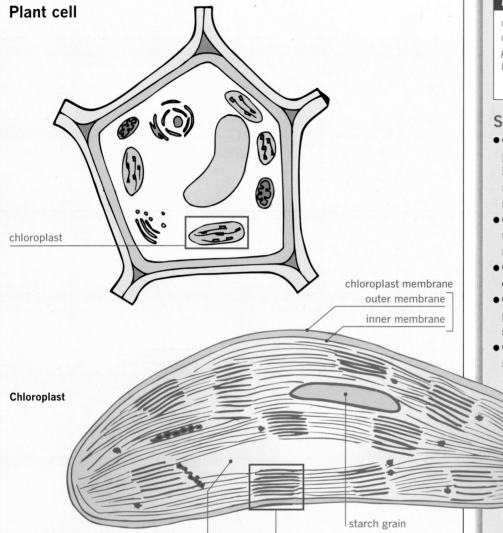

chloroplast

Chloroplast

chloroplast membrane
outer membrane
inner membrane

starch grain

stroma | detail of granum

Detail of granum

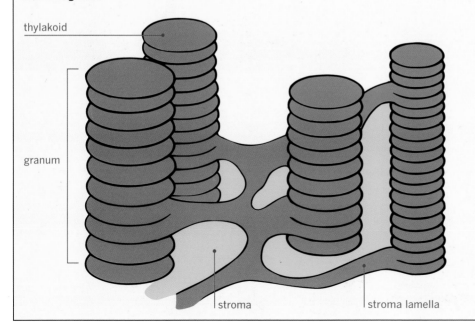

thylakoid

granum

stroma | stroma lamella

Size and distribution

- *Chloroplasts* are found in all photosynthetic plants and are usually large enough to be seen with the light microscope as green disks embedded in the *cytoplasm*.
- Chloroplasts are not present in cells that receive no light, e.g., cells of the root or deep inside plant bodies.
- Chloroplasts are particularly rich in cells in leaves and green stems.
- Chloroplasts are the site of starch production in photosynthesis and of starch storage.
- Chloroplasts are bounded by a double membrane—one derived from the enclosing cell and one from the chloroplast itself.

Grana

- Embedded in the stroma is a complex network of stacked sacs called *grana*.
- The grana consist of interconnected *thylakoids*. Tube-like strands connecting thylakoids from granum to granum are called stroma lamellae.
- Chlorophyll and other pigments that initiate photosynthesis are found on the outer layer of the thylakoids.
- The *light-dependent reaction* takes place in the thylakoids.

Stroma

- Inside the inner membrane is a complex mix of enzymes and water called *stroma*. It is the site of the *light-independent reaction*.

Chemistry of photosynthesis

Key words

glucose	NADP
light-dependent reaction	NADPH
	photosynthesis
light-independent reaction	

Two linked pathways

- *Photosynthesis* is a multistepped process consisting of two linked reaction pathways—the *light-dependent reaction* (LDR) and the *light-independent reaction* (LIR).
- Photosynthesis is usually shown as creating *glucose*, but this is also the starting point for a range of other pathways. Much of the sugar produced will be converted to starch for storage or be respired to produce energy to drive other reactions.

Light-dependent reaction

- This reaction produces chemicals (ATP and NADPH) that contain energy in a form that can be used by the LIR.
- The outputs are shown as electrons (e⁻), which are carried by chemicals that link them to the LIR. The main carrier is the coenzyme *NADP*.

Light-independent reaction

- This reaction uses energy from the LDR to build sugars.
- Carbon dioxide is absorbed by the plant and reduced to form sugar.
- Some of the intermediate products of the reaction can be shunted into other reaction pathways to build fats and even proteins.

Light-dependent reaction (photolysis)

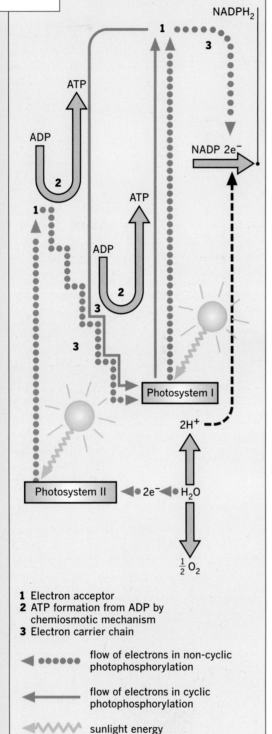

1 Electron acceptor
2 ATP formation from ADP by chemiosmotic mechanism
3 Electron carrier chain

◀ ●●●●●● flow of electrons in non-cyclic photophosphorylation

◀━━━ flow of electrons in cyclic photophosphorylation

〰〰 sunlight energy

◀━━ passage of protons to NADP

⇦ other chemical reactions

Light-independent reaction (carbon fixation)

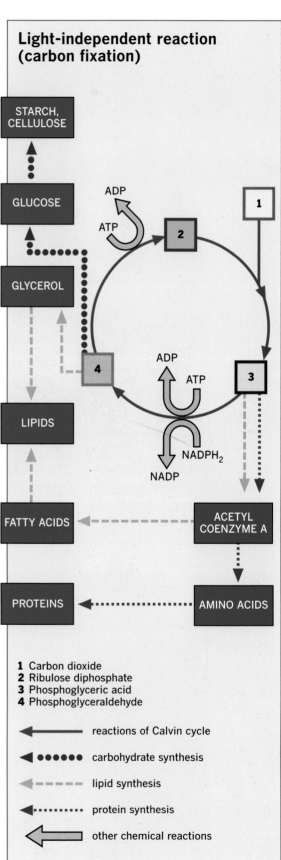

1 Carbon dioxide
2 Ribulose diphosphate
3 Phosphoglyceric acid
4 Phosphoglyceraldehyde

◀━━ reactions of Calvin cycle

◀ ●●●●●● carbohydrate synthesis

◀━ ━ ━ lipid synthesis

◀ ●●●●●● protein synthesis

⇦ other chemical reactions

Summary of aerobic respiration

Key words

adenosine   glycolysis
 triphosphate   Krebs cycle
aerobic   respiration
 respiration
electron
 transfer chain

Mitochondrian

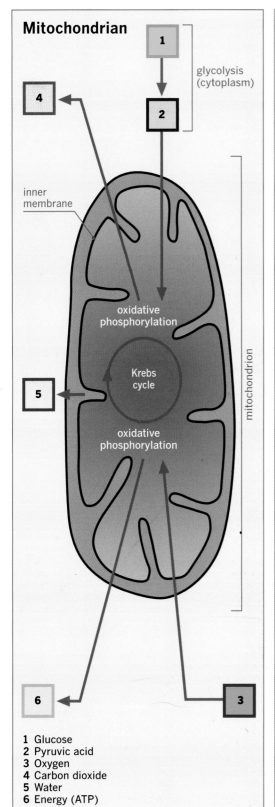

glycolysis
(cytoplasm)

inner
membrane

oxidative
phosphorylation

Krebs
cycle

mitochondrion

oxidative
phosphorylation

1 Glucose
2 Pyruvic acid
3 Oxygen
4 Carbon dioxide
5 Water
6 Energy (ATP)

Simple equation for aerobic respiration
$$C_6H_{12}O_6 + 6O_2 \rightarrow 6CO_2 + 6H_2O + energy\ (38\ ATP)$$

Aerobic respiration

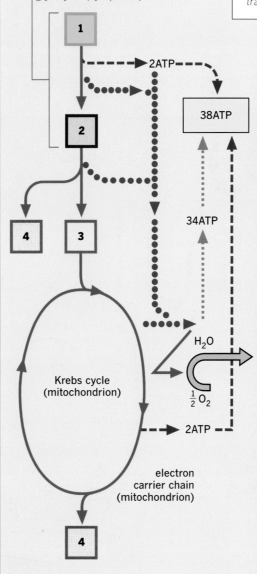

glycolysis (cytoplasm)

2ATP

38ATP

34ATP

H_2O

Krebs cycle
(mitochondrion)

$\frac{1}{2} O_2$

2ATP

electron
carrier chain
(mitochondrion)

1 Glucose
2 Pyruvic acid
3 Acetyl coenzyme A
4 Carbon dioxide

→ glycolysis/Krebs cycle reactions

⇢ ATP produced by substrate-level phosphorylation

⋯→ ATP produced by oxidative phosphorylation

•••→ hydrogen transferred by acceptor to electron carrier chain

⟸ reduction of oxygen to water

Fuel-oxygen systems

- Living things use a fuel–oxygen system to manage energy. Energy is released when the fuel and the oxygen react, and is transferred to other chemical systems that pass it on to other reactions in a cell.
- The energy release and management system in living things is called *respiration*. If oxygen is involved, it is known as *aerobic respiration*.

The "energy currency"

- Glucose releases far too much energy for living things if it reacts with oxygen all at once, as happens in combustion. The respiration system allows the sugar to react in a series of small steps that release smaller amounts of energy. These energy packets are collected by a chemical called *adenosine triphosphate* (ATP).
- ATP passes these packets of energy onto other reactions in the cell. ATP is sometimes called the "energy currency" of the cell.

Three step process

- Aerobic respiration has three main components: *glycolysis*, the *Krebs cycle*, and the *electron transfer chain* (ETC). Glycolysis occurs in the cytoplasm and splits glucose into a smaller molecule. This passes into the mitochondria, where it is further broken down during the Krebs cycle, releasing carbon dioxide and high-energy electrons. The ETC then harvests the energy in these electrons.

Key words

adenosine triphosphate	mitochondrion
cristae	ribosome
Krebs cycle	
matrix	

Size and distribution

- *Mitochondria* are present in all cells with a nucleus. The more metabolically active a cell, the more mitochondria they are likely to have.
- Mitochondria generally have a sausage shape, but some can be almost spherical. They are roughly the size of bacteria, typically about half to a quarter as long as the cell nucleus diameter.

Double membranes

- Like chloroplasts, mitochondria have a double membrane. The outer one is smooth and separates the inside of the mitochondria from the cytoplasm of the cell.
- The inner membrane is folded inward to produce many ridges called *cristae*. These project into the central space of the mitochondrion called the *matrix*. The infolding of the christae provides more surface area for chemical reactions to occur.
- The matrix contains strands of DNA, *ribosomes*, or small granules.

Enzyme systems

- Enzymes floating freely in the matrix are concerned with the *Krebs cycle*—a part of the respiration pathway that produces excited electrons.
- The cristae formed by the infolded inner membrane contain enzymes that handle the transfer of electrons from the Krebs cycle and produce *adenosine triphosphate* (ATP) through a series of complex reactions.

Mitochondrion: structure

Mitochondrion
(part sectioned)

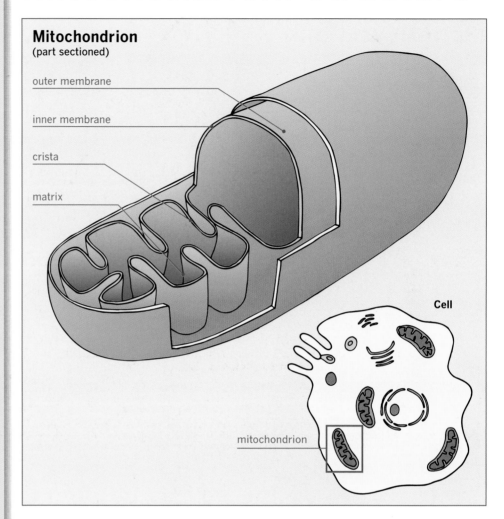

outer membrane

inner membrane

crista

matrix

Cell

mitochondrion

Mitochondrion: section

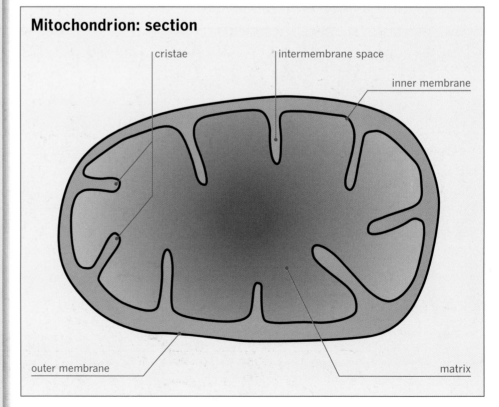

cristae

intermembrane space

inner membrane

outer membrane

matrix

ATP structure

Key words

adenosine
  triphosphate
respiration

ATP structure

Simplified structure
1 Adenine
2 Ribose
3 Phosphate

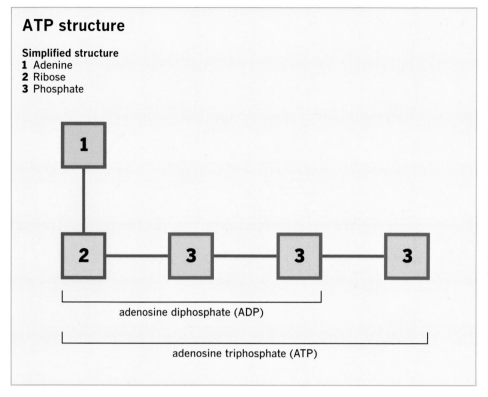

adenosine diphosphate (ADP)

adenosine triphosphate (ATP)

Molecular structure

adenine

NH₂

ribose

OH OH

phosphate

adenosine diphosphate (ADP)

adenosine triphosphate (ATP)

The energy currency

- *Adenosine triphosphate* (ATP) is a molecule that can collect and give out energy when its phosphate groups join or leave the adenosine molecule. You can think of the phosphate groups as "rechargable batteries" or "energy money"—they make other reactions that need energy happen.
- When a phosphate group is released from ATP, the phosphate group attaches itself to a molecule that needs energy to take part in a reaction. The energy in the phosphate groups "passes into" the other molecule, and the reaction can take place.
- Once the energy has been transferred, the phosphate group is released as low energy inorganic phosphate. This can then be reconnected to the adenosine molecule, provided energy is supplied by *respiration*. In this way the "battery" is "recharged."

The phosphate pool

- The energy available to reactions in the cell depends on ATP, and if the concentration of ATP falls, reactions will fail or slow down. Since ATP can be reused many times, this does not happen often. The limiting factor is how quickly the ATP can be recycled from adenosine diphosphate (ADP) and inorganic phosphate.
- The "phosphate pool" is the supply of inorganic phosphate groups in the cell that could be used to build ATP. If this pool "dried up," then the cell would suffer a lack of useful energy.

Key words

adenosine	NAD
triphosphate	NADP
electron transfer	
chain	
Krebs cycle	

Energetic electrons

- The *Krebs cycle* transfers energy into electrons that become "excited." These electrons carry more energy than normal electrons.
- Electrons are difficult to move around the cell, so the cell uses hydrogen ions, which have a positive charge and can "drag" the negatively charged electrons along with them.
- Compounds like nicotinamide adenine dinucleotide (*NAD*) and nicotinamide adenine dinucleotide phosphate (*NADP*) can bind to these hydrogen ions (and so the electrons) to shuttle them between the various parts of the respiration pathway and the start of the *electron transfer chain*.

Redox reactions

- A chemical is oxidized when it gains oxygen or loses an electron. A compound is reduced when it loses oxygen or gains an electron. Reduction involves losing oxygen or gaining an electron.
- Redox reactions usually involve the transfer of energy between chemicals.

Energy transfers

- High energy electrons are fed into the electron transfer chain at one end and pass through a series of redox reactions until they are linked with oxygen to make water (H_2O). Remember that although we talk of electrons moving, we are really moving hydrogen ions.
- At various stages in this process, enough energy is released to build *adenosine triphosphate* (ATP) from adenosine diphosphate (ADP) and inorganic phosphate (Pi).

Electron transfer chain

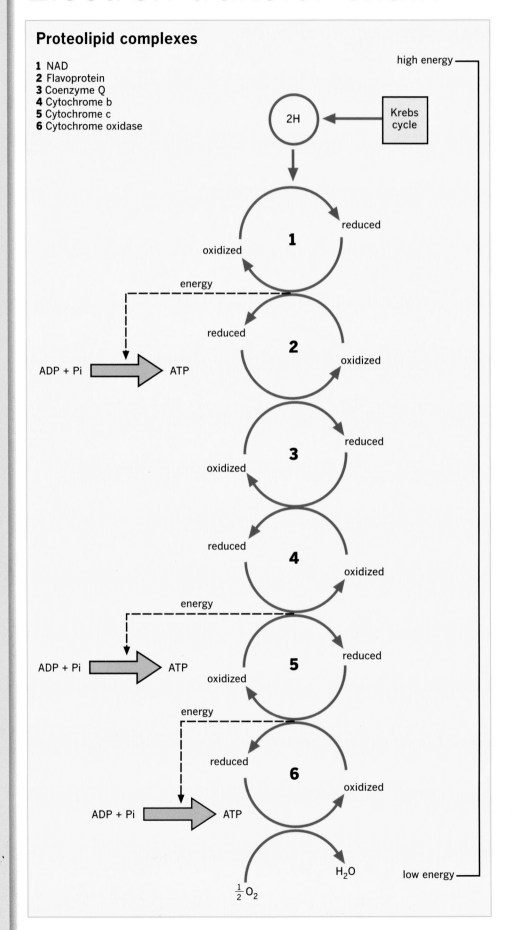

Proteolipid complexes

1 NAD
2 Flavoprotein
3 Coenzyme Q
4 Cytochrome b
5 Cytochrome c
6 Cytochrome oxidase

Anaerobic respiration

Lactic acid fermentation in animals

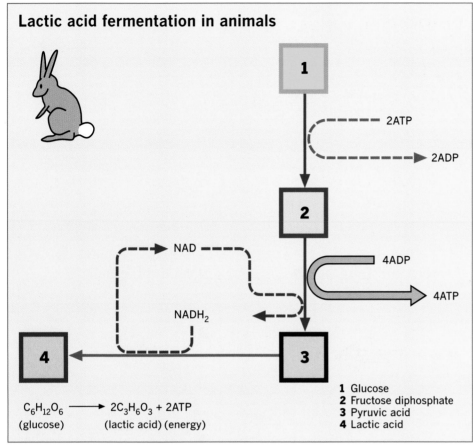

$$C_6H_{12}O_6 \longrightarrow 2C_3H_6O_3 + 2ATP$$
(glucose)   (lactic acid) (energy)

1 Glucose
2 Fructose diphosphate
3 Pyruvic acid
4 Lactic acid

Alcoholic fermentation in yeast

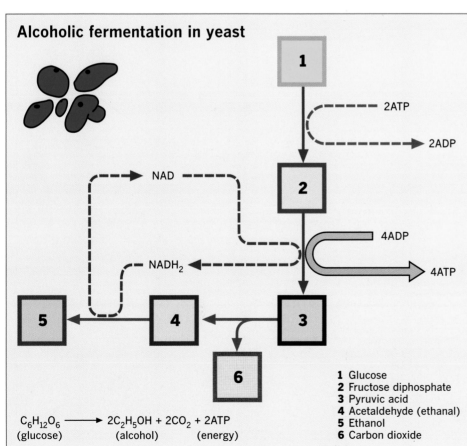

$$C_6H_{12}O_6 \longrightarrow 2C_2H_5OH + 2CO_2 + 2ATP$$
(glucose)   (alcohol)   (energy)

1 Glucose
2 Fructose diphosphate
3 Pyruvic acid
4 Acetaldehyde (ethanal)
5 Ethanol
6 Carbon dioxide

Key words

aerobic respiration	*glucose*
anaerobic respiration	*NAD*
ATP	*NADH*

Anaerobic respiration

- *Anaerobic respiration* does not require oxygen to release energy from sugar. It is less efficient than *aerobic respiration*, producing less energy per gram of *glucose*, so it is usually only used when aerobic respiration is not possible.
- In animals the supply of oxygen to actively respiring cells may not be able to keep up with the demand. The cells will already be respiring as rapidly as possible aerobically but need to produce more energy—perhaps due to excessive stress or physical activity. At this point anaerobic respiration begins, so both forms of respiration are operating at the same time.
- The process converts glucose into pyruvic acid and makes energy in the form of *ATP*.

The "oxygen debt"

- In mammals anaerobic respiration gives a useful extra energy boost in stressful situations. However, it produces toxic lactic acid (see top diagram).
- Once the stress is over and oxygen supplies are plentiful again, the lactic acid must be destroyed. The amount of oxygen needed to do this is called the "oxygen debt."

Alcoholic fermentation

- Anaerobic respiration produces alcohol (ethanol) in yeasts and many other fungi (see bottom diagram). This is the basis of the brewing and baking industries.
- Alcohol is toxic, and yeasts will poison themselves if the alcohol they produce as a waste product of respiration exceeds about seven percent of their environment.

Key words

centromere	gene
chromatid	
chromatin	
chromosome	
DNA	

Visible during division

- *Chromosomes* are large structures found in the nucleus of cells. They are only visible during cell division. They take up certain dyes very well, and so are often treated with these before they are observed with a light microscope. "Chromosome" is Greek for a "colored body."

Chromatids and centromeres

- Chromosomes have three clear parts: two pairs of *chromatids*, which extend from either side of a *cetromere*. The chromatids on one side of the centromere are always the same length, but this can be different from the length of the two chromatids on the other side.
- During cell division, the centromere splits to create chromosomes with single chromatids. These then duplicate to return to pairs of chromatids.

Supercoils

- A chromatid is a coiled spring of protein and deoxyribonucleic acid (*DNA*) called chromatin. The protein and DNA are, in turn, coiled into a spiral.
- The spiral coil is called a supercoil.
- The supercoil unravels when the cell is not dividing so that the enzymes of the nucleus can get easy access to the *genes* in the DNA strand.
- The supercoil condenses during cell division to make it easier to ensure that each daughter cell gets a copy of all of the genes from the parent.

Chromosome structure

Chromosome

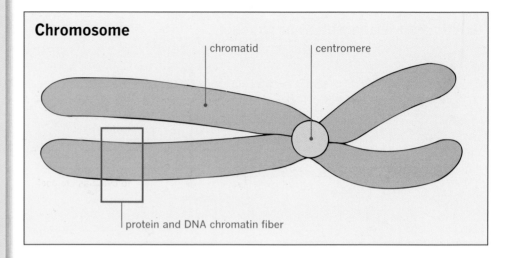

chromatid   centromere

protein and DNA chromatin fiber

Protein and DNA supercoil

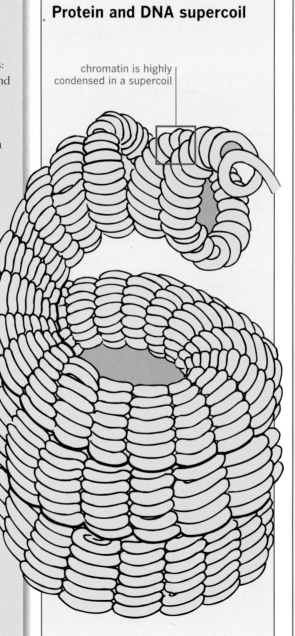

chromatin is highly condensed in a supercoil

DNA double helix

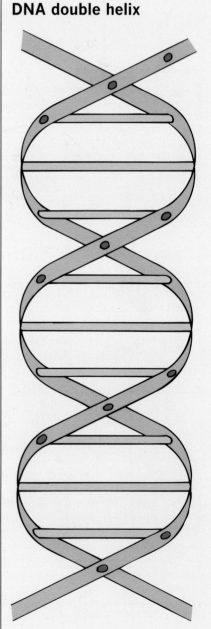

Summary of protein synthesis

Key words

amino acid	transfer RNA
enzyme	translation
messenger RNA	
ribosome	
transcription	

Protein synthesis

- Protein synthesis requires two major processes: *translation* and *transcription*.

Transcription

- Transcription takes place in the nucleus and involves the creation of a molecule of mRNA with a base sequence that mirrors the sequence of the relevant portion of the DNA molecule. This means that a single length of DNA can give rise to many copies of mRNA.
- The mRNA molecules leave the nucleus through a nuclear pore and moves to the ribosomes.

Translation

- Translation is the process of converting information on the messenger RNA (*mRNA*) molecules into a sequence of amino acids. It is catalyzed by *ribosomes*.
- Ribosomes depend on another nucleic acid, called transfer RNA (*tRNA*).
- tRNA has a clover leaf shape with an *amino acid* attached at one end and a triplet of bases revealed at the other end.
- Each tRNA molecule carries a particular amino acid and has a particular triplet revealed.
- When the mRNA molecule threads through the ribosome, tRNA molecules with corresponding triplet codes fall into place. *Enzymes* join the amino acids at the other end together to build the new protein chain.

Protein synthesis

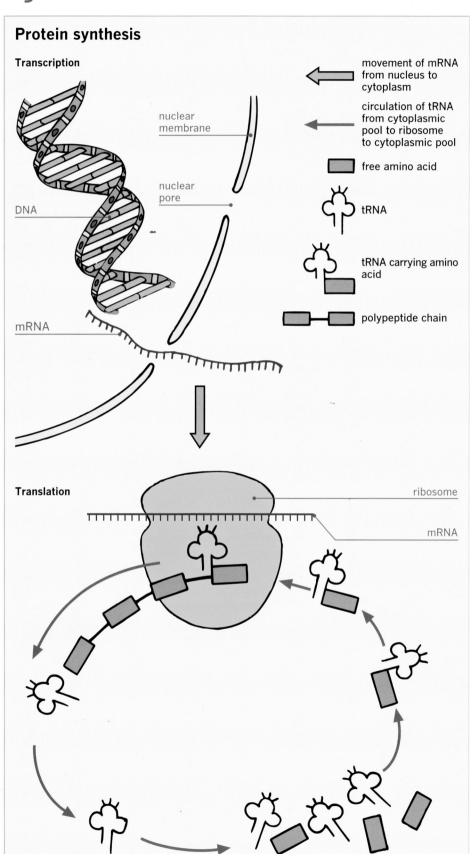

Transcription

movement of mRNA from nucleus to cytoplasm

circulation of tRNA from cytoplasmic pool to ribosome to cytoplasmic pool

free amino acid

tRNA

tRNA carrying amino acid

polypeptide chain

nuclear membrane

nuclear pore

DNA

mRNA

Translation

ribosome

mRNA

Nucleotide units

- A *nucleotide* consists of three parts: a phosphate group, a five-carbon sugar, and an organic base.
- The phosphate–sugar part of the nucleotide joins with other nucleotide molecules to form a strong backbone.
- The complete nucleotide chain is called a nucleic acid. *Deoxyribonucleic acid* or DNA is a nucleic acid.

Organic bases

- There are four possible bases in DNA: adenine, thymine, guanine, and cytosine.
- The nucleotides in a molecule are arranged in a long chain joined by the sugar–phosphate groups. The bases protrude from this backbone.
- If two chains are brought close together, the bases can link up by hydrogen bonds to form a "ladder" where the bases' links act as the rungs. However, the bases can only link up in particular patterns: adenine links with thymine and guanine links with cytosine (see page 41).
- The hydrogen bonds between the base pairs are weaker than the sugar–phosphate links, so that pulling on a DNA molecule splits it down the middle between these bonds.
- If you have one half of a nucleic acid molecule, you can create the other half by joining the correct bases and then bonding them with sugar–phosphate groups. This is how DNA molecules are copied.

Base pairing

Portion of DNA molecule

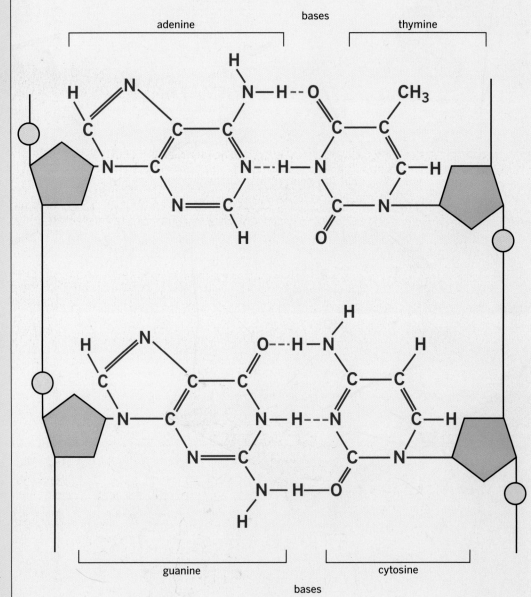

DNA structure

Schematized double helix

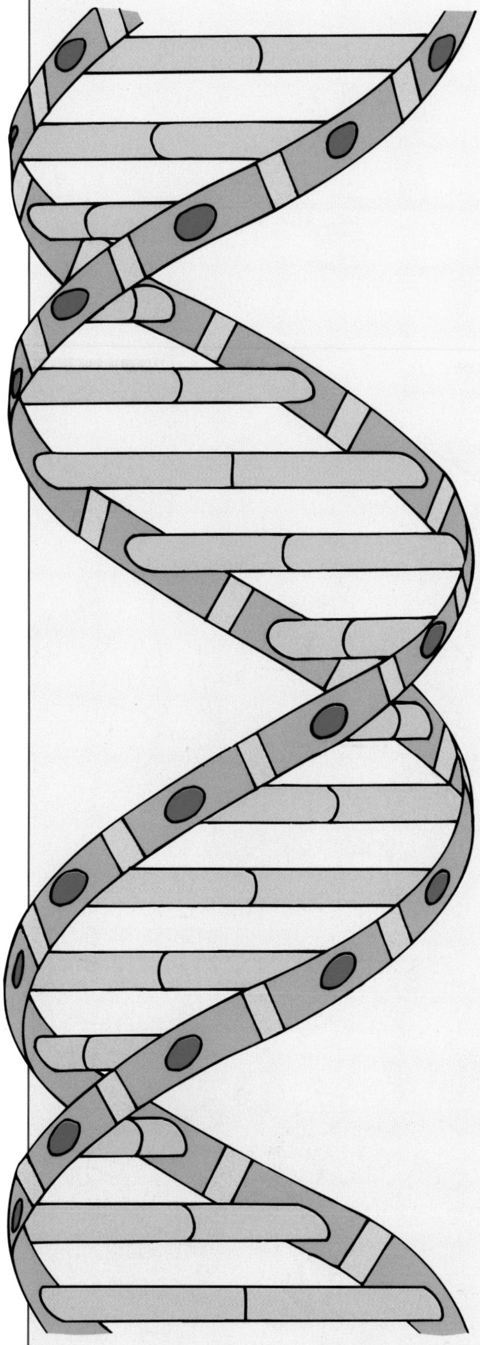

Arrangement of nucleotides in DNA

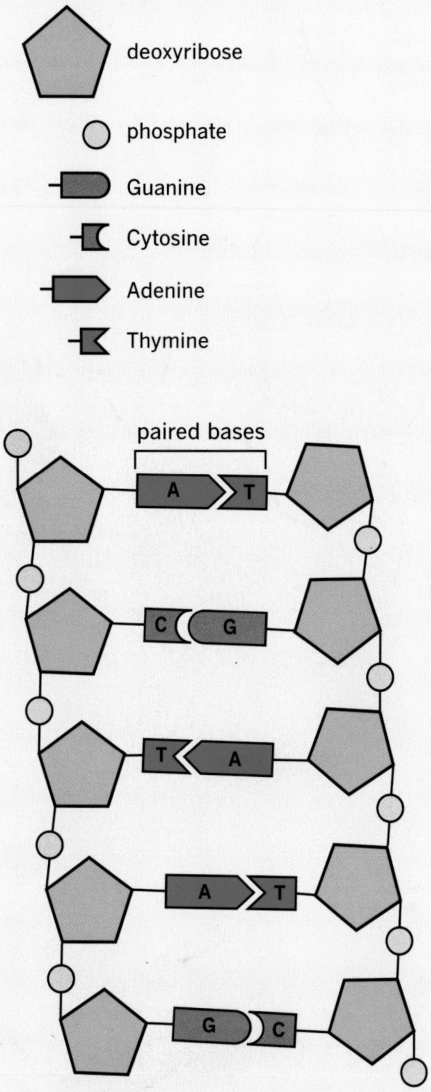
deoxyribose
phosphate
Guanine
Cytosine
Adenine
Thymine
paired bases
A
T
C
G
T
A
A
T
G
C

View from above

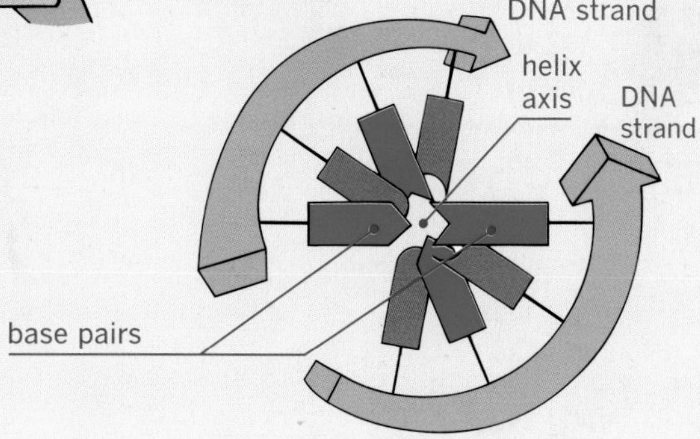
DNA strand
helix axis
DNA strand
base pairs

Key words

amino acid
DNA
nucleotide

Phosphate-sugar backbone

- *DNA* consists of two, intertwined chains of *nucleotides* that form a double helix.
- The backbone of these chains, found on the outside of the helix, is a long sequence of sugar–phosphate groups. These linkages hold the molecule together strongly to make DNA a very resilient molecule. DNA from ancient sources can still be identified long after many other chemicals have decayed beyond recognition.

Information carrier

- The complex structure of DNA allows it to carry and duplicate information in the form of a code. The sequence of bases in a chain can be used to sequence *amino acids* in a protein. This allows the cell to store the blueprint for any protein as a “triplet” code of bases.

DNA replication

Key words

DNA
enzyme
nucleotide

Two possible methods

- *DNA* consists of two intertwined chains of *nucleotides* that form a double helix. Two models have been proposed to explain how DNA is copied: the "new build" or the "semi-conservative" model.
- In the new build model a completely new DNA molecule would be created from scratch. The old DNA molecule would be untouched, but perhaps used as a model to copy.
- The semi-conservative model (see diagram) assumes that the DNA molecule unzips to create two separate but complete nucleotide chains. New bases are added to each of these chains, and these are then linked together by a sugar–phosphate backbone.
- Evidence from radiotracers has shown that the semi-conservative model is correct and that each new DNA molecule contains half of the original molecule.

Enzyme controlled

- The replication, or duplication, of DNA is closely controlled by *enzymes*. This reaction can be quite rapid. In bacteria complete DNA molecules can be copied in fewer than 20 minutes under optimum conditions.

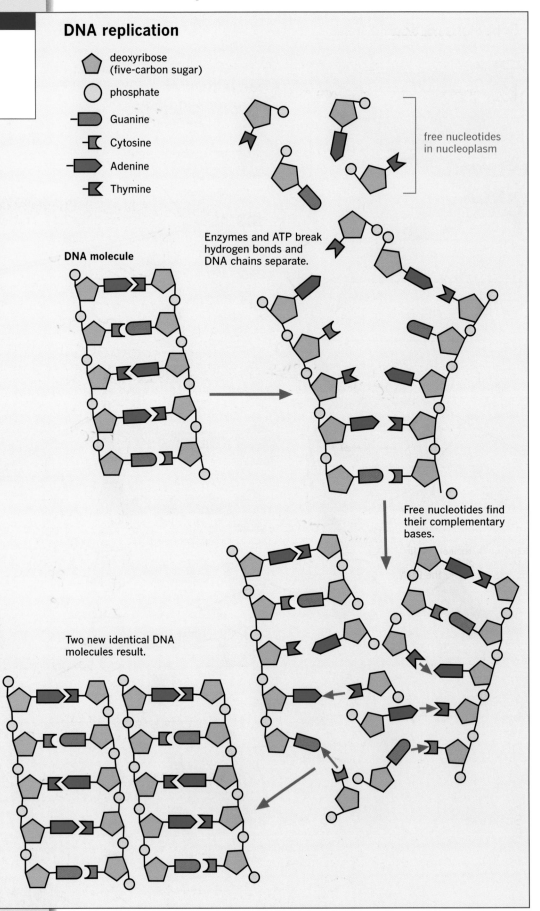

DNA replication

- deoxyribose (five-carbon sugar)
- phosphate
- Guanine
- Cytosine
- Adenine
- Thymine

free nucleotides in nucleoplasm

DNA molecule

Enzymes and ATP break hydrogen bonds and DNA chains separate.

Free nucleotides find their complementary bases.

Two new identical DNA molecules result.

DNA transcription

DNA transcription

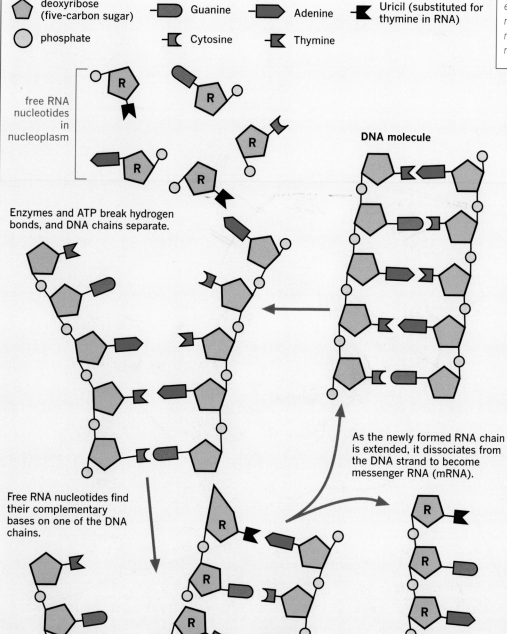

deoxyribose (five-carbon sugar)

phosphate

Guanine

Cytosine

Adenine

Thymine

Uricil (substituted for thymine in RNA)

free RNA nucleotides in nucleoplasm

DNA molecule

Enzymes and ATP break hydrogen bonds, and DNA chains separate.

Free RNA nucleotides find their complementary bases on one of the DNA chains.

As the newly formed RNA chain is extended, it dissociates from the DNA strand to become messenger RNA (mRNA).

Key words

DNA
enzyme
messenger RNA
nucleotide
ribosome

transcription
transfer RNA

Types of nucleic acid

- There are two major groups of nucleic acids: deoxyribonucleic acid (*DNA*) and ribonucleic acid (RNA).
- DNA is always found in the nucleus and has the characteristic double-helical structure.
- RNA has a more variable structure than DNA and has two major forms: *messenger RNA* (mRNA) and *transfer RNA* (tRNA). mRNA moves between the nucleus and the rest of the cell.

Copying the message

- The genes containing essential information for building proteins are kept in the cell nucleus. These genes are coded lengths of DNA.
- The information is copied onto mRNA in a process called *transcription*. This copying is essential to get the information from the store (the DNA) to the *ribosomes*, where the manufacture of proteins occurs.

Building mRNA

- *Enzymes* break open the DNA molecule (top right) at the correct point to reveal the base sequence in the middle of the molecule.
- Individual RNA *nucleotides* can then line up with the DNA using base-matching to ensure they are in the correct order. Enzymes build the mRNA molecule and the mRNA leaves the nucleus. The enzymes are left behind and can be re-used to build more mRNA molecules.

© Diagram Visual Information Ltd.

Key words

polypeptide chain
ribosome
rough
  endoplasmic
  reticulum

smooth
  endoplasmic
  reticulum

Rough endoplasmic reticulum: structure

Endoplasmic reticulum

● The endoplasmic reticulum (ER) is a network of flat open spaces within a cell. The membrane bounding it is continuous with the plasma membrane surrounding the cell. This means materials can pass along the endoplasmic reticulum until they are deep within the cell without having to cross over the plasma membrane.

● There are two types of ER: *smooth endoplasmic reticulum* (SER) and *rough endoplasmic reticulum* (RER).

Rough endoplasmic reticulum

● Both SER and RER are made up of plasma membrane, but RER has small bodies called *ribosomes* attached. These ribosomes made the ER look "studded" or "rough."

● Ribosomes are giant enzyme–RNA complexes concerned with protein manufacture. They consist of two subunits that fit together (top right diagram) and work as one, using information from mRNA to create *polypeptide chains* during protein synthesis.

● These peptide chains pass into the space in the ER to fold and assemble, creating more complex proteins.

Schematic structure of rough endoplasmic reticulum

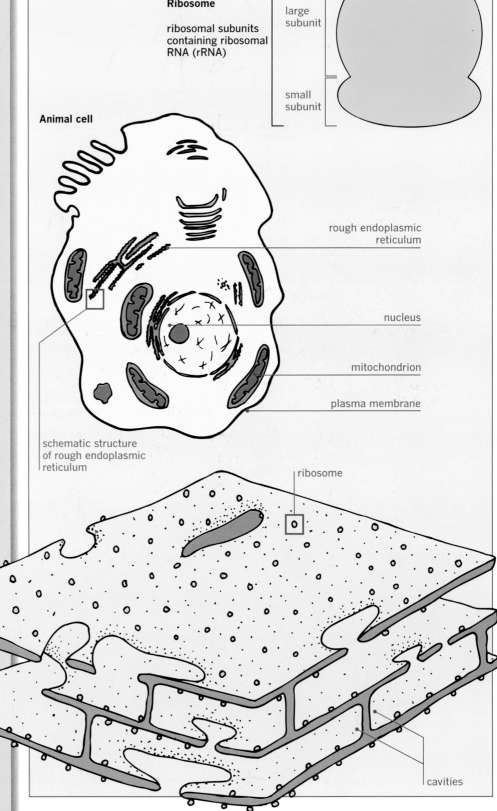

Rough endoplasmic reticulum

Ribosome

ribosomal subunits containing ribosomal RNA (rRNA)

large subunit

small subunit

Animal cell

rough endoplasmic reticulum

nucleus

mitochondrion

plasma membrane

schematic structure of rough endoplasmic reticulum

ribosome

lamellae (layers) —made up of two membranes

cavities

Transfer RNA

Key words

amino acid	transfer RNA
anticodon	
codon	
nucleotide	
polypeptide chain	

Transfer RNA models

Cloverleaf model of tyrosine transfer RNA (tRNA)

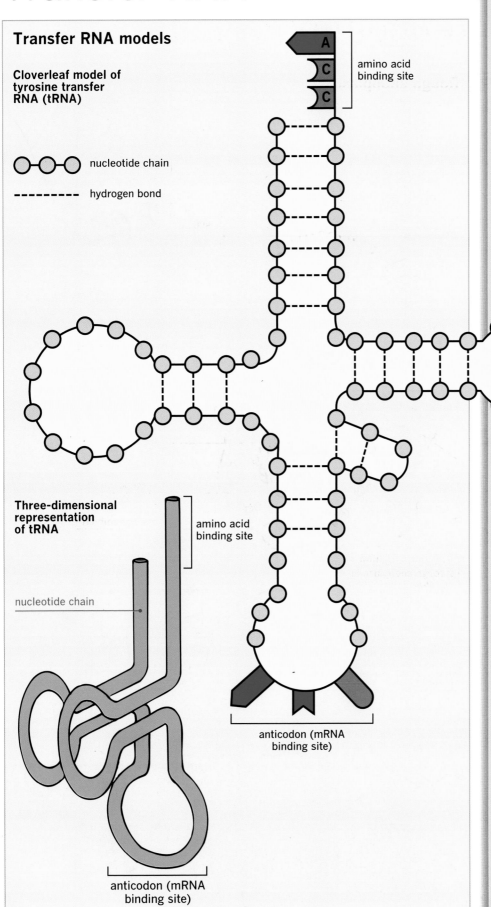

○—○—○ nucleotide chain

- - - - - - - hydrogen bond

amino acid binding site

Three-dimensional representation of tRNA

nucleotide chain

amino acid binding site

anticodon (mRNA binding site)

anticodon (mRNA binding site)

Transfer RNA

● *Transfer RNA* (tRNA) is an essential part of the protein manufacturing process. During translation (see page 46), it transfers a specific *amino acid* to a *polypeptide chain* at the ribosome, where protein is synthesized. In order for this to occur, a specific tRNA molecule must bond with a specific amino acid.

Structure

● The twisted, clover shaped tRNA molecule has two functional sites. At one end of the molecule is a site for amino-acid attachment and *codon* recognition. Condons specify the amino acid to be linked into the polypeptide chain being synthesized. At the other is the *anticodon*, three *nucleotide* bases that are specific for that amnio acid.

● The distance between the amino acid binding site and the anticodon is constant no matter how long the tRNA chain is or how many folds it has.

Anticodons

● There are many different types of tRNA. Each type transfers one particular amino acid to a growing polypeptide chain.

● When messenger RNA (mRNA) enters the ribosome, tRNA anticodons on the tRNA molecule recognize and bind to the appropriate codon on an mRNA molecule, bringing the correct amino acid into sequence for the formation of the polypeptide chain.

Key words

anticodon
codon
messenger RNA
ribosome
transfer RNA

Codons

- Proteins are molecules made of amino acids joined in a particular sequence. If these amino acids are arranged in the wrong order, the protein will not function.
- The sequence of amino acids is coded by a sequence of organic bases in DNA molecules in the nucleus. Each amino acid is coded by a sequence of three bases called a *codon* (see top diagram). So **MET** codes for methionine, **ACC** codes for tryptophan.
- *Messenger RNA* (mRNA) is a copy of the codons on the DNA. The mRNA molecule can pass out of the nucleus to the ribosomes on the endoplasmic reticulum.

Translating the message

- At the ribosome the mRNA acts as a template for other RNA molecules to attach to. These molecules are the *transfer RNA* (tRNA) molecules that carry amino acids needed for protein synthesis.
- A tRNA molecule with an *anticodon* that fits the next available space on the mRNA molecule slots into position. Its amino acid is held in the correct position for enzymes to join it to a growing chain of amino acids formed at the other end of the tRNA molecule.
- Once the amino acid is joined on, it is released from the tRNA, which detaches from the mRNA. The tRNA can be reused when it has had the correct amino acid reattached from the pool in the cell.

Messenger RNA translation

mRNA translation in the cytoplasm

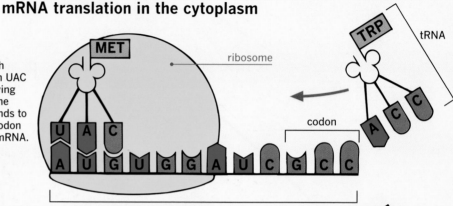

tRNA with anticodon UAC and carrying methionine (MET) binds to correct codon AUG on mRNA.

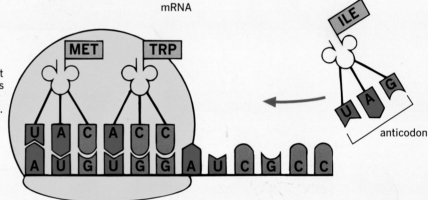

tRNA molecule with the correct anticodon binds to the codon at the second site. It carries tryptophan (TRP).

A peptide bond forms between methionine and tryptophan. The first tRNA molecule returns to the cytoplasm to pick up another methionine molecule. The ribosome shifts, and a third tRNA molecule binds to mRNA.

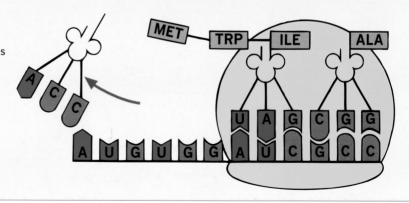

The process is repeated.

Gene control

Key words

DNA
enzyme
operon

Gene induction
ß-galactosidase in *Escherichia coli*

**Operon repressed
(structural gene switched off)**

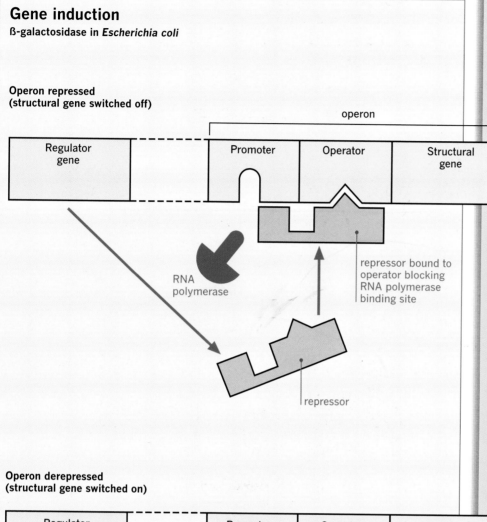

**Operon derepressed
(structural gene switched on)**

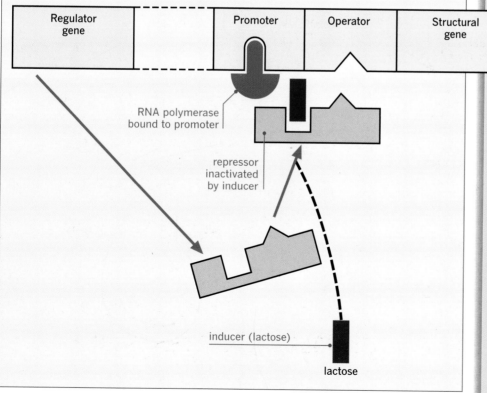

Only when needed

- ß-galactosidase is an *enzyme* involved in the breakdown of lactose. The gene that produces this enzyme is usually switched off, and yet when lactose is found, the gene switches on quickly, and the enzyme is produced.

Gene types

- The gene that produces ß-galactoside consists of two lengths of *DNA*: the regulator gene, and the *operon* containing structural operator and promoter genes.
- The structural gene produces the enzyme when the operator switches it on. The operator, in turn, is controlled by the promoter. The promoter works with an enzyme called RNA polymerase to switch on the operator and the structural gene.
- However, RNA polymerase must be able to link with the promoter for this to happen, and this is normally blocked by a chemical, called a repressor, that binds to the operator.

Blocking the repressor

- The repressor is a molecule produced by the regulator gene. If no lactose is present, the repressor binds to the operator. When lactose is present, it binds with the repressor and prevents it from binding with the operator. This allows RNA polymerase to bind with the promoter and so switch on the structural gene.

Key words

transformation

Pneumococcus

- Pneumococci are a group of bacteria that can cause illness in animals and humans. One particular type can kill mice and has two distinct types: rough (R-type), which does not kill, and smooth (S-type), which is always fatal.
- Rough and smooth refer to the outer coat of the Pneumococcus organisms.

Dead bacteria

- Dead bacteria cannot cause illness. Experiments with heat-killed bacteria in mice showed this.
- When heat killed S-type bacteria were injected into mice with live R-type bacteria, the mice died. Live R-type do not kill mice, so the S-type must have influenced them in some way. The R-type were said to be transformed by the dead S-type.

The active component

- Further work looked at what component in the S-type bacteria was producing the *transformation*.
- S-type bacteria were killed, and the various components separated. Different mice were injected with different extracts from the S-type bacteria along with live R-types.
- The only mice that died had been injected with DNA from the S-type. This showed that it was the DNA that had the power to transform the R-type bacteria.

Transformation

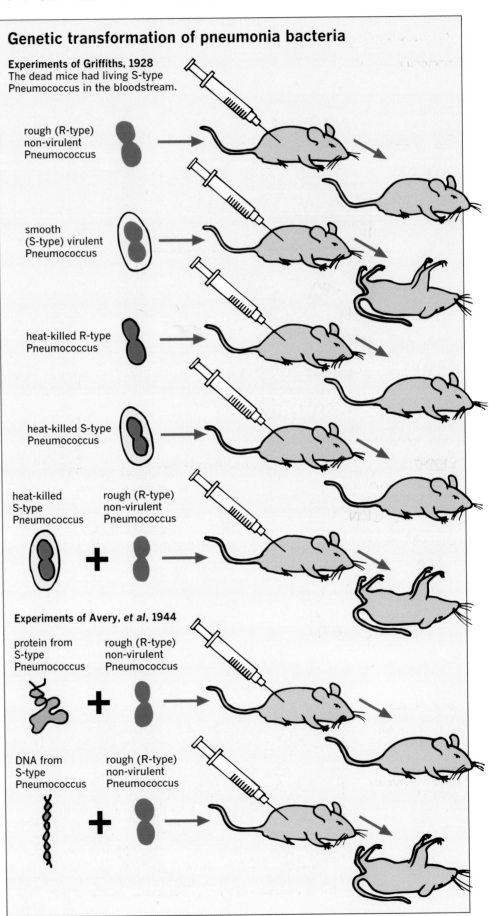

Genetic transformation of pneumonia bacteria

Experiments of Griffiths, 1928
The dead mice had living S-type Pneumococcus in the bloodstream.

rough (R-type) non-virulent Pneumococcus

smooth (S-type) virulent Pneumococcus

heat-killed R-type Pneumococcus

heat-killed S-type Pneumococcus

heat-killed S-type Pneumococcus   rough (R-type) non-virulent Pneumococcus

Experiments of Avery, *et al*, 1944

protein from S-type Pneumococcus   rough (R-type) non-virulent Pneumococcus

DNA from S-type Pneumococcus   rough (R-type) non-virulent Pneumococcus

Genetic engineering

Key words

plasmid
restriction
 enzyme

Transferring genes

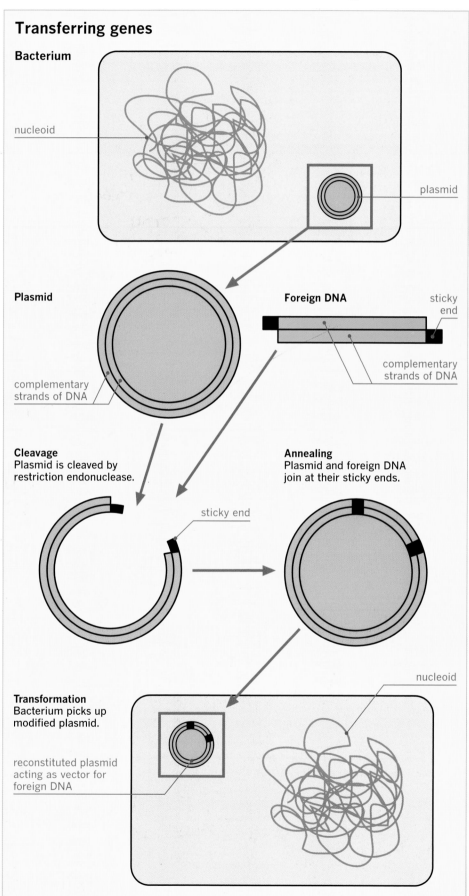

Bacterium

nucleoid

plasmid

Plasmid

complementary
strands of DNA

Foreign DNA

sticky
end

complementary
strands of DNA

Cleavage
Plasmid is cleaved by
restriction endonuclease.

sticky end

Annealing
Plasmid and foreign DNA
join at their sticky ends.

Transformation
Bacterium picks up
modified plasmid.

reconstituted plasmid
acting as vector for
foreign DNA

nucleoid

Bacterial chromosomes

- Bacteria do not have a nucleus. Their
DNA is found in a compacted mass
called the nucleoid. Bacteria also
contain a *plasmid*, a small DNA
molecule that can be transferred from
one cell to another. Plasmids are
commonly used in genetic
engineering to transfer genes.

Sticky ends

- The two strands in the DNA helix of
the plasmid are "mirror images" of
each other. Where one side has
adenine the other has thymine; where
one has cytosine the other has
guanine.
- *Restriction enzymes*, which recognize
specific, short nucleotide sequences,
can cut the plasmid to produce a gap
with "sticky ends." These enzymes do
not cut straight across the DNA
strand—they split the two strands
apart so that one end sticks out
beyond the other. Because the single
strands of DNA have complementary
bases, they can bind to a portion of
DNA with appropriate bases
protruding from their "sticky ends."

Plasmids

- Careful use of restriction enzymes
allows genetic engineers to cut out
lengths of DNA with sticky ends that
correspond to the gaps in a broken
bacterial DNA. The foreign genes can
then be added and the DNA rejoined
to make a circular plasmid.
- The plasmid can be inserted into
another bacterium where it can be
expressed. In this way, for example,
the gene responsible for producing
the hormone insulin can be spliced
into a bacterium.

Key words

anaphase	mitosis
centromere	prophase
chromatid	telophase
chromosome	
gamete	
interphase	
metaphase	

Cell division

● All living cells divide. There are two methods of division: *mitosis*, which produces copies of the original cell, and meiosis which is only used to produce *gametes*, the reproductive cells in plants and animals.

Interphase

● Cells do not divide all of the time—they are present in a state called *interphase*. In interphase, the DNA in the chromatin threads is dividing and multiplying to produce copies of all the genes in the cell—but this process is invisible.

Mitosis

● Mitosis is a continuous process that involves four main stages.

● In *prophase*, chromatin is condensed into short, thick *chromosomes*. Each chromosome has duplicated and now consists of two sister *chromatids* visibly connected at their *centromeres*. The nuclear envelope disintegrates, and the nucleolus disappears.

● In *metaphase* the chromosomes arrange themselves around the equator of the cell. Microtubules form the mitotic spindle.

● *Anaphase* begins when the centromere in the chromosome divides and starts to move to opposite ends of the cell.

● By *telophase* the chromosomes are at opposite ends of the cell, and a new nuclear membrane begins to form. It ends when the cell pinches in to produce daughter cells.

Uses of mitosis

● Mitosis produces daughter cells that are genetically identical to the parent cell. The growth and repair of multicellular organisms require mitosis to produce new cells.

Mitosis in an animal cell

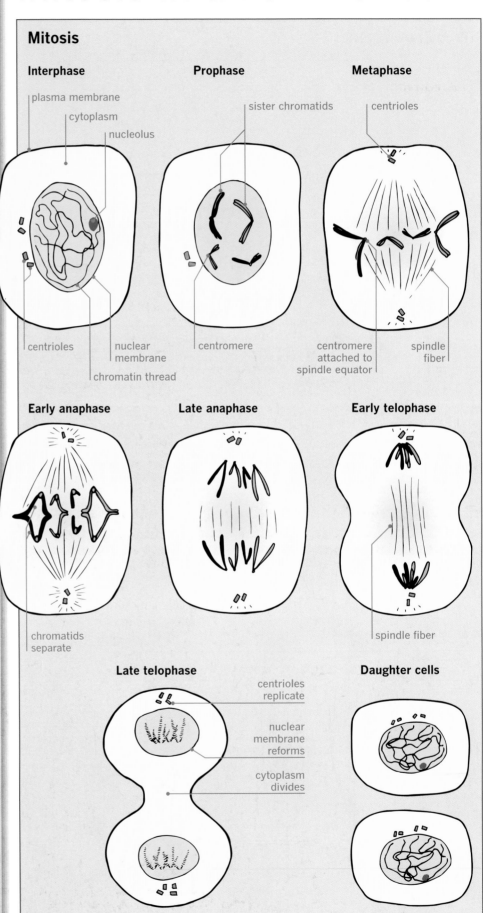

Mitosis

Interphase
- plasma membrane
- cytoplasm
- nucleolus
- centrioles
- nuclear membrane
- chromatin thread

Prophase
- sister chromatids
- centromere

Metaphase
- centrioles
- centromere attached to spindle equator
- spindle fiber

Early anaphase
- chromatids separate

Late anaphase

Early telophase
- spindle fiber

Late telophase
- centrioles replicate
- nuclear membrane reforms
- cytoplasm divides

Daughter cells

Asexual reproduction: fission

Key words

clone
cyst
fission
mitosis
pseudopodium

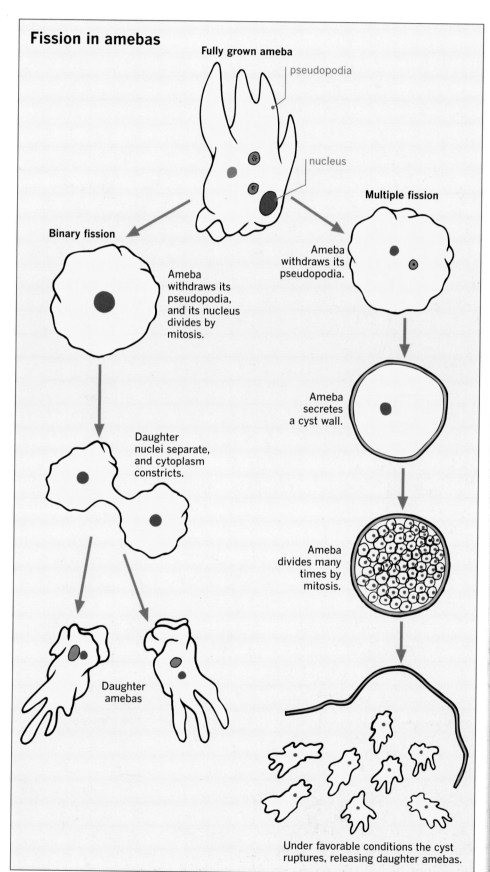

Fission in amebas

Fully grown ameba

pseudopodia

nucleus

Binary fission

Multiple fission

Ameba withdraws its pseudopodia, and its nucleus divides by mitosis.

Ameba withdraws its pseudopodia.

Ameba secretes a cyst wall.

Daughter nuclei separate, and cytoplasm constricts.

Ameba divides many times by mitosis.

Daughter amebas

Under favorable conditions the cyst ruptures, releasing daughter amebas.

Two types of fission

- *Fission* is the splitting of a parent cell into a number of daughter cells. In binary fission two cells are produced. In multiple fission many more daughters are produced.
- The daughters produced by fission are genetically identical to the parent, i.e. they are *clones*.

Binary fission

- In *Amoeba proteus* (ameba), binary fission begins when the *pseudopodia* (false feet) are withdrawn to make a slightly more spherical shape.
- The nucleus divides by *mitosis* to produce two identical nuclei. These move to opposite ends of the cell.
- The ameba constricts around the middle and forms two daughter cells.

Multiple fission

- In multiple fission the ameba withdraws its pseudopodia to form a more spherical shape as in binary fission but then secretes a wall around the cell to form a *cyst*.
- The cyst can survive harsher conditions than the normal ameba cell.
- Inside the cyst the ameba divides multiple times by mitosis to produce many small daughter cells. These daughters are released when the cyst wall breaks.

© Diagram Visual Information Ltd.

Key words

clone
starch
tuber

Vegetative propagation

- In vegetative propagation a plant will produce daughters that are genetically identical to the parent. These *clones* are produced without any sexual process and develop from roots, stems, or leaves.

Potato tubers

- Potato plants form fleshy stems in the roots that act as a store for *starch*. These organs, called *tubers*, can grow into new plants if separated from the parent plant.
- In the second half of the growing season, parts of the root will swell as starch is deposited in them. This starch acts as an energy store for the plant.
- At the end of the growing season, the aerial parts of the potato wilt and die, leaving the tubers underground protected from frost. In the next season the tubers will use their starch to provide energy to develop into new potato plants.

Strawberry runners

- Strawberry plants produce shoots that grow out from the side of the plant horizontally. These above ground stems are called runners.
- Where runners touch the ground, they develop their own roots and aerial shoots. These develop into a new strawberry plant.
- Over time the original runner can decay to produce a completely independent plant.

Asexual reproduction: vegetative propagation

Potato reproduction

1 A shoot grows from a lateral bud.

2 The shoot forms leaves, and roots grow.

3 Side stems grow out and swell up into tubers.

4 Food made in the leaves is stored in the tubers.

5 The leaves, stem, and old tuber die, but new tubers remain dormant in the soil.

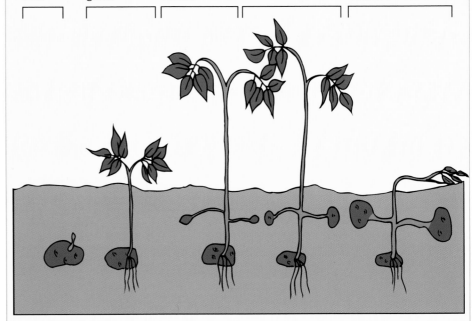

Strawberry reproduction

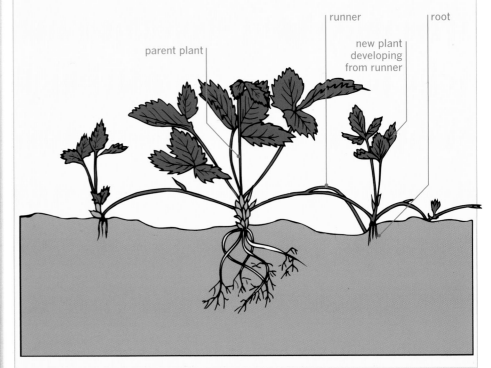

parent plant

runner

root

new plant developing from runner

Meiosis: first division

Meiosis I

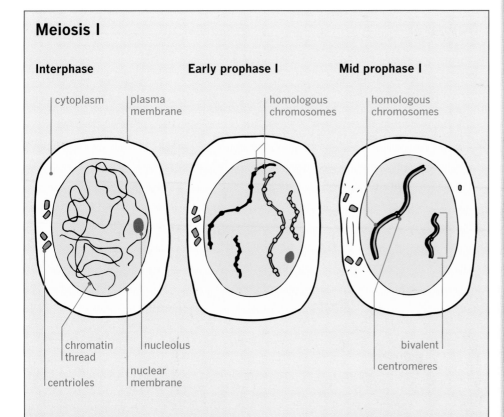

Interphase

- cytoplasm
- plasma membrane
- chromatin thread
- nucleolus
- nuclear membrane
- centrioles

Early prophase I

- homologous chromosomes

Mid prophase I

- homologous chromosomes
- bivalent
- centromeres

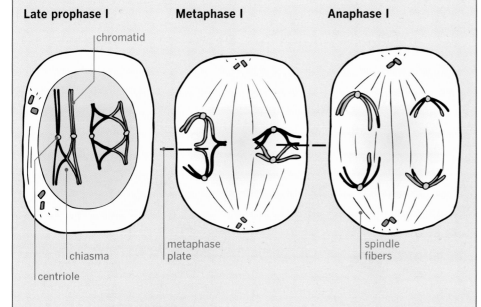

Late prophase I

- chromatid
- chiasma
- centriole

Metaphase I

- metaphase plate

Anaphase I

- spindle fibers

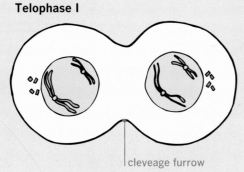

Telophase I

- cleveage furrow

Key words

anaphase	homologous
chiasma	chromosome
chromatid	interphase
gamete	meiosis
gene	prophase
haploid	telophase

Meiosis

- *Meiosis* is a two-stage form of cell division used only in the sex organs to produce gametes.
- Meiosis differs from mitosis in that during prophase genetic material may be exchanged between the chromatids.

Meiosis I

- Interphase in meiosis is identical to interphase in mitosis (see page 50).
- In early prophase I, homologous chromosomes, which have the same genes but may have different alleles, are attached along their lengths in a process called synapsis.
- Synapsis is completed in mid-prophase I, and the chromosomes are said to be bivalent, a reference to the fact that two chromosomes are united.
- In late prophase I, chromosomes may exchange segments of genetic information at locations called chiasmata (see page 55).
- During prophase, the centrioles, when present, begin migrating to the two poles of the cell.
- In metaphase I, the chiasmata slip apart, and the chromosome pairs align on either side of the metaphase plate.
- During anaphase I, spindle fibers pull the chromosomes toward each pole of the cell, and the cell elongates in preparation for division.
- During telophase I, spindle fibers disappear, a cleavage furrow forms, and the cell splits. Each daughter cell now haploid. It has half the number of chromosomes as the parent.

Key words

anaphase II	haploid
centriole	meiosis
centromere	metaphase II
chromatid	prophase II
chromosome	telophase II
gamete	zygote

Gamete formation

- *Meiosis* II, is the mitotic division of the *haploid* cells produced in meiosis I.

Second stage: cell division

- In *prophase II*, *chromatids* shorten and thicken into visible *chromosomes*. *Centrioles* (when present) move to the poles of the cell, spindle fibers form, and the chromosomes move toward the equator of the cell.
- In *metaphase II*, the chromosomes line up along the metaphase plate.
- In *anaphase II*, the *centromeres* divide to produce four separate chromatids from the original two chromosomes. These sister chromatids move toward opposite ends of the cells.
- *Telophase II* doubles the number of cells without a corresponding increase in the number of chromosomes so each new cell has only one chromatid. These haploid daughter cells have half the number of chromosomes found in the parent cell.
- These cells develop further into functional *gametes*.

Meiosis: second division

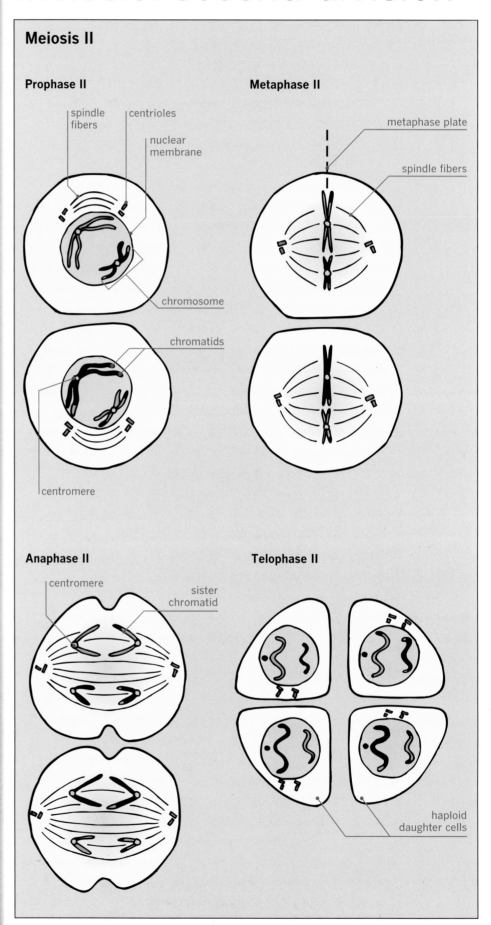

Meiosis II

Prophase II

spindle fibers — centrioles — nuclear membrane — chromosome — chromatids — centromere

Metaphase II

metaphase plate — spindle fibers

Anaphase II

centromere — sister chromatid

Telophase II

haploid daughter cells

Crossing over and genetic variation

Key words

allele   meiosis
chiasma
chromatid
gamete
homologous
  chromosome

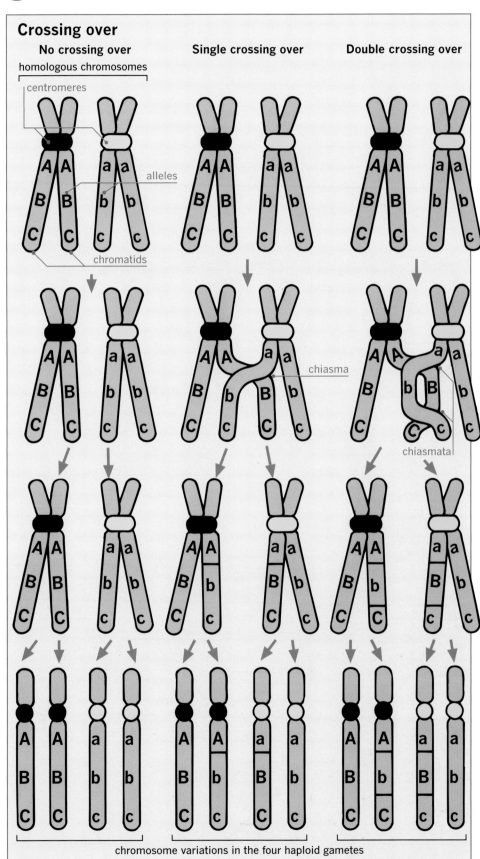

Crossing over

| No crossing over | Single crossing over | Double crossing over |

homologous chromosomes

centromeres

alleles

chromatids

chiasma

chiasmata

chromosome variations in the four haploid gametes

Homologous chromosomes

- *Homologous chromosomes* have the same genes in the same positions but may have different variants, or *alleles*, of the same gene.
- The gene for eye color in humans always resides at a particular place, called a locus, on a chromosome. However, there are a number of different forms (alleles) for this gene, for example blue, brown, or green.

Crossing over

- Crossing over occurs when one length of *chromatid* is exchanged for the equivalent length on a homologous chromosome.
- Crossing over occurs during the first division in *meiosis*. This ensures that new arrangements of alleles are produced during the process that leads to the formation of *gametes*.
- The further apart two genes are on a chromosome, the more likely they are to be separated and remixed during a crossover.

Crossed shapes

- Crossing over occurs when *chiasmata* form, temporarily joining the chromatids of homologous chromosomes together at a particular point.
- When the chiasmata break apart, the chromatids can be re-attached to the broken end of a different chromatid. In this way lengths of chromatid can be exchanged.

Flower structure

© Diagram Visual Information Ltd.

Key words

anther	ovule
carpel	seed
fruit	stamen
gamete	stigma
ovary	style
pistil	

Flowers and fruits

- Flowers are the sexual organs of a group of plants known as angiosperms. They are responsible for producing *seeds* enclosed in structures that aid in their dispersal. The combinations of seeds and these structures are called *fruits*.

Sequences of rings

- All flowers have the same basic structure—a series of rings or whorls arranged on each other on a highly condensed stem called the receptacle.
- The lowest ring looks like simple leaves or bracts and is the sepal.
- The next ring up includes the petals. In insect-pollinated flowers, the petals are often brightly colored and may produce scent, which attracts insects.
- Inside the ring of petals are the male parts of the flower. These are the *stamens*. The final ring is the female part called the *pistil* or *carpel*.

Stamens and carpels

- The stamens are arranged in a ring and consist of *anthers*, which produce pollen grains containing the male *gamete*, supported on a filament.
- The female part of the flower in the innermost ring is composed of the *stigma* and *style*. It is often so highly modified that it does not resemble a ring.
- The female gametes are completely enclosed in the *ovule* located in the *ovary*, which is found as the lowest part of the carpel.

Vertical section through flower

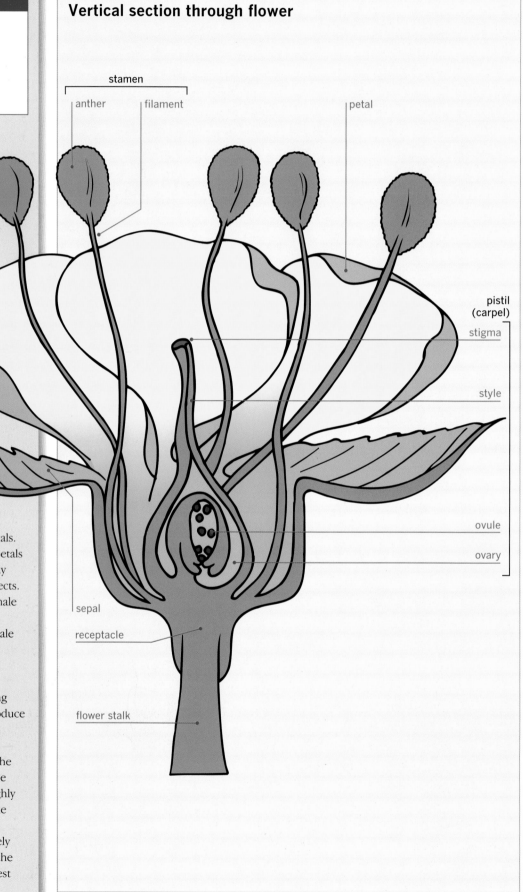

stamen

anther   filament

petal

pistil (carpel)

stigma

style

ovule

ovary

sepal

receptacle

flower stalk

Mature stamen

Key words

anther	stamen
dehiscence	
gamete	
meiosis	
pollen	

Stamen

Flower: vertical section

anther before dehiscence: external view

anther after dehiscence: external view

Anther before dehiscence: external view

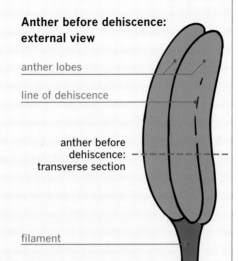

anther lobes

line of dehiscence

anther before dehiscence: transverse section

filament

Anther before dehiscence: transverse section

tapetum

vascular bundle

outer fibrous layer

inner fibrous layer

pollen mother cell (microspore mother cell) dividing by meiosis

line of dehiscence

anther lobes containing pollen sacs

pollen sacs

Anther after dehiscence: transverse section

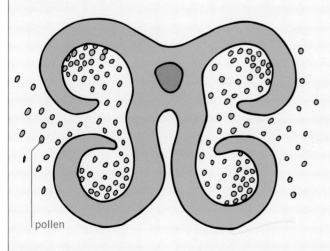

pollen

Anther after dehiscence: external view

anther after dehiscence: transverse section

The male gametes

- *Anthers* are the part of the flower that produce the male *gametes*, which are contained in *pollen*. A special form of cell division called *meiosis* is required for this process.

Gross structure

- A *stamen* consists of an anther fixed on top of a filament. The filament is attached to the stalk of the flower below the ring of female parts.
- The anther itself has four chambers or pollen sacs arranged around the filament. A bundle of vascular tissue carries water and organic materials to the anther to support the developing pollen.

Microscopic structure

- A layer of cells called the tapetum lines the inside of each pollen sac and nourishes the growing pollen grain. Cells from this tapetum pass into the space in the middle of the sac and divide by meiosis to form pollen grains—often in tetrads or groups of four.
- A tissue outside the pollen sac is supplied with fibrous elements that stress the anther as it dries out—an essential part of the mechanism for the release of the mature pollen.
- When the pollen cells are mature, the anther begins to dry out. This causes the cells to shrink as they lose water. This sets up strains in the tissues of the anther walls, which eventually split to release the pollen. This splitting is called *dehiscence*.

Key words

dehiscence	pollen
generative	
nucleus	
haploid	
meiosis	

Pollen development

- *Pollen* develops pollen sacs from cells that undergo *meiosis* to produce *haploid* cells, cells that contain single chromosomes rather than the pairs of chromosomes found in most body cells (see microspore mother cell diagram).
- Since pollen grains are produced by meiosis, each one is unique, with a slightly different genetic makeup than all other grains produced by the plant.
- Pollen grains are microspores—this means they have very little storage material in them—unlike eggs.

Pollen: external structure

- The outer wall of a pollen grain is a tough waterproof structure called the exine. It is often highly sculpted (see bottom diagram).
- A number of pores exist in the exine. The pollen tube that forms during pollen germination grows out of one of these pores.

Pollen: internal structure

- The internal structure of a pollen grain is fairly simple. It is bounded by the intine, or inner wall, and contains two nuclei: the *generative* (sperm) *nucleus* and the tube nucleus.
- The tube nucleus controls the production of a pollen tube (see page 59). This structure grows out through a pore in the exine and passes between the cells of the stigma and style of the carpel.
- The generative nucleus passes down this tube toward the female nucleus found in the ovule. When it unites with the female nucleus, the first cell of the new plant has formed.

Pollen formation

Pollen formation

Anther before dehiscence: transverse section

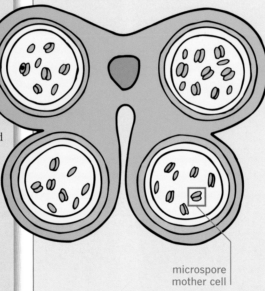

microspore mother cell

Anther after dehiscence: transverse section

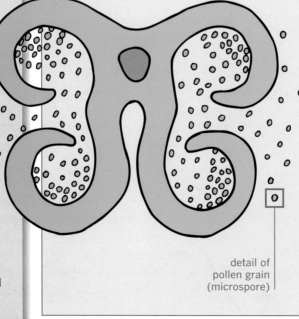

detail of pollen grain (microspore)

Microspore mother cell

First meiotic division produces two cells.

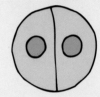

Second meiotic division produces four haploid microspores.

Pollen grains

Detail of pollen grain

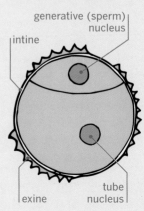

generative (sperm) nucleus

intine

exine

tube nucleus

Pollination

Key words

anther
carpel
pollen
stamen
stigma

Types of pollination

Insect (entomophilous) pollination

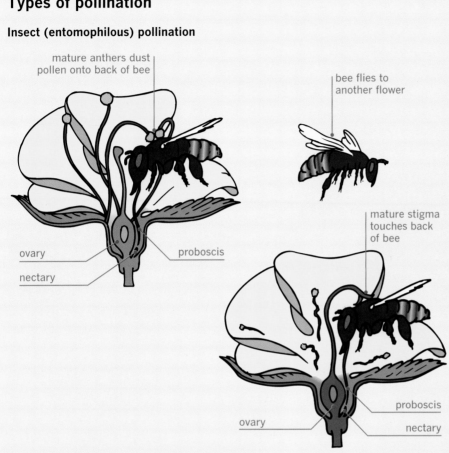

mature anthers dust pollen onto back of bee

bee flies to another flower

mature stigma touches back of bee

ovary

nectary

proboscis

ovary

proboscis

nectary

Wind (anemophilous) pollination

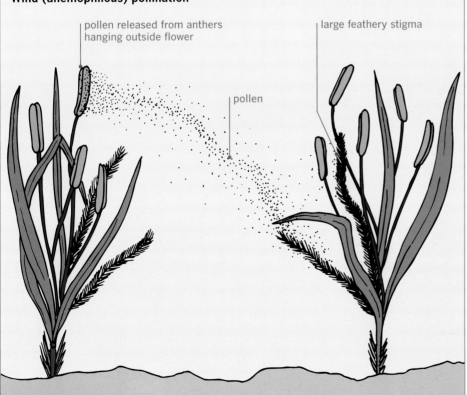

pollen released from anthers hanging outside flower

large feathery stigma

pollen

Types of pollination

- Pollination is the transfer of *pollen* from a male *anther* to a *stigma* of the female *carpel*.
- Pollen is received by the stigma, which arises out of the ovary.
- There are two major forms of pollination: insect pollination and wind pollination.

Insect pollination

- Many insects use their proboscus to collect nectar from flowers for food. Nectar is a solution of sucrose in water produced by glands, called nectaries, at the base of petals.
- While the insect is collecting the nectar, pollen from anthers can be dusted on to its body. When this insect visits another flower looking for nectar, the pollen is transferred to the stigma, thereby pollinating it.
- Insect-pollinated flowers tend to have ostentatious petals, scent, and nectar, and are often highly adapted to attract particular types of insect.

Wind pollination

- Plants that use wind pollination produce extremely large amounts of pollen, which blow onto the stigmas of other plants.
- Wind-pollinated plants tend to have large numbers of inconspicuous flowers with *stamens* and large, feathery stigmas that hang outside of the flower.

Key words

embryo sac	micropyle
endosperm	pollen
fertilization	triploid
gamete	
generative nucleus	

Fertilization and pollination

- Pollination is the transfer of *pollen* from the male anther to the female stigma. *Fertilization* then occurs when the male *gamete* from a pollen grain fuses with the female gamete in the ovule.

Pollen tube development

- Pollen grains contain two nuclei: the tube nucleus and the *generative* (sperm) *nucleus* containing the male gametes. When a pollen grain begins to grow, it forms a pollen tube, which conducts the nuclei from the pollen grain to the *embryo sac*. The tube nucleus controls the growth of the pollen tube.
- The embryo sac is contained within the ovule of the carpel. It is surrounded by thin membranes called integuments, which have a small opening at the bottom called the micropyle. The pollen tube enters the ovule by way of the *micropyle*.

Fertilization

- During the movement of the generative nucleus down the pollen tube, it has divided by mitosis. The pollen tube thus delivers two generative nuclei to the micropyle at the base of the carpel.
- The nuclei pass across into the embryo sac. One of the generative nuclei fuses with the female nucleus in the embryo sac. This will become the first cell of a new plant.
- The other generative nucleus fuses with two polar bodies produced by meiosis to form the endosperm (food storage material) which has a *triploid* number.

Plant fertilization

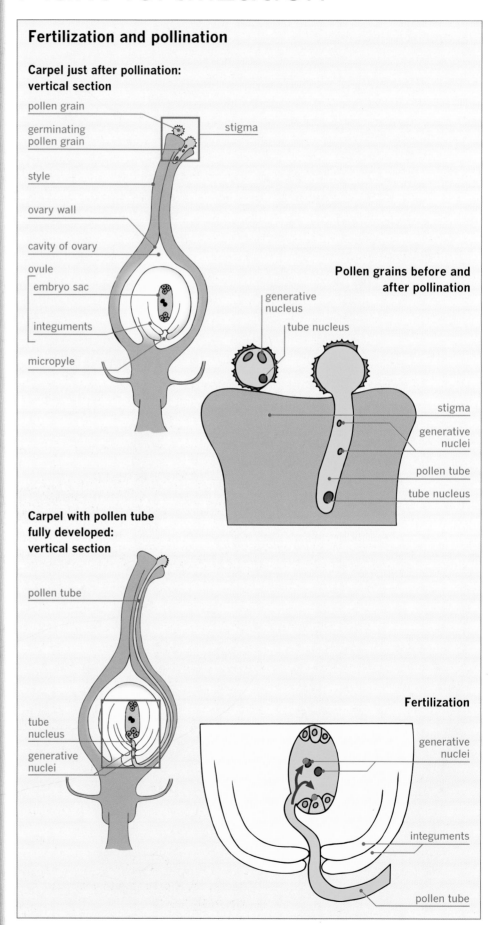

Fertilization and pollination

Carpel just after pollination: vertical section

- pollen grain
- germinating pollen grain
- stigma
- style
- ovary wall
- cavity of ovary
- ovule
- embryo sac
- integuments
- micropyle

Pollen grains before and after pollination

- generative nucleus
- tube nucleus
- stigma
- generative nuclei
- pollen tube
- tube nucleus

Carpel with pollen tube fully developed: vertical section

- pollen tube
- tube nucleus
- generative nuclei

Fertilization

- generative nuclei
- integuments
- pollen tube

Seed development

Key words

embryo sac
generative
  nucleus
zygote

Seed development

Carpel after fertilization: vertical section

Development after fertilization

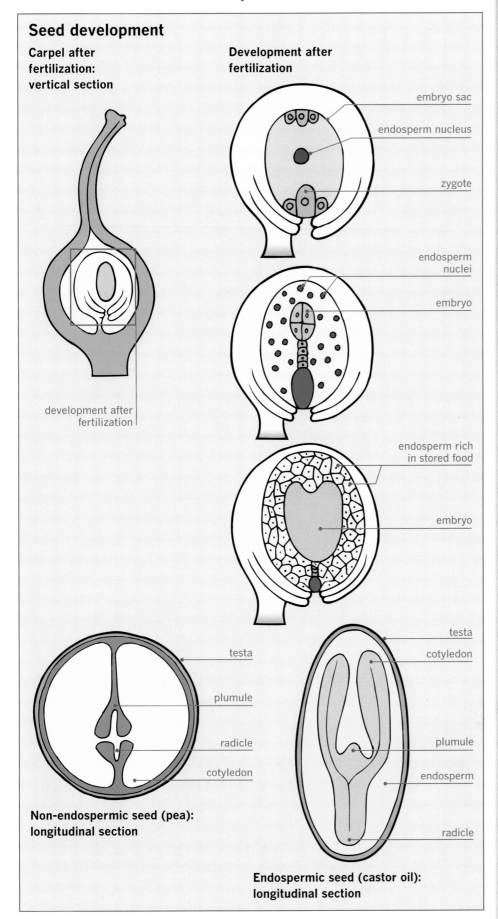

development after fertilization

embryo sac

endosperm nucleus

zygote

endosperm nuclei

embryo

endosperm rich in stored food

embryo

testa

cotyledon

plumule

endosperm

radicle

testa

plumule

radicle

cotyledon

Non-endospermic seed (pea): longitudinal section

Endospermic seed (castor oil): longitudinal section

Seeds and fruit

- The seed develops from the fertilized *embryo sac*. It starts with the *zygote*, which is the first cell of the new individual created when the *generative* (sperm) *nucleus* and the egg nucleus fuse. Repeated division produces a multicelled embryo plant.
- The fruit develops from the remains of the ovary wall. Fruits show many adaptations to aid the dispersal or eventual germination of the seed.

Endospermic seeds

- At fertilization, the pollen tube delivers two generative nuclei (male gametes) to the embryo sac (see page 60). One nucleus fuses with the female nucleus and will become the new plant. The other fuses with the polar bodies and develops into endosperm tissue that acts as a food store for the growing zygote. This endosperm takes up most of the space within the seed.
- As the embryo grows, it will develop two lobes, called cotyledons. These are embryonic leaves that store a large amount of food obtained by digesting and absorbing the endosperm tissue.

- The integuments that had surrounded the embryo sac (see page 60) toughen and become the seed coats (testa) (bottom diagram).
- The developing root is called the radicle and the developing stem the plumule.

Non-endospermic seeds

- In non-endospermic seeds the growing embryo takes up most of the space. The cotyledons become swollen and filled with materials that act as the food store for the growing plant until photosynthesis takes place.

© Diagram Visual Information Ltd.

Key words

epididymis	testis
gamete	vas deferens
seminiferous	
tubule	
spermatozoon	

Anatomy

- The *testes* are the organs that produce sperm, the *gametes* in human males. They also produce the male hormone testosterone. They hang outside the body in the scrotum.

- *Seminiferous tubules* in the testes are lined with cells that divide by meiosis to produce *spermatozoa*. Sperm pass from the testis into a convoluted tube called the *epididymis*, and from there into another tube, the *vas deferens* (sperm duct). A healthy male can produce millions of spermatozoa every day between puberty and old age.

- Sperms are dormant while they are stored in the epididymis and only become active when mixed with secretions from the seminal vesicles along the vas deferens. This seminal fluid combines with the sperm, prostatic fluid from the prostate gland, and mucus secreted by the Cowper's glands to form semen, which is discharged from the urethra during ejaculation.

Ejaculation

- The penis is normally flaccid or soft, but when excited, blood is pumped into it at high pressure making it larger and stiffer. This also allows sperm to pass from the testis to the outside world in an ejaculation.

Human reproductive system: male

Male reproductive system

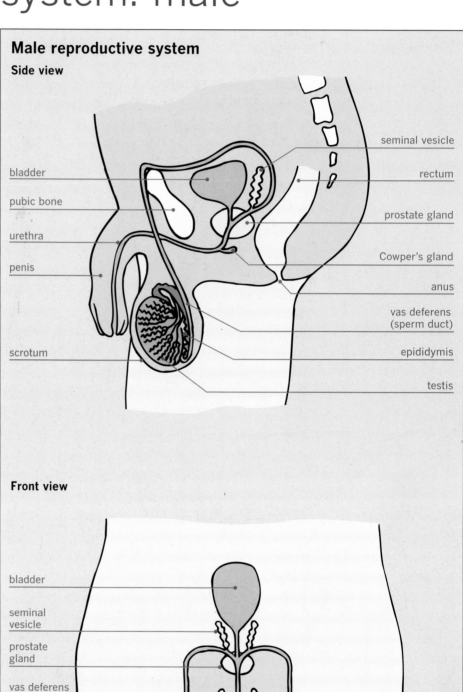

Side view

- bladder
- pubic bone
- urethra
- penis
- scrotum
- seminal vesicle
- rectum
- prostate gland
- Cowper's gland
- anus
- vas deferens (sperm duct)
- epididymis
- testis

Front view

- bladder
- seminal vesicle
- prostate gland
- vas deferens (sperm duct)
- epididymis
- scrotum
- foreskin
- testis

Human reproductive system: female

Key words

cervix
fallopian tube
ovary
uterus

Female reproductive system

Side view

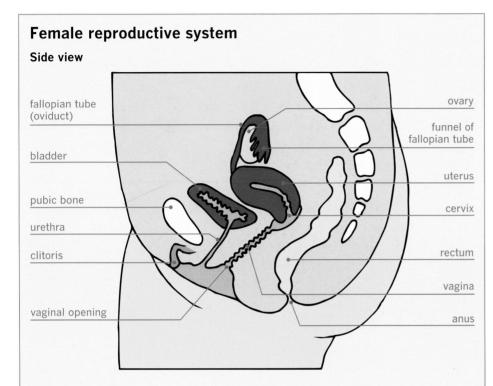

- fallopian tube (oviduct)
- bladder
- pubic bone
- urethra
- clitoris
- vaginal opening
- ovary
- funnel of fallopian tube
- uterus
- cervix
- rectum
- vagina
- anus

Front view

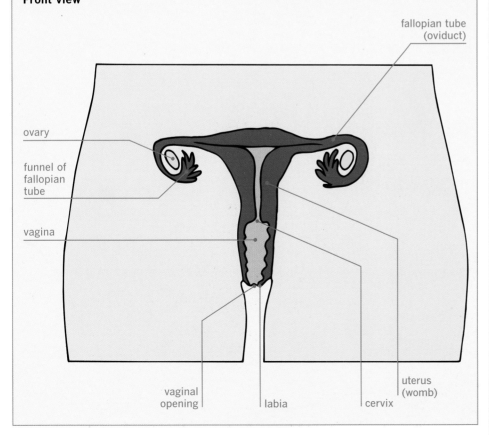

- ovary
- funnel of fallopian tube
- vagina
- fallopian tube (oviduct)
- vaginal opening
- labia
- cervix
- uterus (womb)

Anatomy

- Unlike the male, the organs that produce the gametes in females are found deep inside the body. These are the *ovaries*. There are two of them found above the bladder in the abdominal cavity.
- A tube called a *fallopian tube* (oviduct) connects each ovary to the top of the *uterus*. Eggs produced by the ovaries pass down this tube.
- The uterus is a thick-walled structure sealed by the *cervix* at the lower end. Roughly the shape and size of a small pear when the woman is not pregnant, it can swell to many times this in the final stages of pregnancy.
- The cervix leads from the uterus into the vagina, which connects with the outside world.

External structures

- The external structures of the reproductive system in females are simpler than the male. The opening of the vagina is bounded by a number of flaps of tissue called the labia. The clitoris is an area that is particularly sensitive.
- The bladder connects to the outside via the urethra in this area as well.

Key words

epididymis
seminiferous
 tubule
spermatozoon
testis

Testis anatomy

- *Seminiferous tubules* are very long tubes found in the *testes* of male mammals. They all drain into the *epididymis*, which is a wider, convoluted tube that rests on the back edge of the testis. Mature but inactive *spermatozoa* are stored here until they are passed out of the body through the vas deferens and urethra during an ejaculation.
- Seminiferous tubules have a space in the middle where growing spermatozoa can develop and mature. Between these tubules are other tissues (Leydig cells) that nourish them and produce the hormone testosterone, which maintains the secondary sexual characteristics of males (facial hair, etc.).

Sperm production

- Sperm production is affected by temperature and is most effective at slightly below body temperature—which is why the testes hang outside the body.
- Studies have suggested that many males are producing less sperm than previous generations. The wearing of tight pants and underwear that hold the testes close to the body has been suggested as a cause of this change. Another possible cause is the presence in the environment of pollutants that are similar to female hormones.

Spermatogenesis: testis

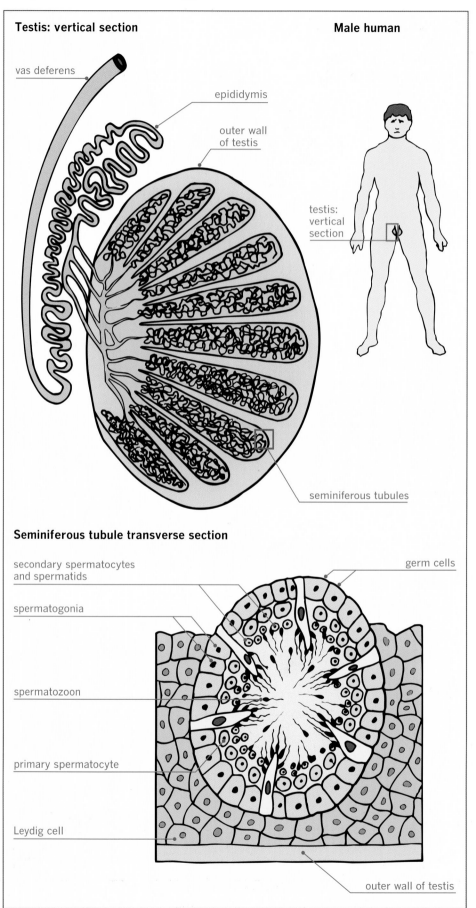

Testis: vertical section

Male human

vas deferens

epididymis

outer wall of testis

testis: vertical section

seminiferous tubules

Seminiferous tubule transverse section

secondary spermatocytes and spermatids

spermatogonia

spermatozoon

primary spermatocyte

Leydig cell

germ cells

outer wall of testis

Spermatogenesis: sperm

Spermatogenesis: schematic

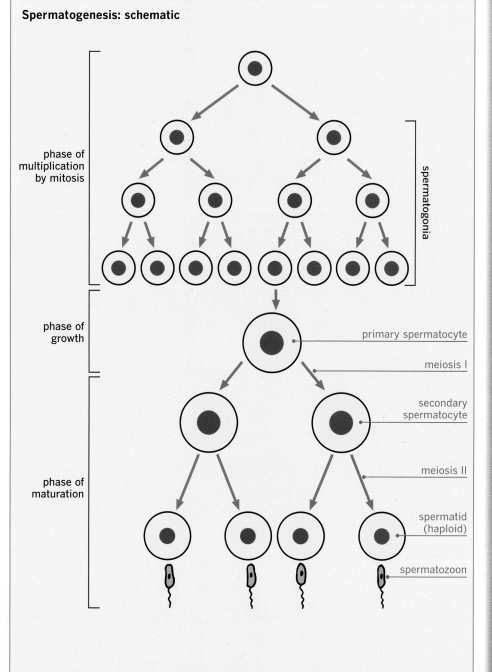

phase of multiplication by mitosis

spermatogonia

phase of growth

primary spermatocyte

meiosis I

phase of maturation

secondary spermatocyte

meiosis II

spermatid (haploid)

spermatozoon

Spermatozoon

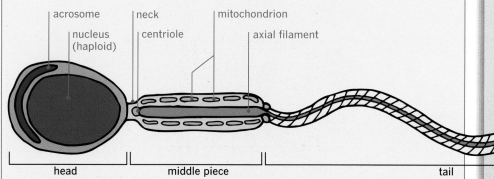

acrosome

nucleus (haploid)

neck

centriole

mitochondrion

axial filament

tail sheath

head   middle piece   tail

Sperm formation

- Spermatogenesis is the name given to the process of producing sperm.
- Cells lining the *seminiferous tubules* in the testes divide in the first instance by *mitosis* to form spermatogonia. These then develop into cells called primary spermatocytes.
- A single primary spermatocyte divides by *meiosis* to produce four *haploid* cells called *spermatids*.
- The spermatids mature into *spermatozoa*—the male gametes— by growing a tail and reducing the amount of cytoplasm surrounding the nucleus to a minimum. The spermatozoa are stored in the center of the seminiferous tubules and *epididymis* until released (see page 64).

Sperm structure

- Spermatozoa consist of a single haploid nucleus in the head with a tail behind it that can move and so propel the sperm toward the ovum produced by the female.
- The acrosome at the front of the head contains a package of *enzymes* that are able to digest the outer skin of the egg, thereby allowing the nucleus to pass into the cell.
- A collection of *mitochondria* surround the filaments of the tail in the middle part of the spermatozoa. These provide energy in the form of ATP, which allows the tail to thrash sideways to drive the sperm forward.

Key words

gamete	ovary
germ cell	ovum
meiosis	primary oocyte
mitosis	secondary oocyte
oogonium	

Oogenesis

- Oogenesis is the name given to the process by which *ova* are formed.
- Human females produce eggs regularly, roughly every 30 days, from puberty to menopause. All of these eggs develop from *germ cells* (*gametes*) in the two *ovaries*.
- Germ cells initially divide by *mitosis* to produce *oogonia*, cells that develop into *primary oocytes* (immature ova). At a woman's birth, there are hundreds of thousands of primary oocytes present in the ovarian tissues.

Meiotic division

- The next stage in the process is the production of *secondary oocytes* by *meiosis*. These cells are haploid—they have half the chromosomes of their parent cells. One of these haploid cells will develop into the ovum; the other three will be enclosed within the vitelline membrane surrounding this cell.
- The ovum is a large cell with a good supply of cytoplasm that helps to act as a food store for the first few critical days of development.
- The other nuclei become the polar bodies, redundant cells that remain much smaller than the ovum.
- The vitelline membrane can be digested by enzymes in the acrosome of the sperm to allow the sperm nucleus to enter. Once one sperm has entered, the membrane is modified to prevent entry of other nuclei.
- Around the outside of the vitelline membrane is a clear area of mucilage called the zona pellucida.

Oogenesis: meiotic division

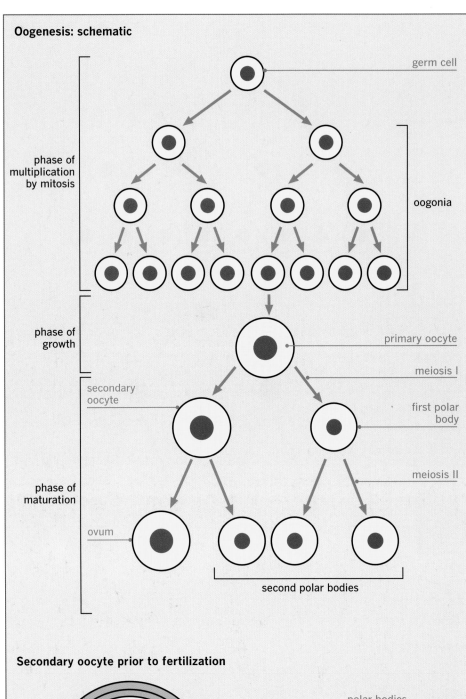

Oogenesis: schematic

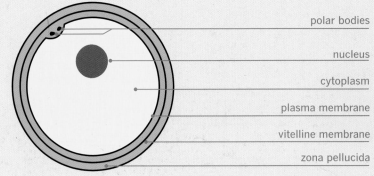

Secondary oocyte prior to fertilization

Oogenesis: ovarian cycle

Human female

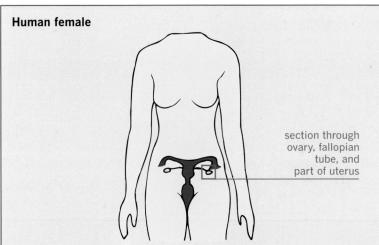

section through ovary, fallopian tube, and part of uterus

Maturation of Graafian follicle inside human ovary: schematic

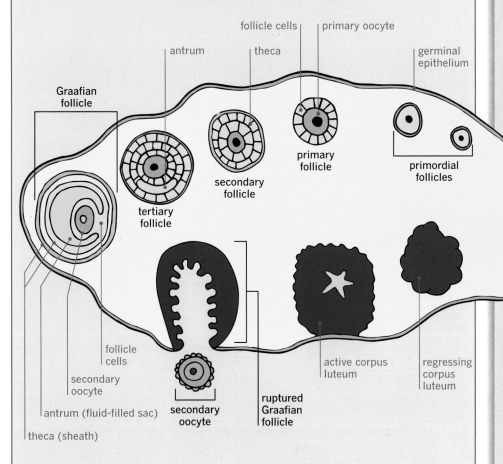

Key words

fallopian tube	uterus
hormone	
ovary	
ovum	
pituitary gland	

The ovarian cycle

- The production of human eggs is controlled by *hormones*. These act on tissues in the *ovaries* to switch on processes that, in turn, produce hormones that regulate the cycle.
- Hormones produced by the *pituitary gland* in the brain cause the development of primordial follicles into primary follicles. These go through various stages until a mature Graafian follicle is formed.
- A Graafian follicle contains a mature *ovum*, and it moves to the edge of the ovary where it ruptures to release the ovum and form a yellow body called the corpus luteum. The egg passes down the *fallopian tube* toward the *uterus*.
- The corpus luteum produces a hormone called progesterone, which prevents development of further ova.
- If the egg is fertilized and the woman becomes pregnant, the corpus luteum lasts for up to four months. If no pregnancy occurs, it degenerates after about two weeks. Hormones from the pituitary cause the maturation of another follicle, and the whole process begins again.

The ovarian cycle
Follicular phase: days 1–14.
Primordial follicles develop into primary and then secondary follicles; these secrete the hormone estrogen. Development proceeds through the tertiary follicle to the Graafian follicle.

Ovulation
The Graafian follicle ruptures, releasing the secondary oocyte.
Luteal phase: days 14–28.
The corpus luteum is formed from the ruptured follicle. It secretes the hormones progesterone and estrogen, finally shrinking to become a scar.

© Diagram Visual Information Ltd.

Key words

cervix
semen
uterus

Preparing for coitus

- Coitus, or sexual intercourse, occurs when a man inserts his erect penis into the vagina of a woman. The penis is kept erect by blood that floods into spongy tissue in the penis at high pressure.
- As sperm is released, it is mixed with secretions from the seminal vesicles, prostate, and Cowper's glands (see page 62) to produce *semen*. Semen is a mixture of sperm and a liquid containing sugar that gives the sperm energy to swim.
- At the same time, the walls of the vagina produce secretions that help to lubricate the penis.

Intercourse

- The man inserts his penis into the woman's vagina. The head of the penis reaches near the *cervix*, which is the base of the *uterus* projecting slightly into the vagina.
- The male climax (the orgasm) occurs when semen containing sperm is forcefully ejected from the penis into the vagina. The female climax produces increased secretions from the vagina as well as contractions of the uterus and vagina.

Conception

- Conception occurs when a spermatozoon fuses with the egg. This must occur in the fallopian tubes. Consequently, sperm must swim from the vagina up through the uterus.

Sexual intercourse

Human sexual intercourse

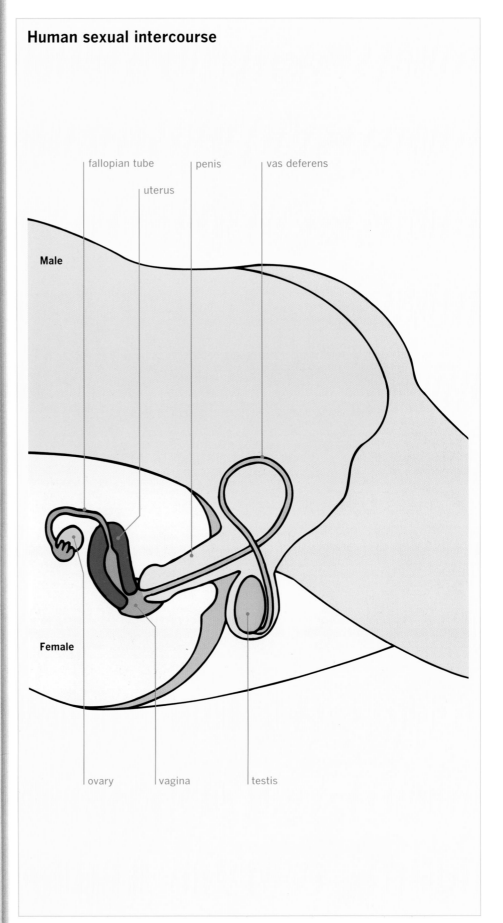

fallopian tube   penis   vas deferens

uterus

Male

Female

ovary   vagina   testis

Human fertilization

Key words

cervix
fertilization
mitosis
sperm
zygote

Female human

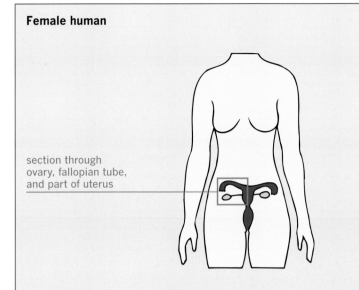

section through ovary, fallopian tube, and part of uterus

Section through ovary, fallopian tube, and part of uterus

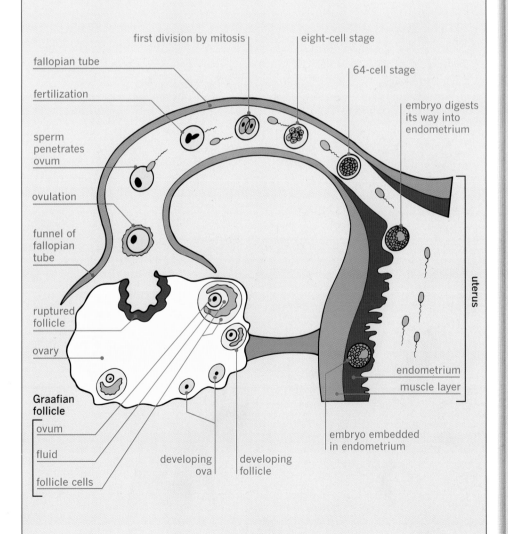

first division by mitosis

eight-cell stage

64-cell stage

fallopian tube

fertilization

embryo digests its way into endometrium

sperm penetrates ovum

ovulation

funnel of fallopian tube

ruptured follicle

ovary

Graafian follicle

ovum

fluid

follicle cells

developing ova

developing follicle

embryo embedded in endometrium

uterus

endometrium

muscle layer

Site of fertilization

- During intercourse *sperm* is deposited in the vagina at the *cervix*, the entrance to the uterus.
- *Fertilization* must occur high up in the fallopian tube so that the ovum can divide by *mitosis* before it attaches itself to the uterus.
- The sperm must swim up through the uterus to reach this point. Chemical gradients guide the sperm towards the egg. This must occur within 72 hours of ejaculation, or the sperm will be non-viable.

Egg formation

- The egg is released when the Graafian follicle, the fluids-filled vesicle within the ovary containing the ovum, ruptures at the surface of the ovary. The funnel of the fallopian tube guides the egg into the tube where it starts its journey downward.

Fertilization

- The nucleus from one sperm penetrates the egg and fuses with the egg nucleus to form the first cell of the *zygote*. This then divides repeatedly by mitosis to form a pair of cells and then again to form a ball of eight cells and so on. By the time a 64-cell ball has been formed, it enters the uterus.
- This ball of cells then has to embed itself in the endometrium, the wall of the uterus. Further development can then occur.

© Diagram Visual Information Ltd.

Key words

contraception
embryo
fallopian tube
gamete
vas deferens

Types of contraception

- Contraception covers all of the technologies that prevent a viable *embryo* from forming or surviving.
- There are three main types of contraception: barrier methods, sterilization, and the intrauterine device.

Barrier methods

- Barrier methods prevent viable sperm from meeting a viable egg.
- A condom is a thin membrane of latex that fits over the erect penis. The sperm cannot pass through this barrier, and the penis and condom are removed from the vagina after ejaculation.
- The diaphragm is a rubber cap that fits over the cervix and prevents sperm entering. The diaphragm must be left in place after intercourse for some time.

Sterilization

- Sterilization prevents viable *gametes* from meeting by cutting the tubes carrying them from the gonads (testes or ovary) to the opposite gender. Male sterilization cuts the *vas deferens*. Female sterilization cuts the *fallopian tubes*. Sterilization is effectively permanent.

Intrauterine devices (IUDs)

- Intrauterine devices, sometimes called coils, prevent fertilized eggs from embedding in the endometrium. Once fitted, IUDs normally remain in place for months or years.

Contraception

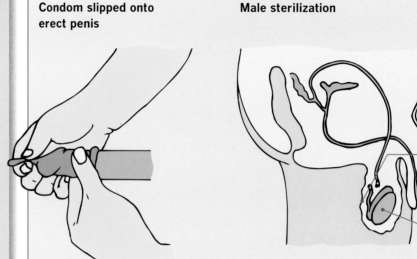

Condom slipped onto erect penis

Male sterilization

vas deferens

testis

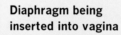
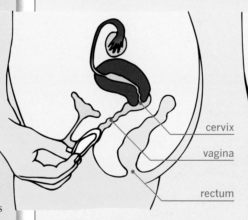

Diaphragm being inserted into vagina

cervix

vagina

rectum

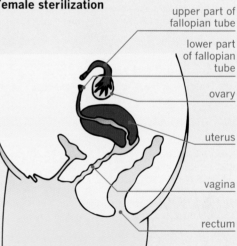

Female sterilization

upper part of fallopian tube

lower part of fallopian tube

ovary

uterus

vagina

rectum

Diaphragm in place

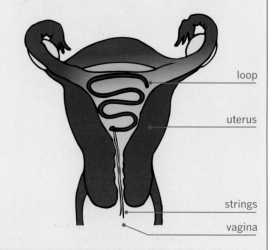

Intrauterine device

loop

uterus

strings

vagina

Twins

Key words

embryo
genotype
ovary

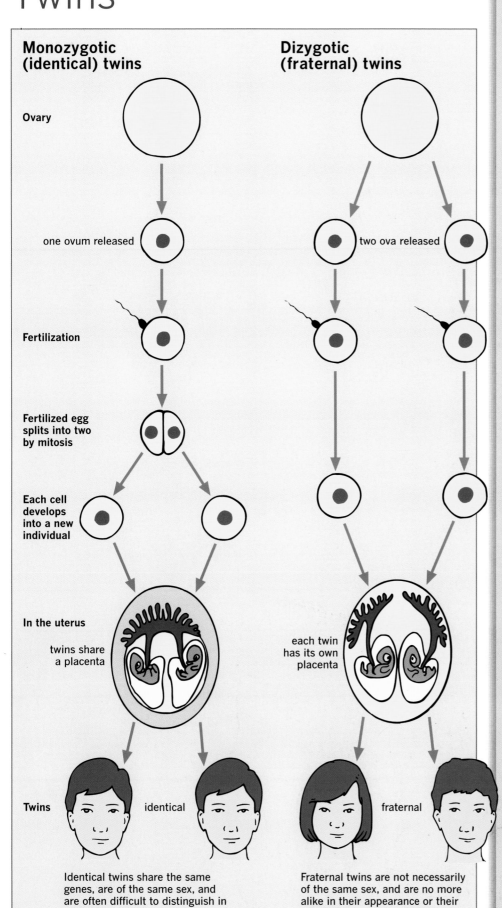

Monozygotic (identical) twins

Ovary

one ovum released

Fertilization

Fertilized egg splits into two by mitosis

Each cell develops into a new individual

In the uterus

twins share a placenta

Twins — identical

Identical twins share the same genes, are of the same sex, and are often difficult to distinguish in their appearance.

Dizygotic (fraternal) twins

two ova released

each twin has its own placenta

fraternal

Fraternal twins are not necessarily of the same sex, and are no more alike in their appearance or their genes than ordinary siblings.

Types of twins

- There are two types of twins: fraternal or dizygotic twins and identical or monozygotic twins.
- Other forms of multiple births (triplets, quads etc.) fall into the same two categories.

Identical twins

- Sometimes a fertilized ovum splits by mitosis into two cells, each of which develops into a separate *embryo*.
- Since identical twins come from the same egg and sperm, they are genetically identical.
- Identical twins are much rarer than fraternal twins and are always the same gender. Fertility treatments do not increase the chances of identical twins.

Fraternal twins

- Sometimes more than one egg is released from the *ovaries* at the same time. If all of these eggs are fertilized, more than one embryo can be formed.
- Since fraternal twins (and other multiple births) develop from separate eggs and sperms, they have different *genotypes* (genetic combinations) and are only as similar as other brothers or sisters of the same age from the same parents.
- Fraternal twins can be different genders. Some modern fertility treatments increase the rate of multiple egg production and so are more likely to produce multiple births.

Key words

amnion
fetus
placenta

Fetal development

The first trimester

- The first trimester covers the first three months after conception. Most of the key structures are laid down during this period.
- Teratogenic chemicals (chemicals that produce birth deformities) are most dangerous during this time.
- By the end of the first trimester the *fetus* can be recognized as male or female. It has a well-developed *placenta* linking it to the mother. The fluid-filled sac called the *amnion* has formed and surrounds the growing fetus with a bag of waters to protect it from mechanical damage. The fetus will be about 3 inches (80 mm) long by the end of this stage.

The second trimester

- Development continues during the second trimester, and by 20 weeks the fetus is able to produce digestive enzymes and move itself. Mothers will feel kicks from the baby by this stage.

The third trimester

- During the third trimester the fetus continues to grow in size. Most of the key body parts have developed by this stage, and babies born during this time can normally survive outside the mother, although they will be small and will need special care.
- By the end of the third trimester, the baby is ready to be born. It will now weigh approximately 7 or 8 pounds (3–4 kg). The placenta will weigh almost as much.

**Fetus at 6 weeks
0.5 inches (12 mm)**

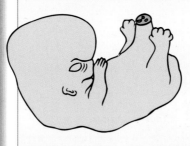

Uterus at 6 weeks

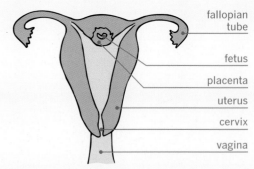

fallopian tube

fetus

placenta

uterus

cervix

vagina

**Fetus at 10 weeks
2.4 inches (60 mm)**

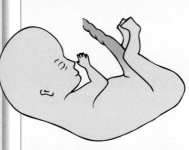

Uterus at 10 weeks

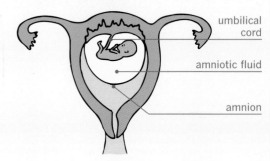

umbilical cord

amniotic fluid

amnion

Uterus at 20 weeks

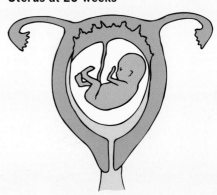

**Fetus at 20 weeks
9.8 inches (250 mm)**

Full-term fetus

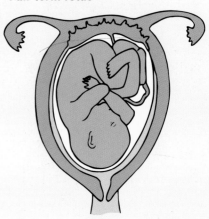

Placenta

Key words

amnion	villus
fetus	
placenta	
umbilical cord	
uterus	

Fetus in the uterus

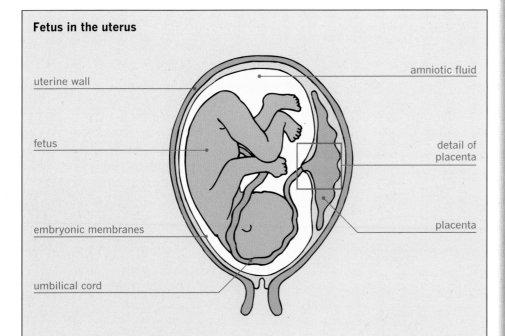

uterine wall

amniotic fluid

fetus

detail of placenta

embryonic membranes

placenta

umbilical cord

Detail of placenta

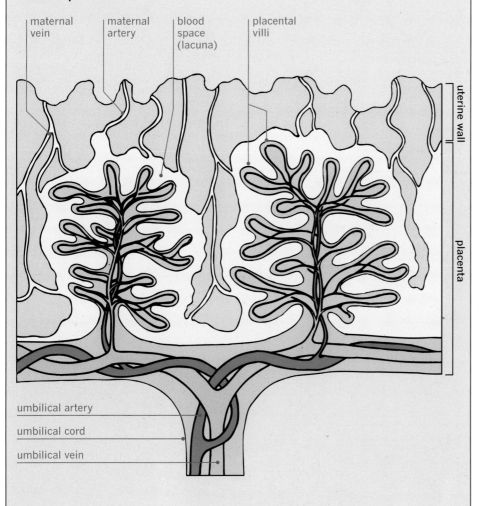

maternal vein

maternal artery

blood space (lacuna)

placental villi

uterine wall

placenta

umbilical artery

umbilical cord

umbilical vein

Source of the placenta

- The *placenta* is an organ that develops from cells from the *fetus* and the wall of the *uterus*. Despite this, the blood supplies and cells of fetus and mother are kept separate, although chemicals can pass easily across the barrier.

Function of the placenta

- The placenta supplies the growing fetus with oxygen and food, and removes waste products such as carbon dioxide.
- The placenta allows this exchange but also keeps the fetus and mother separate—they are separate individuals. If cells leak across the barrier, they will produce a rapid and potentially fatal immune response.

Structure of the placenta

- The placenta connects the fetus to the mother by the *umbilical cord*, which contains an artery and a vein.
- The *amnion* is a structure created by the placenta that covers the fetus in a bag of amniotic fluid. When this bursts—the waters break—it is a sign that the birth is close.
- Blood from the mother fills large spaces called lacunae, *villi* from the fetus penetrate. This gives a very large surface area across which exchange takes place while keeping the blood from each individual separate.

Key words

cervix
fetus
uterus

Presentation of the fetus

- The head is the heaviest part of the *fetus*, and toward the end of pregnancy it will fall to rest against the inside of the *cervix*. The dropping of the head into this position is visible as the mother's shape changes slightly.
- During the late stages of pregnancy, the mother will also start to feel contractions. These are muscle movements in the *uterus* wall as it prepares to expel the baby.

Labor

- The stage prior to birth is called labor. It can last from as little as an hour to a few days. Labor extending beyond 48 hours is a sign of potential problems.
- During labor the waters break (this is the bursting of the amniotic membrane), and the cervix begins to open or dilate.

Birth

- When the baby is ready to be born, the cervix is dilated sufficiently to let the head pass through. The baby's head will rotate slightly to fit more easily through the cervix.
- After the head and shoulders have passed through the cervix, the rest of the body normally follows quickly.
- The last stage is the delivery of the placenta, which typically follows moments after the baby's birth.

Birth

First stage of labor

1 Cervix starts to flatten

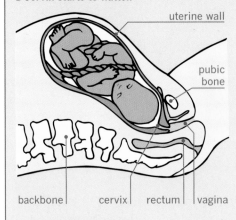

2 Cervix flattens completely

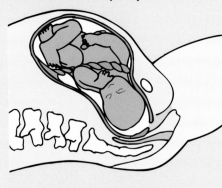

3 Cervix partially opens

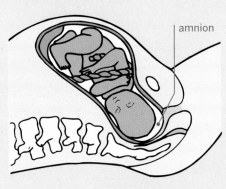

4 Cervix fully opens; amnion breaks

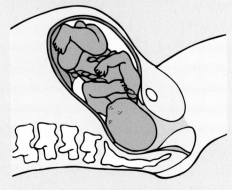

Second stage of labor

5 Head rotates

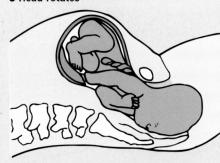

6 Head is born, shoulders and rest of body follow

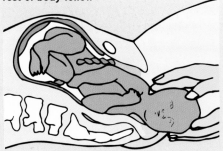

Third stage of labor

7 Delivery of placenta

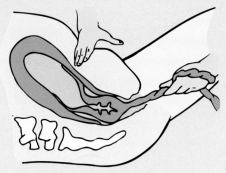

Variation

Key words

continuous
  variation
discontinuous
  variation

Height in human males as an example of continuous variation

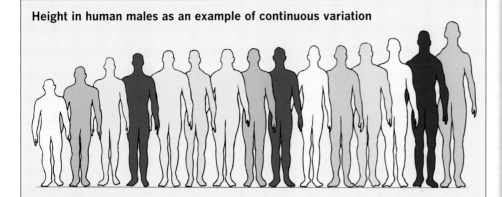

Bar graph of continous variation in height

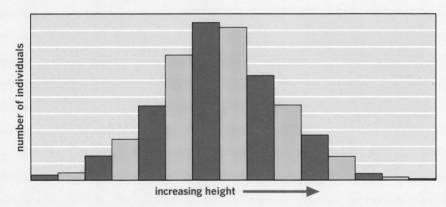

number of individuals

increasing height

Discontinuous variation in humans

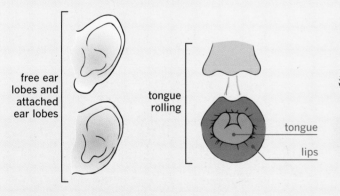

free ear lobes and attached ear lobes

tongue rolling

tongue

lips

female and male

Discontinuous variation in peas

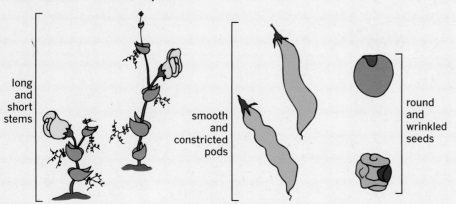

long and short stems

smooth and constricted pods

round and wrinkled seeds

Types of variation

- The term "variation" is used to describe differences between members of the same species.
- There are two types of variation: continuous and discontinuous.

Continuous variation

- Height and weight are examples of *continuous variation*. This type of variation is produced by the action of multiple genes, and there are no clear groups or classes to put individuals into. Individuals in a population show a complete spectrum of values between two extremes.
- To investigate continuous variation, biologists assign classes to the data, e.g., all values between 60 and 64 inches in height, values between 64 and 68 inches etc. The frequency of individuals within these arbitrary classes can be plotted.

Discontinuous variation

- Eye and hair color in mammals, ability to roll the tongue or taste certain chemicals in humans, and flower color in peas are examples of *discontinuous variation*. Discontinuous variation is produced by the action of single or a small number of genes.
- Discontinuous variation can easily be sorted into groups or classes and can be displayed by histograms.

Key words

dominant
genotype
homozygous
phenotype
recessive

Monohybrid crosses

- A monohybrid cross is a cross between two organisms that differ by only one inherited characteristic controlled by a single gene with two forms.
- The *genotype* is the combination of genes in an organism. The *phenotype* is the physical characteristics of an organism produced by the expression of its genotype.
- In certain types of pea, the height of the adult plant, one aspect of its phenotype, is controlled by a single gene with two forms: tall and short.
- If an organism has two forms of the same gene at the same time, the *dominant* form is expressed. The *recessive* form is present but not visible in the adult form of the plant.

First generation (F₁)

- Pure (*homozygous*) breeding plants of the two forms (tall and short) are crossed. The seeds produced by this cross are then collected and sown to produce the first generation or F₁.
- All of the plants in the F₁ generation are tall. This shows that the tall gene is dominant to the short gene.

Second generation (F₂)

- If the F₁ plants are allowed to self-pollinate and the seeds produce plants, the plants produced are the F₂.
- The ratio of tall:short plants in the F₂ generation is 3:1.
- The genotypes TT, Tt, tT all produce tall plants because a dominant tall gene is present. Only the tt genotype produces a short plant. This explains why tall plants are three times more likely than short plants.

Monohybrid cross: peas

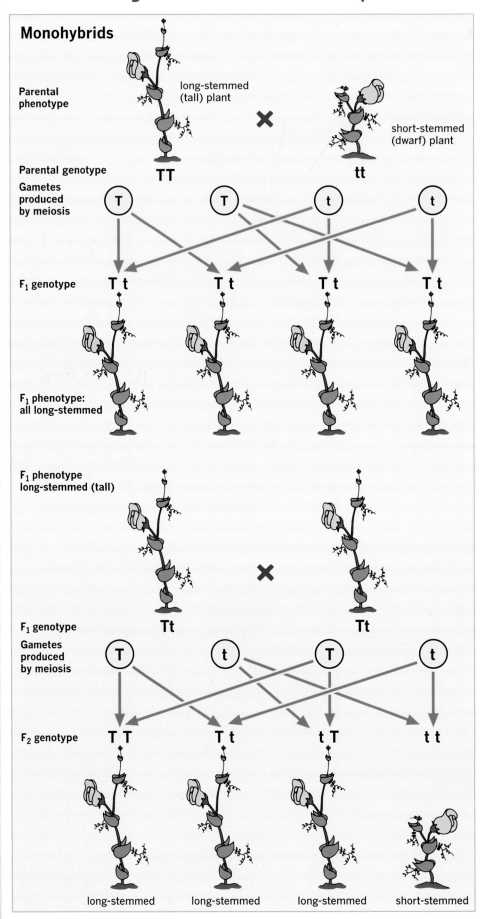

Dihybrid cross: guinea pigs

Key words

allele
dominant
genotype
phenotype

Dihybrids

The F₁ guinea pigs have two different alleles for each of the two characters (i.e., coat color and coat length) symbolized as BbSs. They are said to be dihybrids.

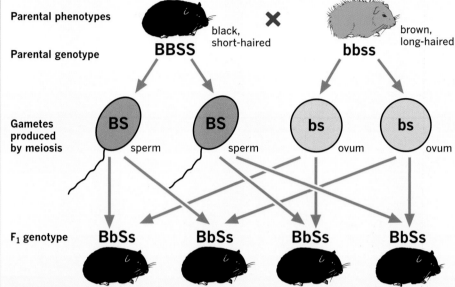

Parental phenotypes — black, short-haired × brown, long-haired

Parental genotype — BBSS × bbss

Gametes produced by meiosis — BS (sperm), BS (sperm), bs (ovum), bs (ovum)

F₁ genotype — BbSs, BbSs, BbSs, BbSs

F₁ phenotype: all black, short-haired

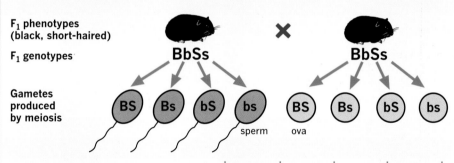

F₁ phenotypes (black, short-haired)

F₁ genotypes — BbSs × BbSs

Gametes produced by meiosis — BS, Bs, bS, bs (sperm); BS, Bs, bS, bs (ova)

Punnett square showing possible offspring in the F₂ generation

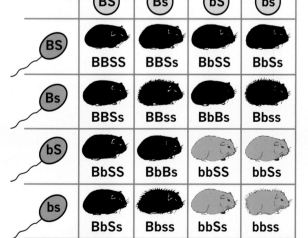

	BS	Bs	bS	bs
BS	BBSS	BBSs	BbSS	BbSs
Bs	BBSs	BBss	BbSs	Bbss
bS	BbSS	BbSs	bbSS	bbSs
bs	BbSs	Bbss	bbSs	bbss

F₂ phenotype ratios

9 : 3 : 3 : 1

black, short-haired : black, long-haired : brown, short-haired : brown, long-haired

Dihybrid crosses

- Dihybrid crosses are crosses that look at the inheritance of two independent characteristics, each of which is controlled by a single gene that exists in two forms.
- The coat of guinea pigs is controlled by two genes: black/brown color and long/short length.

First generation (F₁)

- In the first generation the *phenotype* was entirely black short-haired guinea pigs. This shows that black is *dominant* to brown and short is dominant to long hair.

Second generation (F₂)

- When the F₁ generation was allowed to cross breed, the F₂ *genotypes* were in the ratio 9:3:3:1 of black, short-haired:black, long-haired:brown, short-haired:brown, long-haired.
- The distribution of genotypes showed that the genes were inherited independently, with the rules for monohybrid crosses, which look at one characteristic, operating on each gene pair separately.

Key words

allele	phenotype
dominant	
genotype	
heterozygous	
homozygous	

Dominance

- Genes exist in pairs. Where both members (*alleles*) of the pairs are the same, the individual is said to be *homozygous*. If the two alleles are different, the individual is said to be *heterozygous*.
- In heterozygous individuals, one allele is usually *dominant* and the other is recessive. This means that when a single dominant allele is present, the *phenotype* produced will be identical to that of an individual with two dominant alleles. In effect, the recessive allele is hidden and can only be detected by breeding with another heterozygous organism.
- In codominance, the differing alleles both have an effect on the phenotype.

Coat color in shorthorns

- Coat color in shorthorn cattle is controlled by a single pair of genes that show codominance.
- Cattle that breed true for red coats have the *genotype* RR. Cattle that breed true for white coats have the genotype WW.
- If an RR individual is crossed with a WW individual, the F_1 will be RW. Both genes are expressed, giving a roan coat with red and white hairs in it.
- Crossing the RW individuals produces an F_2 with the ratio 1 red:2 roan:1 white. The red and white coats are homozygous, while the roans are heterozygous.

Codominance

Codominance and coat color

- The F_1 phenotype is intermediate with respect to the parental phenotypes.
- Neither parental allele (R or W) can exert its dominance over the other.

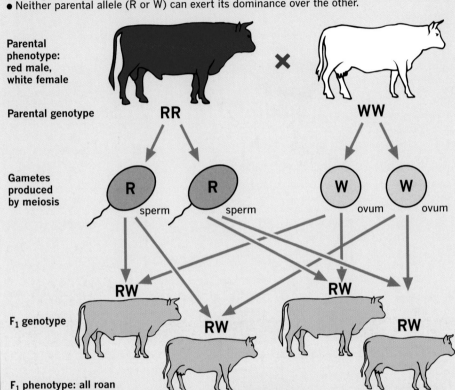

Parental phenotype: red male, white female

Parental genotype RR × WW

Gametes produced by meiosis — R sperm, R sperm, W ovum, W ovum

F_1 genotype RW RW RW RW

F_1 phenotype: all roan

- Shorthorns with two identical alleles (i.e., RR or WW) have coats with solid red or white, respectively.
- Their progeny (the F_1 individuals) have dissimilar alleles (i.e., RW), and have a phenotype that is intermediate with respect to the parental phenotypes.
- Their coat has white hairs intermingled with the colored hairs, giving a roan appearance.
- Mating between F_1 individuals can bring the parental alleles together in certain offspring, and so the solid coat color reappears.

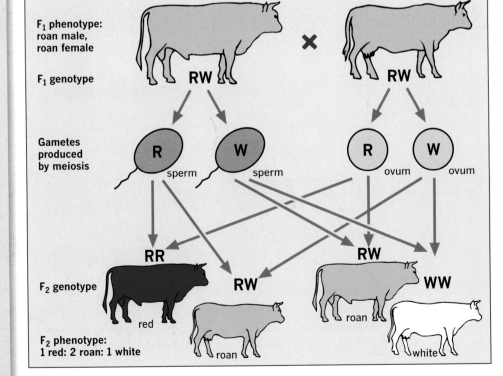

F_1 phenotype: roan male, roan female

F_1 genotype RW × RW

Gametes produced by meiosis — R sperm, W sperm, R ovum, W ovum

F_2 genotype RR RW RW WW

F_2 phenotype: 1 red: 2 roan: 1 white

red   roan   roan   white

Karyotype preparation

Karyotype preparation

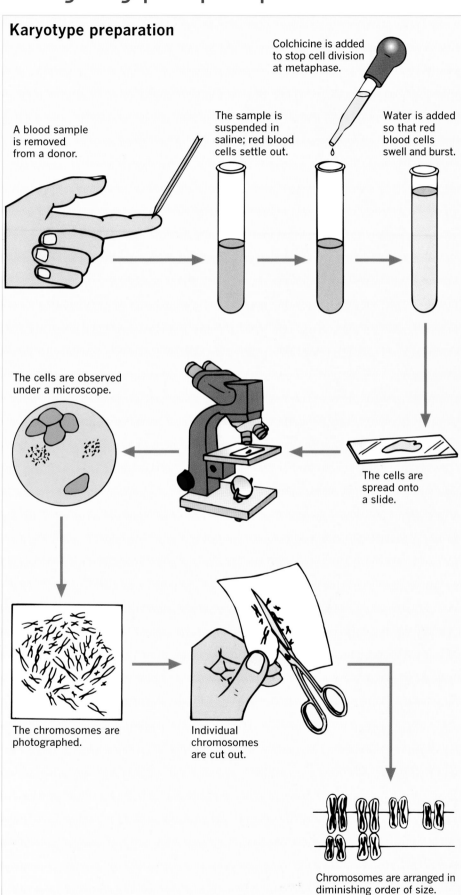

Colchicine is added to stop cell division at metaphase.

A blood sample is removed from a donor.

The sample is suspended in saline; red blood cells settle out.

Water is added so that red blood cells swell and burst.

The cells are spread onto a slide.

The cells are observed under a microscope.

The chromosomes are photographed.

Individual chromosomes are cut out.

Chromosomes are arranged in diminishing order of size.

Key words

chromosome
diploid
karyotype
metaphase

Karyotypes

- The *karyotype* is a picture of the physical form of the *chromosomes* found in normal body cells in a species.
- Karyotypes usually show pairs of chromosomes corresponding to the *diploid* number for the species. The diploid number is the number of chromosomes in a normal cell. Where organisms have more than two sets of chromosomes (e.g., wheat plants have six), the karyotype is more complicated.

Colchicine

- After a sample of *metaphase* cells (usually blood cells) has been extracted from an organism, it is poisoned with colchicine. Colchicine interferes with cell division, causing it to stop at metaphase, when all of the chromosomes are visible.
- The poisoned cells are broken open and placed on a slide—often with a dye to stain the chromosomes to make them easier to see.

Sorting the karyotype

- A microscope with a camera attachment is used to photograph a selection of cells that show the chromosomes.
- The photograph is cut up so that the chromosomes spread randomly within a dividing cell can be arranged in pairs on a piece of paper. Only one cell is used to create the karyotype, but photographs of other cells can provide useful extra information if some of the chromosomes are overlapping and obscuring each other.

Key words

centromere
chromatid
chromosome
karyotype

Chromosomes

- *Chromosomes* are structures made of DNA and protein. They are normally invisible in the cell but shorten and thicken during cell division to become visible as small X-shaped bodies.
- The "limbs" of the X are called *chromatids*. The point where they join, the center of the X, is called the *centromere*.

Human karyotype

- A *karyotype* is a picture of the chromosomes as they appear during cell division. Karyotypes are normally arranged to show similar chromosomes in groups or series.
- The human karyotype shows 22 pairs of chromosomes and one "pair" that consists of two chromosomes that are the same in females (XX) but slightly different in males (XY).
- The "pair" of chromosomes that are different in males and females are called the sex chromosomes and deal with the inheritance of gender in humans. All of the chromosomes that are not sex chromosomes are called autosomes.

Human chromosomes

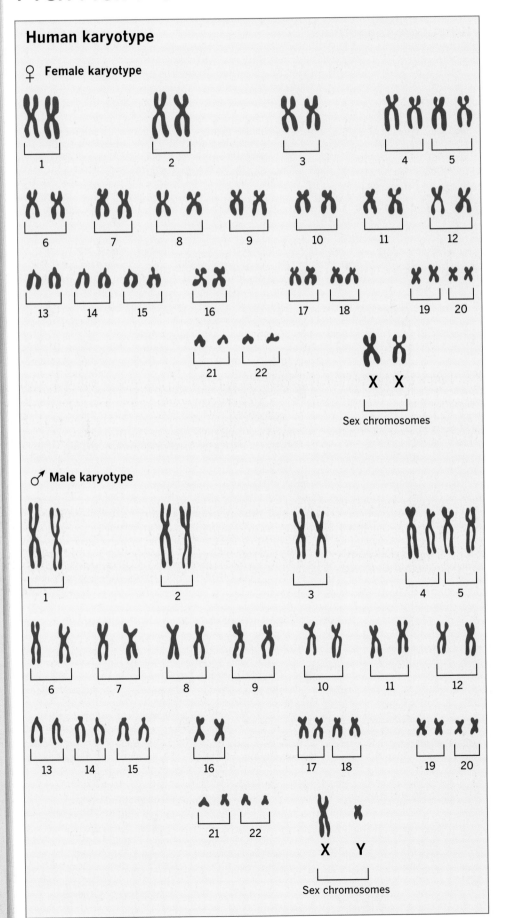

Human karyotype

♀ Female karyotype

♂ Male karyotype

Human sex inheritance

Key words

chromosome
gamete
genotype
phenotype

Sex inheritance

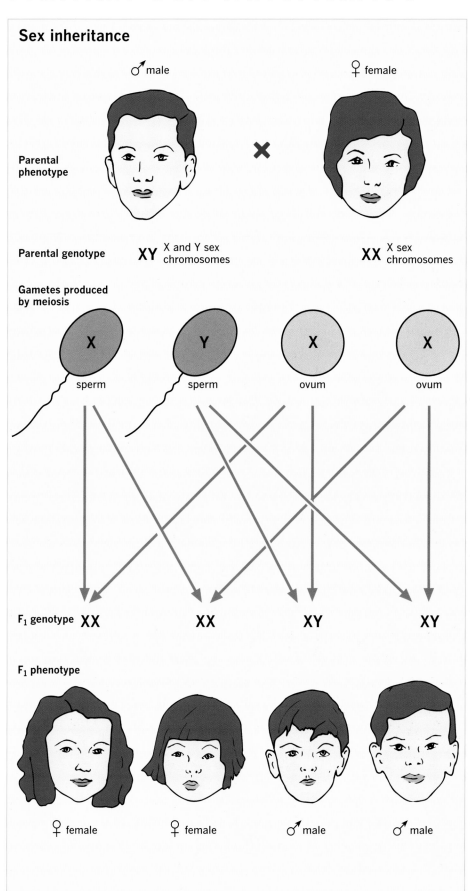

Parental phenotype

♂ male ✕ ♀ female

Parental genotype XY X and Y sex chromosomes XX X sex chromosomes

Gametes produced by meiosis

X sperm Y sperm X ovum X ovum

F₁ genotype XX XX XY XY

F₁ phenotype

♀ female ♀ female ♂ male ♂ male

Sexual characteristics

- There are many characteristics that define "maleness." Some are structures that are not present in females, e.g., penis, testes. Some are slight differences in structures that exist in both genders, e.g., facial hair.
- Such a large package of characteristics cannot be controlled by a single gene. However, all of these characteristics are inherited as a package that implies they are linked together in some way.

The sex chromosomes

- One pair of *chromosomes* is different in males and females. These are the sex chromosomes and contain the package of genes that determine whether an individual is male or female.
- Females have two X chromosomes while males have one X and a shorter Y chromosome.

Sex inheritance

- A male will produce *gametes* that contain one chromosome from each homologous pair found in normal body cells. This means that half of the gametes will have a single X chromosome and half will have the corresponding Y chromosome.
- Females, with two X chromosomes, only produce gametes with X.
- If a sperm carrying an X chromosome joins with an egg, it produce XX—a female cell. A sperm containing a Y chromosome would produce XY—a male.

Human sex linkage: hemophilia

Key words

factor VIII

The sex chromosomes

- Females have two X chromosomes while males have one X and a shorter Y chromosome. Genes on these chromosomes are described as sex-linked.
- Traits such as colorblindness and hemophilia are sex linked.

Hemophilia

- Hemophilia is a condition in which blood does not clot. This leads to serious bleeding following even small cuts. Hemophilia is caused by a lack of a blood chemical called *factor VIII*. The gene that codes for factor VIII is on the X chromosome (H_x).
  The Y chromosome, which is shorter, is missing the corresponding part.

Carriers and sufferers

- A woman with a faulty gene on one X chromosome (^hX) will produce factor VIII. She will not suffer from the illness but could pass it on to her offspring through the damaged gene on one X chromosome.
- The shorter Y chromosome has no space for the factor VIII gene. If a male has the defective gene on his single X chromosome, he suffers from the disease.
- Males get an X chromosome from their mother and a Y chromosome from the father. A father cannot pass on the faulty factor VIII gene because he does not pass on an X chromosome.

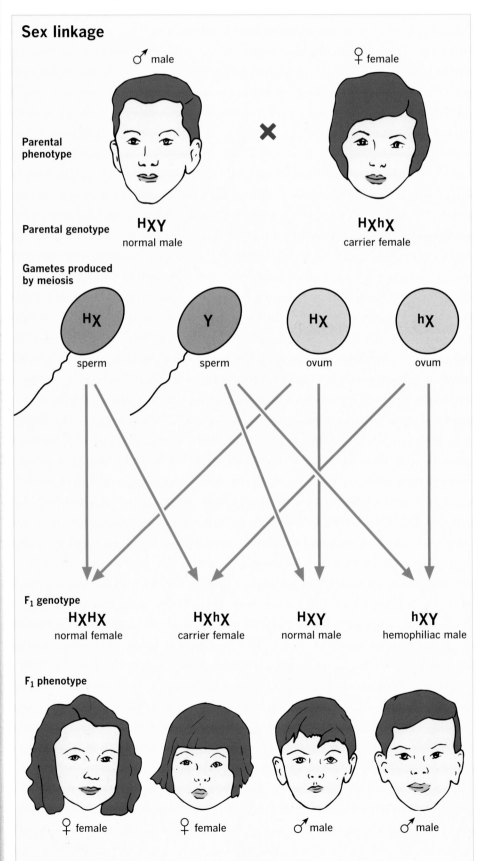

Sex linkage

♂ male   ✕   ♀ female

Parental phenotype

Parental genotype
H_XY
normal male

$H_X{}^hX$
carrier female

Gametes produced by meiosis

H_X sperm   Y sperm H_X ovum ^hX ovum

F_1 genotype
H_XH_X
normal female

$H_X{}^hX$
carrier female

H_XY
normal male

^hXY
hemophiliac male

F_1 phenotype

♀ female   ♀ female   ♂ male   ♂ male

Amniocentesis

Key words

amnion
Down syndrome
fetus

Amniocentesis

Sample of amniotic fluid, including cells

placenta

uterine wall

fetus

amniotic fluid

umbilical cord

amnion

cervix

vagina

syringe

Amniotic fluid centrifuged

supernatant (soluble liquid)

cells

Cells grown in nutrient solution

culture dish

Chromosomal analysis

Down syndrome karyotype

Cultured cells

Biochemical analysis

The amniotic fluid

● The growing *fetus* is protected by fluid produced by a membrane called the *amnion*. This amniotic fluid contains fetal cells floating freely around in it.

Amniocentesis

● Around the 16th week of pregnancy, a fine needle is inserted into the amniotic sac and a small sample of fluid containing some fetal cells is withdrawn. The technician carrying out this procedure uses ultrasound imaging to direct the needle—if it were to scratch the fetus, it could cause potentially serious complications for both mother and child. For this reason, the benefits to be gained from the procedure must be weighed carefully against the risks.

Analysis of fluid

● The amniotic fluid sample is centrifuged to separate out the floating cells. These are cultured and can be tested for a variety of abnormalities. One of the commonest tests is for *Down syndrome*.

● In Down syndrome the cells of the fetus have 47 chromosomes instead of 46. The extra chromosome is found with the 21st chromosome. As the baby develops, a number of problems arise. He or she will grow slowly and fail to reach full adult development either physically or mentally.

Key words

allele
dominant
gene
genotype

Multiple alleles

- *Alleles* are different forms of the same *gene*. So the gene for the major ABO blood groups in humans exists in three forms or alleles: A, B, and O.
- A and B are both *dominant* to O. If the A gene is present, the red blood cells will have a protein on their outer surface called protein A. In genetic diagrams the dominant allele is usually shown with a capital letter and the corresponding recessive factor is shown with a lowercase letter.
- If the B gene is present, the proteins on the red blood cells will be type B.
- If the O gene is present, the blood cells will not contain either of these proteins.

Inheritance of blood groups

- The blood groups of the ABO system are determined by three major alleles: A, B, and O. Both A and B are dominant (I^A, I^B), while O is recessive (i^O).
- The ABO alleles follow the standard rules for a monohybrid cross—a cross in which only one pair of traits is considered. If a parent with AA (blood group A) is crossed a parent with BB (blood group B), the offspring will be AB. This means that they will have both protein type A and type B on their red blood cells. They will belong to blood group AB.
- If a parent is AO, he or she will be blood group A because A is dominant to O. If this parent is crossed with someone with *genotype* BO, the offspring will distribute themselves in the same ratio as: one AB: one AO: one OB: one OO. This gives the individual a 25 percent chance of being blood group AB, A, B, or O.

Inheritance of blood groups

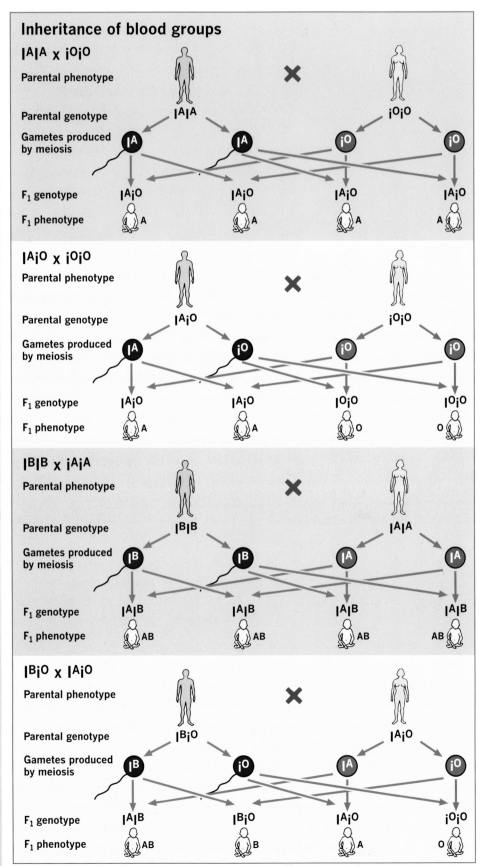

Inheritance of blood groups

Chromosome mutation: types

Key words

chromosome
gene

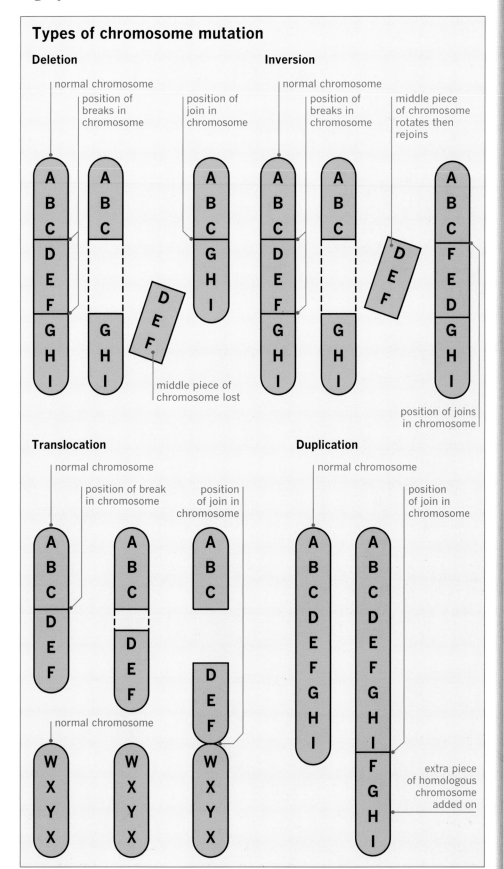

Types of chromosome mutation

Deletion

normal chromosome

position of breaks in chromosome

position of join in chromosome

middle piece of chromosome lost

Inversion

normal chromosome

position of breaks in chromosome

middle piece of chromosome rotates then rejoins

position of joins in chromosome

Translocation

normal chromosome

position of break in chromosome

position of join in chromosome

normal chromosome

Duplication

normal chromosome

position of join in chromosome

extra piece of homologous chromosome added on

Chromosome mutations

- *Chromosome* mutations involve complete packages of *genes* rather than individual genes. For this reason their effects can be very far-reaching.

Deletion

- In deletion, a portion of a chromosome is lost. This affects the coding of proteins that use the DNA sequence as well as other amino acids that are supposed to be coded from the sequence.

Inversion

- In inversion, a portion of the chromosome is reversed. This affects the order of the bases in the genetic code, usually making it impossible to read successfully.

Translocation

- Translocation involves a piece of DNA within a chromosome being moved to a different position or even a different chromosome. This effectively shuffles the genes available to an organism— possibly producing improved varieties.

Duplication

- In duplication, a portion of DNA in a chromosome is copied and re-inserted into the chromosome. Since there is no increase in the number of genes, the effects of duplication tend to be small.

Key words

chromosome
genotype
mutation

Chromosome mutations

● *Chromosome* mutations involve complete packages of genes rather than individual genes. For this reason their effects can be very far-reaching.

● Some *mutations* involve adding or removing a complete chromosome. These are usually lethal, although the sex chromosomes (XY) seem to be able to suffer from these sorts of mutations and still produce viable, if damaged, offspring.

Klinefelter's syndrome

● Individuals are male but possess an extra X chromosome to be XXY. Their sexual development is defective, and they are often sterile—unable to produce sperm. They may have enlarged breasts and abnornmal body proportions.

Triple X syndrome

● Individuals with triple X syndrome possess an extra X chromosome to give them a *genotype* of XXX. The extra chromosome in this instance seems to have very little effect.

Turner's syndrome

● The ovum that produced an individual with Turner's syndrome was formed without an X chromosome. If this ovum meets a sperm containing an X chromosome, a viable female is formed, although she is almost always infertile. If the ovum meets a sperm with a Y chromosome, a viable embryo cannot be formed.

Chromosome mutation: syndromes

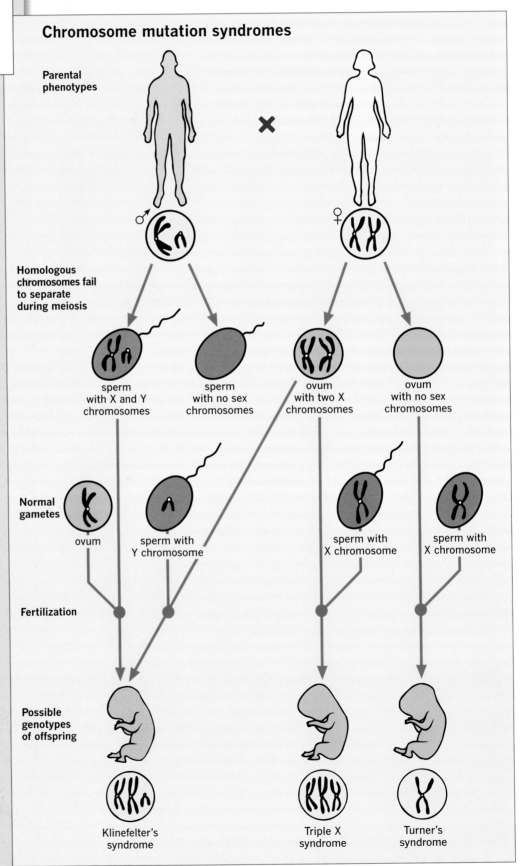

Chromosome mutation syndromes

Parental phenotypes

Homologous chromosomes fail to separate during meiosis

sperm with X and Y chromosomes

sperm with no sex chromosomes

ovum with two X chromosomes

ovum with no sex chromosomes

Normal gametes

ovum

sperm with Y chromosome

sperm with X chromosome

sperm with X chromosome

Fertilization

Possible genotypes of offspring

Klinefelter's syndrome

Triple X syndrome

Turner's syndrome

Gene mutation: types

Key words

codon
gene
mutation
polypeptide chain

Types of genetic mutation

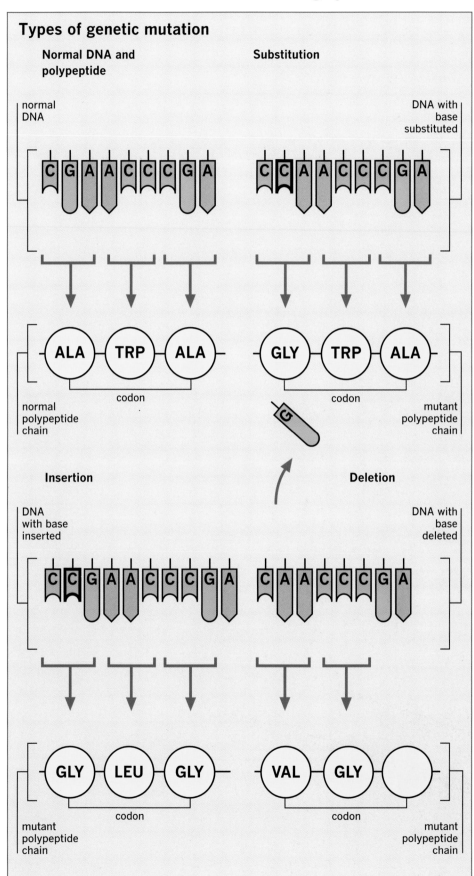

Normal DNA and polypeptide

normal DNA

C G A A C C C G A

ALA — TRP — ALA

codon

normal polypeptide chain

Substitution

DNA with base substituted

C C A A C C C G A

GLY — TRP — ALA

codon

mutant polypeptide chain

Insertion

DNA with base inserted

C C G A A C C C G A

GLY — LEU — GLY

codon

mutant polypeptide chain

Deletion

DNA with base deleted

C A A C C C G A

VAL — GLY —

codon

mutant polypeptide chain

Gene mutations

- Gene *mutations* involve changes in the base sequence (the order of nucleotide bases) of the DNA of a *gene*. Almost all of these changes will be harmful and lead to a malfunction of the gene. Sometimes they can produce a new gene, which produces a characteristic that is better suited to the environment.
- Gene mutations fall into three categories: substitution, insertion, and deletion.

Substitution

- In a substitution mutation a single base is changed for another one. Since the single base only figures in one *codon*, the damage is limited to changing one amino acid in a *polypetide chain*. This could be significant if the amino acid were in a critical place on the chain or had a very specific function in the molecule.

Insertion

- Insertion involves adding a base to a sequence of DNA. The extra base will disrupt all of the subsequent codons because they will now be out of sequence.

Deletion

- Deletion removes a single base. This also disrupts all subsequent codons because the "gaps" between the codons are now in the wrong place.

Key words

codon
polypeptide chain

Sickle-cell anemia

- Sickle-cell anemia is a disease of the red blood cells caused by an error in one triplet of one of the *polypeptide chains* in beta (β) hemoglobin.
- Sufferers from sickle-cell anemia have red blood cells that are irregular shapes, often crescent moon or sickle shapes, which cannot carry oxygen as well as normal blood cells. This leads to a general lack of energy in the sufferer. Their abnormal shape also means that they tend to get stuck in small blood vessels, leading to painful clots.

Glutamine to valine

- The sickle-cell mutation involves a single triplet substitution from CTC (Cytosine/Thymine/Cytosine) to CAC (Cytosine/Adenine/Cytosine). This change leads to the amino acid valine (VAL) being added to the polypeptide chain in place of glutamine (GLU). This change leads, in turn, to other problems with the three-dimensional shape of the hemoglobin formed, and therefore with its functionality.
- Since the gene mutation is a base substitution, only one of the *codons*, and so one of the amino acids, is affected. In certain areas of the world, sickle-cell anemia offers a degree of protection against the malaria parasite.

Gene mutation: sickle-cell shape

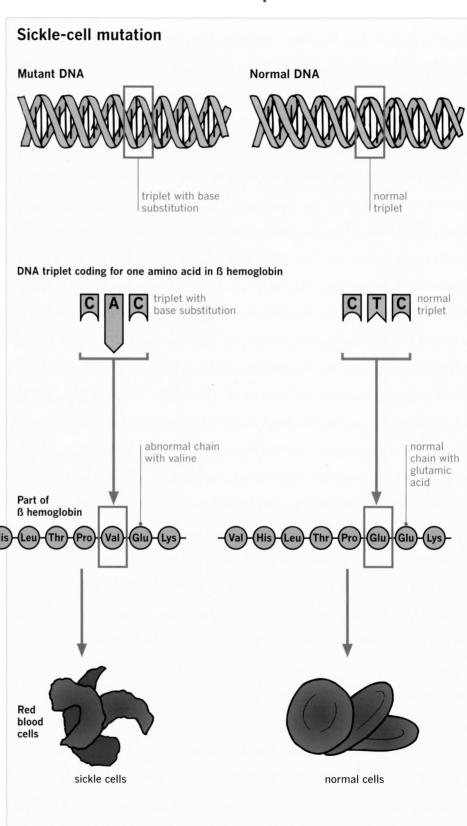

Sickle-cell mutation

Mutant DNA

Normal DNA

triplet with base substitution

normal triplet

DNA triplet coding for one amino acid in ß hemoglobin

| C | A | C | triplet with base substitution

| C | T | C | normal triplet

abnormal chain with valine

normal chain with glutamic acid

Part of ß hemoglobin

–Val–His–Leu–Thr–Pro–Val–Glu–Lys–

–Val–His–Leu–Thr–Pro–Glu–Glu–Lys–

Red blood cells

sickle cells

normal cells

Gene mutation: sickle-cell anemia

Key words

hemoglobin
heterozygous
homozygous
polypeptide chain
recessive

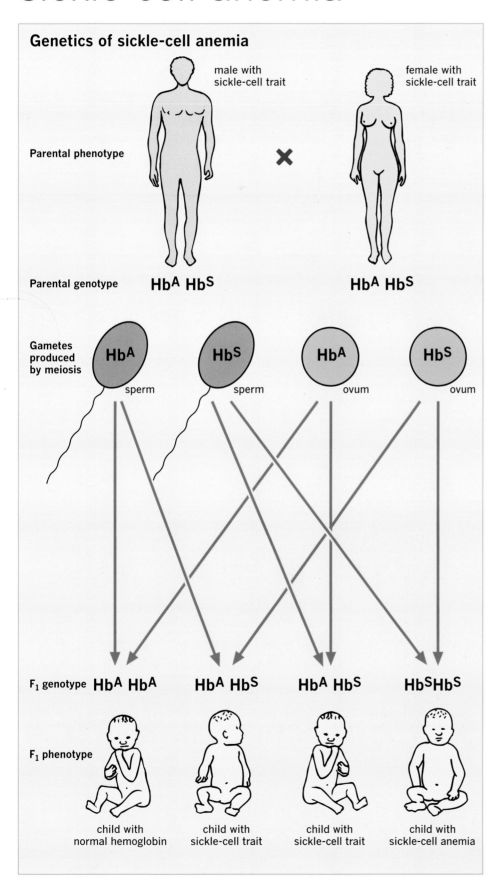

Genetics of sickle-cell anemia

male with sickle-cell trait

female with sickle-cell trait

Parental phenotype

✕

Parental genotype $Hb^A Hb^S$ $Hb^A Hb^S$

Gametes produced by meiosis Hb^A sperm Hb^S sperm Hb^A ovum Hb^S ovum

F_1 genotype $Hb^A Hb^A$ $Hb^A Hb^S$ $Hb^A Hb^S$ $Hb^S Hb^S$

F_1 phenotype

child with normal hemoglobin   child with sickle-cell trait   child with sickle-cell trait   child with sickle-cell anemia

Sickle-cell anemia and trait

- Sickle-cell condition is caused by a defective gene for the protein beta *hemoglobin*. The defect is a single base, which leads to valine being substituted for glutamine in the *polypeptide chain*.
- If an individual has two sickle genes ($Hb^S Hb^S$), they will suffer form the full condition and exhibit symptoms.
- A *heterozygous* individual with only one sickle gene ($Hb^A Hb^S$) will show sickle-cell trait. In sickle-cell trait, symptoms are not visible, and the blood can appear normal except in conditions of low oxygen (e.g., airplanes, some surgical procedures), when complications can occur.

Inheritance of sickle-cell gene

- The sickle-cell gene is a *recessive* allele inherited following all the normal rules for monohybrid crosses. The gene is not sex-linked and is equally common in men and women.
- A *homozygous* normal parent (Hb^A, Hb^A) crossed with a homozygous sickled parent ($Hb^S Hb^S$) will produce offspring that are heterozygous and will have sickle-cell trait ($Hb^A Hb^S$).
- In order to produce children with the full sickle-cell condition, both of the parents must possess at least one sickle-cell allele (e.g., two parents with sickle-cell trait).
- Sickle-cell genes are more common in Africans and their descendants than other racial groups.

© Diagram Visual Information Ltd.

Key words

fossil record
species

Evidence for evolution: primitive and advanced

Primitive and advanced

- Primitive characteristics are characteristics that existed prior to a more advanced form that developed from it. Primitive does not always mean simpler, as some forms of development occur that involve loss of structures and complexity. Primitive and advanced can only be used when referring to particular pairs of characteristics, and a characteristic may be primitive in one relationship but advanced in another.

Increase in size

- The development of the modern horse is well-documented through the *fossil record*. A gradual increase in body size is noticeable over millions of years as primitive forms gave rise to larger, more advanced *species*.

Decrease in complexity

- As the body size increased from the smallest *Hyracotherium* of the Eocene era (roughly 50 million years before present) to the largest *Equus* (the modern horse), there was a parallel fall in complexity of forefoot bones.
- The entire weight of the horse is now borne on the third digit, with the other digits much reduced in size and importance.

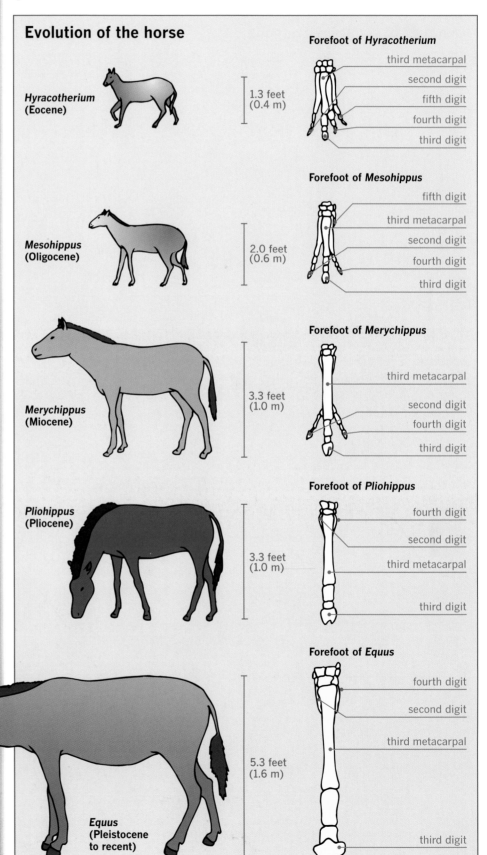

Evolution of the horse

Hyracotherium (Eocene) — 1.3 feet (0.4 m)

Forefoot of *Hyracotherium*
- third metacarpal
- second digit
- fifth digit
- fourth digit
- third digit

Mesohippus (Oligocene) — 2.0 feet (0.6 m)

Forefoot of *Mesohippus*
- fifth digit
- third metacarpal
- second digit
- fourth digit
- third digit

Merychippus (Miocene) — 3.3 feet (1.0 m)

Forefoot of *Merychippus*
- third metacarpal
- second digit
- fourth digit
- third digit

Pliohippus (Pliocene) — 3.3 feet (1.0 m)

Forefoot of *Pliohippus*
- fourth digit
- second digit
- third metacarpal
- third digit

Equus (Pleistocene to recent) — 5.3 feet (1.6 m)

Forefoot of *Equus*
- fourth digit
- second digit
- third metacarpal
- third digit

Evidence for evolution: adaptive radiation

Key words

species

Adaptive radiation of Darwin's finches

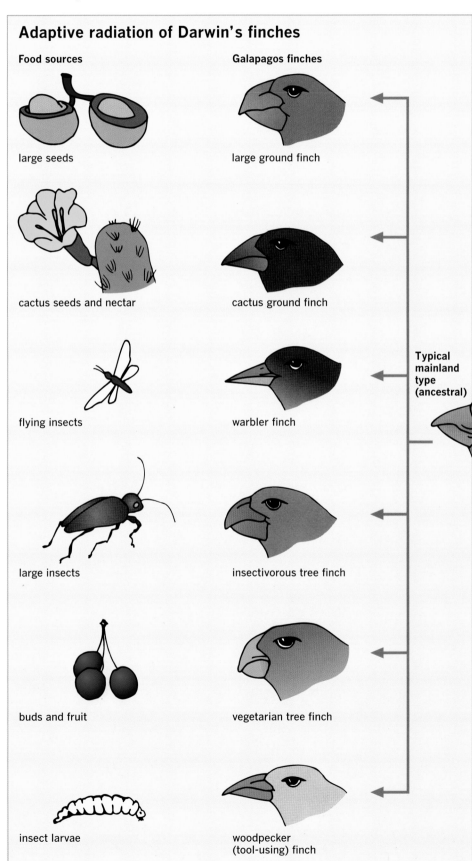

Food sources

large seeds

cactus seeds and nectar

flying insects

large insects

buds and fruit

insect larvae

Galapagos finches

large ground finch

cactus ground finch

warbler finch

insectivorous tree finch

vegetarian tree finch

woodpecker (tool-using) finch

Typical mainland type (ancestral)

Adaptive radiation

- Adaptive radiation occurs when a single primitive form of a *species* develops into a wider range of advanced forms, each of which is adapted to particular environmental conditions.
- One of the best-documented examples of adaptive radiation is provided by Darwin's finches from the Galapagos Islands.

Galapagos Islands

- The Galapagos Islands are a remote group of islands in the Pacific Ocean 600 miles due west of Ecuador. Each island has its own microclimate with different flora and fauna.

Darwin's finches

- The biologist Charles Darwin visited the Galapagos Islands in the nineteenth century. He noticed that each island had its own local type of finches. They were adapted to eat the food available on their particular island. All of the finches were slightly different from each other and from the primitive finch found on the mainland of South America.
- Darwin suggested that certain individuals on each island had a survival advantage if they were better at eating the locally available food. Over many generations these local finches increased in number, and because they were isolated from the finches on the other islands, eventually became a separate species.

Key words

continental drift

Continental drift

- The landmasses on Earth's surface are constantly moving. They are carried by immense forces generated by convection currents in the liquid rock in the mantle of the planet.

- Scientists can observe these movements using satellite images that show, for example, that the North American and Eurasian landmasses are moving apart by approximately one centimeter every year. This movement is called *continental drift*.

- By plotting these movements backward, we can reconstruct the landmasses as they were millions of years ago. At one point 250 million years ago, all the continents were combined in a single landmass called Pangaea (Greek for "all land"). Over millions of years, this broke up into our present-day continents.

Fossil relatives

- The Mesosaurus is a type of lizard that is now extinct. Its fossils are found only in South America and South West Africa.

- This surprising fact is easily explained by continental drift. When Mesosaurus was alive, South West Africa and South America must have been joined.

- This is evidence for a single species on a single landmass rather than two identical species having to evolve separately—a far less likely scenario.

Evidence for evolution: continental drift

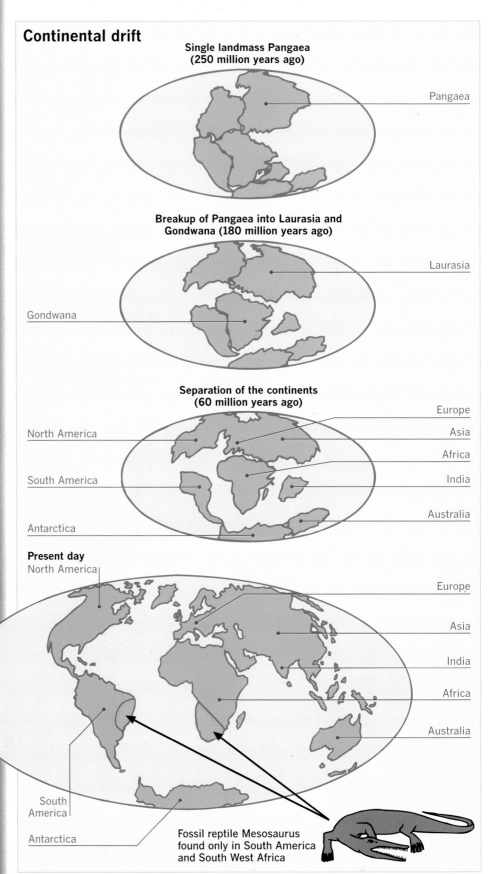

Continental drift

Single landmass Pangaea (250 million years ago)

Pangaea

Breakup of Pangaea into Laurasia and Gondwana (180 million years ago)

Laurasia

Gondwana

Separation of the continents (60 million years ago)

Europe
Asia
Africa
India
Australia

North America
South America
Antarctica

Present day
North America

Europe
Asia
India
Africa
Australia

South America
Antarctica

Fossil reptile Mesosaurus found only in South America and South West Africa

Classification of living organisms

Key words

bacterium
chlorophyll
photosynthesis
virus

Tree diagram of living organisms

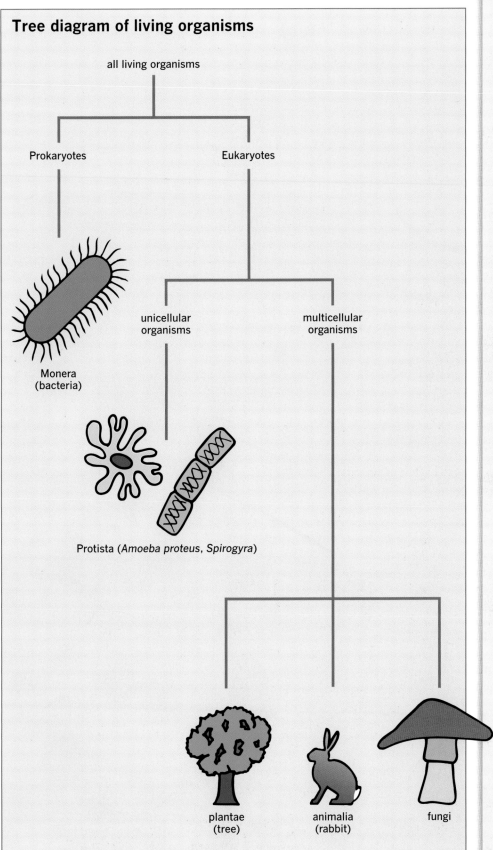

all living organisms

Prokaryotes

Eukaryotes

unicellular organisms

multicellular organisms

Monera (bacteria)

Protista (*Amoeba proteus, Spirogyra*)

plantae (tree)

animalia (rabbit)

fungi

Prokaryotes

- Prokaryotes are the simplest living organisms and include all living things without a proper membrane-bound nucleus. All prokaryotes are microscopic, and they include *bacteria* and *viruses*.

Eukaryotes

- Eukaryotes are organisms with membrane-bound structures present in their cells. The most obvious of these structures is the nucleus.
- Eukaryotes can be single or multicellular and are more complex than prokaryotes.

Types of eukaryote

- Eukaryotes can be split into four main groups: unicellular organisms, fungi, plants, and animals.
- Eukaryotic unicellular organisms include the Protista and a range of microscopic algae.
- The fungi are plantlike organisms that do not possess *chlorophyll* and depend on organic matter from other organisms for food. Many fungi are important in decomposition and decay in the environment.
- Plants are organisms that carry out *photosynthesis*. They typically have cellulose-rich cell walls.
- Animals depend on plants or other animals for food. They do not possess cell walls or chlorophyll. Almost all animals are multicellular.

Kingdom Monera: Bacteria

Key words

bacterium	plasma
cytoplasm	membrane
mesosome	plasmid
organelle	ribosome
photosynthesis	

Classification

- *Bacteria* are prokaryotes and so are unicellular organisms that do not possess membrane-bound *organelles*. All are microscopic. Some carry out *photosynthesis* while others require an external source of organic matter and are involved in decomposition and decay.
- Bacteria are sorted into groups depending on their cell shape and how these cells stick together.

Cellular structure

- Bacteria contain a single large molecule of DNA that floats freely within the *cytoplasm* of the cell. Other smaller circles of DNA called *plasmids* also exist and can pass between bacteria to carry genes between types.
- The outer surface of the cell is sometimes covered by a slime layer. Inside this is a cell wall.
- Sometimes present is a flagellum— a long, whiplike structure that can thrash about to propel the cell forward. Smaller hairs called pili behave in a similar way.
- The *plasma membrane* is found inside the cell wall. It has a number of processes called *mesosomes* that protrude into the center of the cell. They are associated with the synthesis of DNA and the secretion of proteins.
- Other structures include *ribosomes* (site of protein synthesis), and food reserves—oil globules (fat stores) and starch grains (food stores).

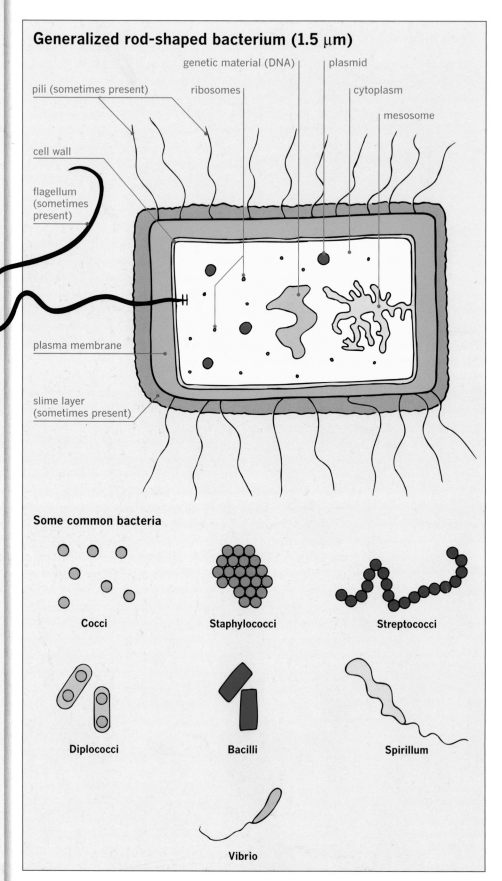

Generalized rod-shaped bacterium (1.5 μm)

genetic material (DNA)
plasmid
pili (sometimes present)
ribosomes
cytoplasm
mesosome
cell wall
flagellum (sometimes present)
plasma membrane
slime layer (sometimes present)

Some common bacteria

Cocci

Staphylococci

Streptococci

Diplococci

Bacilli

Spirillum

Vibrio

Kingdom Protista: *Amoeba*

Key words

contractile   pseudopodium
  vacuole
exocytosis
nucleus
organelle

Typical ameba

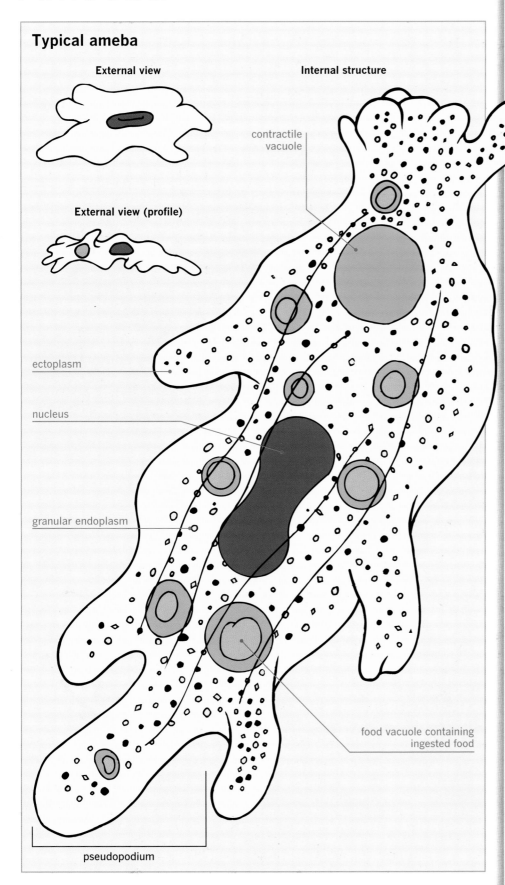

External view

Internal structure

External view (profile)

contractile
vacuole

ectoplasm

nucleus

granular endoplasm

food vacuole containing
ingested food

pseudopodium

Classification

- Protists are eukaryotes and so possess membrane-bound *organelles*—specialized regions in the cell that carry out particular functions.
- Protists have a fully developed *nucleus*, but despite this, all are unicellular, microscopic organisms.
- The genus *Amoeba* is an example of a non-photosynthetic protist that eats smaller microorganisms.

Cellular structure

- Amebas are microscopic, in the size range 0.0004–0.004 inches (10–100 microns), and are usually invisible to the naked eye. A few of the largest species are just visible.
- An ameba has a single nucleus and a simple *contractile vacuole*, which pumps fluid from within the cell to the outside by alternately filling and then contracting. It functions in maintaining osmotic equilibrium, regulating the body's salt and water balance
- An ameba is bounded by a plasma membrane, and its shape can change as cytoplasm contained within the cell flows forward. The cell bulges outward in some places to create a *pseudopodium*.
- Amebas feed by throwing pseudopodia around a prey organism and engulfing it in a vacuole. Enzymes are then secreted into this vacuole to digest the food and allow it to be absorbed into the ameba. Indigestible remains are ejected from the cell by *exocytosis*.
- The endoplasm, the cytoplasm near the ameba's nucleus, is highly granular, but the area immediately below the cell membrane is clear: this is called the ectoplasm.

Key words

buccal cavity	vacuole
cilium	
nucleus	
organelle	
osmoregulation	

Classification

- Protists are eukaryotes and so possess membrane-bound *organelles*, including a fully-developed *nucleus*. All protists are unicellular microscopic organisms.
- A *Paramecium* is a water-dwelling, non-photosynthetic microorganism that ingests small algae and bacteria for food.

Cellular structure

- A *Paramecium* is covered with small hair-like structures called *cilia*. These beat in coordinated patterns to drive the *Paramecium* through the water. Trichocysts are the structures embedded in the cell that produce the cilia.
- The oral groove, a deep groove in the surface of the *Paramecium*, leads from the oral vestibule to the *buccal cavity* (the oral region) and cytosome (mouth), where food can be engulfed to form a food *vacuole*. Enzymes are released into this vacuole to digest the food and allow it to be absorbed into the cell. Cilia beat to create currents that push food into this area. After digestion, the vacuoles fuse with the cytoproct, which empties the cell's waste material to the outside.
- The nucleus in *Paramecium* is complex, with two components: the macronucleus, which controls most of the functions of the cell, and the smaller micronucleus, which is concerned with reproduction.
- *Osmoregulation*, the regulation of the body's salt and water balance, depends on contractile vacuoles that collect excess water in the cell and then burst to expel it.

Kingdom Protista: *Paramecium*

Paramecium

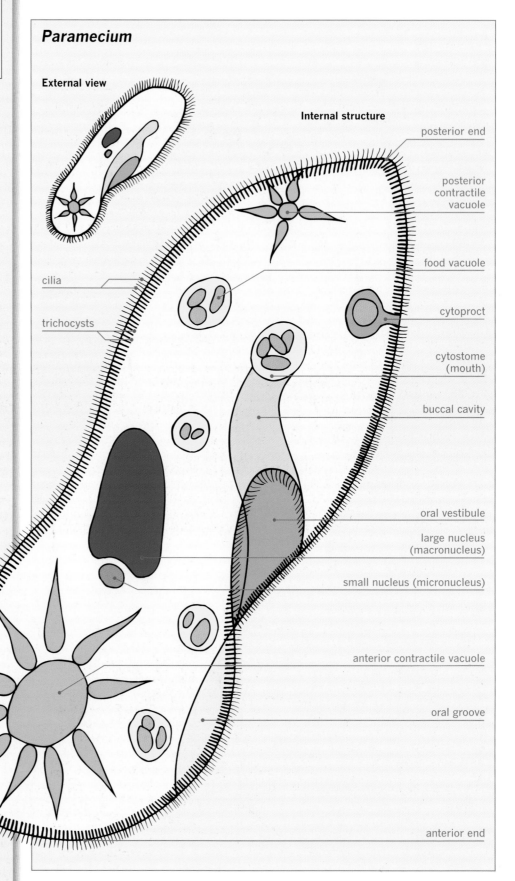

External view

Internal structure

- cilia
- trichocysts
- posterior end
- posterior contractile vacuole
- food vacuole
- cytoproct
- cytostome (mouth)
- buccal cavity
- oral vestibule
- large nucleus (macronucleus)
- small nucleus (micronucleus)
- anterior contractile vacuole
- oral groove
- anterior end

Kingdom Protista: *Spirogyra*

© Diagram Visual Information Ltd.

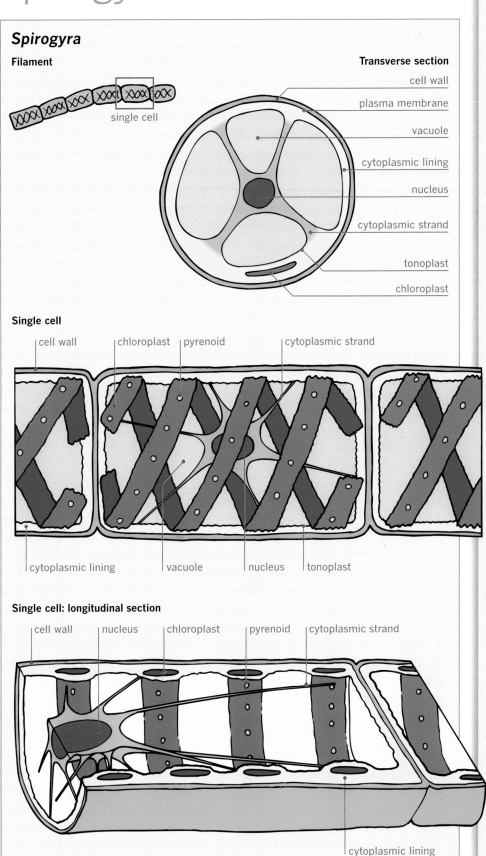

Spirogyra

Filament

single cell

Transverse section

cell wall
plasma membrane
vacuole
cytoplasmic lining
nucleus
cytoplasmic strand
tonoplast
chloroplast

Single cell

cell wall   chloroplast   pyrenoid   cytoplasmic strand

cytoplasmic lining   vacuole   nucleus   tonoplast

Single cell: longitudinal section

cell wall   nucleus   chloroplast   pyrenoid   cytoplasmic strand

cytoplasmic lining

Key words

cellulose   vacuole
chloroplast
cytoplasm
photosynthesis
pyrenoid

Classification

● The *Spirogyra* is unusual in that it is a multicellular protist and can form large mats of intertwined filaments (top left diagram) clearly visible to the naked eye.

Cellular structure

● The most noticeable component in the *Spirogyra* cell is the large spiralled *chloroplast* that runs around the periphery of the cell immediately inside the cell wall. The presence of the chloroplast means that *Spirogyra* can carry out *photosynthesis*.

● *Pyrenoids* are small structures embedded in the chloroplast that are concerned with the formation of starch.

● The cell wall of *Spirogyra* is made up of *cellulose*, a complex carbohydrate that stiffens the cell wall. Inside this are the plasma membrane and a thin layer of *cytoplasm* surrounding a central *vacuole* enclosed by a membrane called the tonoplast.

● The large nucleus is suspended in the center of the cell by strands of cytoplasm.

Multicellular protists

● *Spirogyra* cells join end to end to create long filaments that are clearly visible with the naked eye. Growth of the filament occurs when a cell divides into two. Any cell in a filament is able to do this.

Kingdom Fungi: *Rhizopus*

Key words

enzyme
mycelium
organic matter
photosynthesis
spore

Classification

- Fungi cannot carry out *photosynthesis*. *Enzymes* secreted by the fungus digest *organic matter* externally before it is absorbed into the cell. Many fungi have complex reproductive structures that are often the only part of the organism visible to the naked eye.
- *Rhizopus* is a mold that grows on damp bread and other foods. It is seen as a white network of fine hairs, often with very small black pinheads.

Structure

- The main body of the fungus is a network of tiny interconnected threads called hyphae. Hyphae are tubular structures that can branch and fuse to produce a network called a *mycelium*.
- Fungi do not have true cells: hyphae are cut up into cell-like sections, but the cross walls do not fully join in the middle to separate these parts.
- The large surface area provided by the mycelium allows both the rapid secretion of enzymes to break down food substrates and the absorption of the products into the body.
- Certain hyphae are specialized to produce *spore*-containing bodies called sporangia. The sporangia are often black in color. These burst when ripe to release single-celled spores that float on the air until they find a suitable place to grow. Here they produce another mycelium.

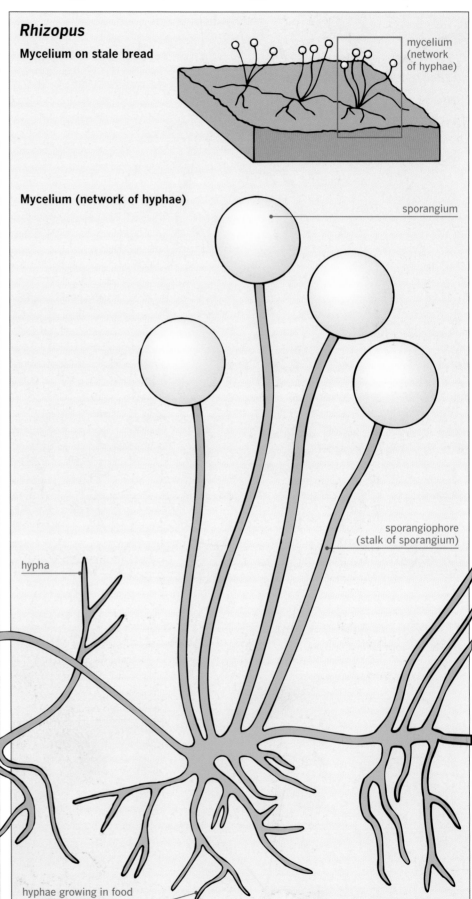

Rhizopus
Mycelium on stale bread

mycelium (network of hyphae)

Mycelium (network of hyphae)

sporangium

sporangiophore (stalk of sporangium)

hypha

hyphae growing in food

Kingdom Plantae: classification

Tree diagram of Plantae

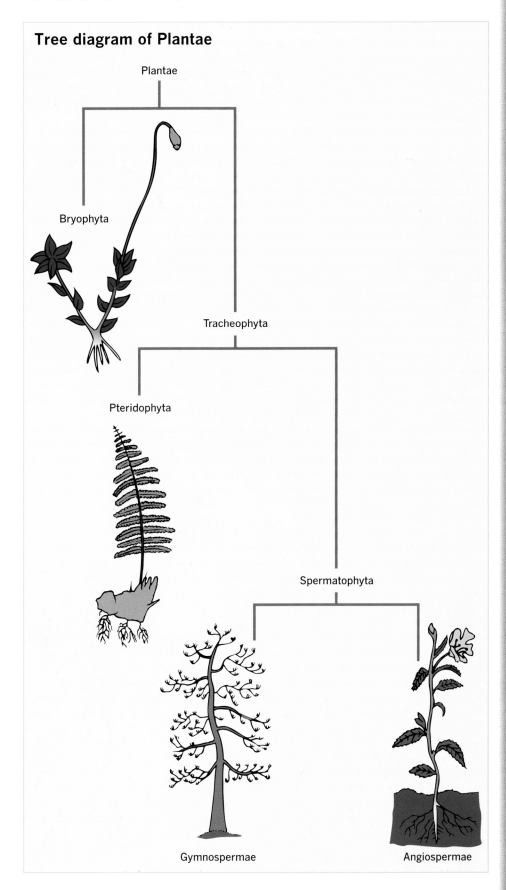

Plantae

Bryophyta

Tracheophyta

Pteridophyta

Spermatophyta

Gymnospermae

Angiospermae

Key words

cellulose
chlorophyll
spore

Plantae

- Members of the Plantae all share a number of features: they all possess *cellulose* cell walls. The majority also possess *chlorophyll* and have vessels or tubes inside their bodies to carry water.
- Most are multicellular, and some are very large.
- The Kingdom Plantae is divided into Bryophyta, which lack anatomical differentiation between leaves and roots, and Tracheophyta, which are characterized by the presence of vascular tissue and the differentiation of parts into roots, stems, and leaves. Tracheophyta, in turn, are divided into Pteriodophyte, plants that reproduce by spores, and Spermatophyta, plants that produce seeds.

Bryophyta

- These are the mosses and are primitive plants that are small (they never grow more than a few centimeters high) and can only survive in damp areas. They reproduce by *spores*.

Pteridophyta

- These are the ferns and are larger than mosses but are still confined to fairly damp places. They reproduce by spores.

Gymnospermae

- The gymnospermae include coniferous trees and include some very large plants. They produce seeds but do not have full-developed flowers.

Angiospermae

- These are called the flowering plants since they have both true flowers and seeds and fruits. They are the most successful and advanced plants and can survive a huge range of conditions.

Key words

gamete	zygote
gametophyte	
photosynthesis	
spore	
sporophyte	

Bryophyta

● Members of the bryophyta are small, simple green plants that carry out *photosynthesis*. They are restricted to require water for reproduction. They include the liverworts and the mosses.

Liverworts

● Liverworts consist of a flattened branching structure called a thallus, which has no obvious division into leaves and stems. Root-like structures called rhizoids grow out of the lower surface to anchor the plant and to take up nutrients.

● The sexual parts of liverworts are contained in inconspicuous structures known as antheridia (male) and archegonia (female). These develop on separate plants and are borne on stalked antheridiophores and archegoniophores, respectively. Fertilization takes place when raindrops splash sperm to female plants. The sperm swim down the canal in the archegonium to the chamber containing the egg. The resulting *zygote* begins the sporophyte generation. *Spores* subsequently develop and are dispersed by air currents. Once they settle in a moist environment, they germinate, and the gametophyte generation begins again.

Mosses

● Mosses have clearly identified stems with leaves attached.

● Reproduction involves sporophyte and gametophyte generations. The tiny sporophyte (spore-producing moss plant) is attached to the top of the moss gametophyte (gamete plant). It consists of a seta (slender stalk) and a terminal capsule (sporangium), which produces spores. As the sporophyte dries out, the capsule releases its spores, which will grow into a new generation of gametophytes upon germination.

Kingdom Plantae: Bryophyta

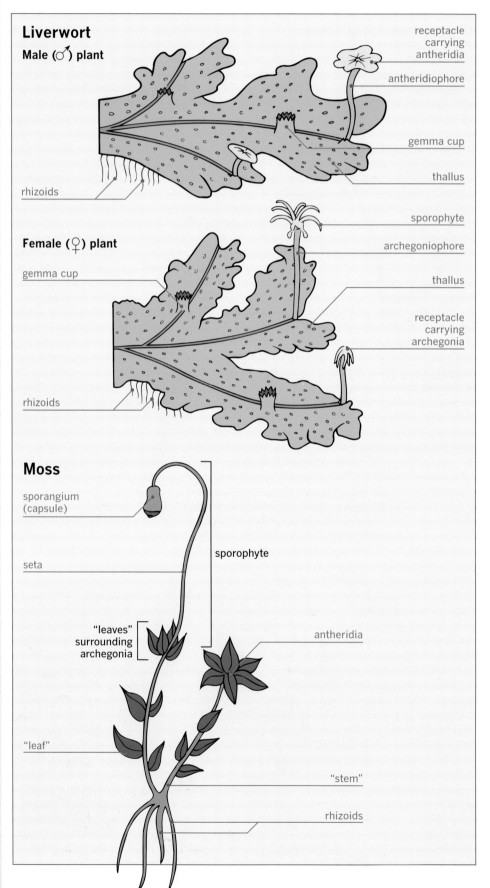

Liverwort

Male (♂) plant

- receptacle carrying antheridia
- antheridiophore
- gemma cup
- thallus
- rhizoids

Female (♀) plant

- gemma cup
- sporophyte
- archegoniophore
- thallus
- receptacle carrying archegonia
- rhizoids

Moss

- sporangium (capsule)
- seta
- sporophyte
- "leaves" surrounding archegonia
- antheridia
- "leaf"
- "stem"
- rhizoids

Kingdom Plantae: Pteridophyta

Key words

bilateral
 symmetry
gamete
gametophyte
spore

sporophyte
zygote

Typical pteridophyte

Sporophyte: external view

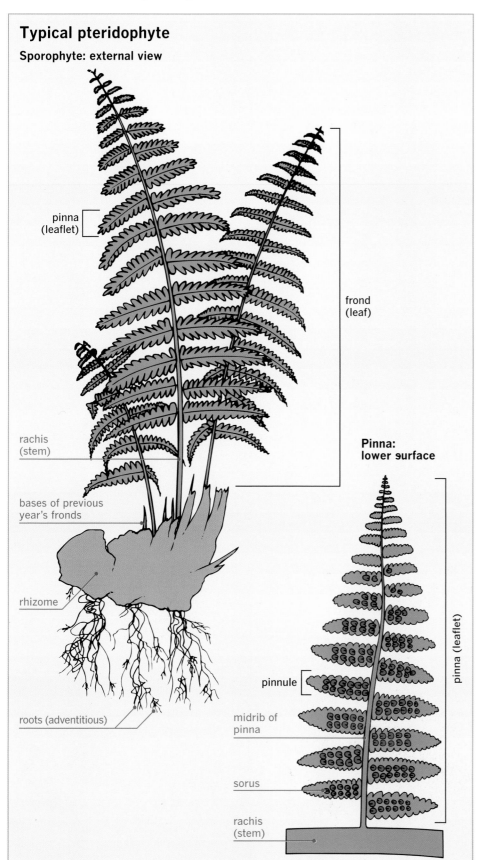

pinna
(leaflet)

frond
(leaf)

rachis
(stem)

bases of previous
year's fronds

rhizome

roots (adventitious)

**Pinna:
lower surface**

pinna (leaflet)

pinnule

midrib of
pinna

sorus

rachis
(stem)

Pteridophyta

- Members of the Pteridophyta range from small clubmosses to very large tree ferns, which can grow to 9 feet (approx. 3 m) with fronds that stretch up to 6 feet (approx. 2 m) in length.
- All pteridophytes are restricted to damp areas, although they are able to survive drier conditions than liverworts and mosses.

Adult form

- The typical form for a pteridophyte is a central rhizome (a horizontal underground stem) with long fronds growing out of it. The fronds support flat leaves, which grow out from a central stalk. The leaves are *bilaterally symmetrical* with a central stalk and flat leaflets called pinna on either side.

Reproduction

- The visible fern plant is the *sporophyte* generation. It produces *spores* from sporangia borne on the underside of the leaf. These sporangia are called sori and produce spores that resemble a rusty brown powder.
- The spores produced by the sori will develop into the *gametophyte* generation, which gives rise to reproductive cells. This plant is very small and requires very damp conditions to survive. If these conditions are available, it will develop and produce *gametes* that will fuse to produce a *zygote* (a fertilized ovum), if gametes of the other gender are available. This zygote then grows to produce an adult fern.

Key words

diploid
secondary
  thickening
seed

Seed plants

- Gymnospermae are plants that produce true *seeds*. These seeds are different from the spores produced by mosses and ferns because they are *diploid*—they contain pairs of chromosomes—and develop directly into adult plants.
- Gymnosperms are able to survive drier conditions than bryophytes and pteridophytes and are found in many harsh environments.
- Gymnosperms are divided into three main groups: coniferous plants like pines, fernlike plants called cycads, and a small and rare group of highly specialized plants called gnetales.

Adult form

- Pines and cycads both show *secondary thickening* in their stems, which means that they can form tall, strong structures. The woody stems give rise to branches that grow out from the sides and, in turn, produce smaller branches.
- Growth occurs at the apical bud at the apex or terminal position on the branch.
- The leaves of all gymnosperms are waxy and resist water loss well.

Reproduction

- Gymnosperms produce enclosed seeds held in cones. Male and female cones are separate structures. The female cones tend to be woody and are covered by ovuliferous scales, which protect the developing seeds. In the mature cone, the scales curl to release the seeds.
- Cones that do not separate open up so that the seeds, which are equipped with a wing to aid dispersal by the wind, are released.

Kingdom Plantae: Gymnospermae

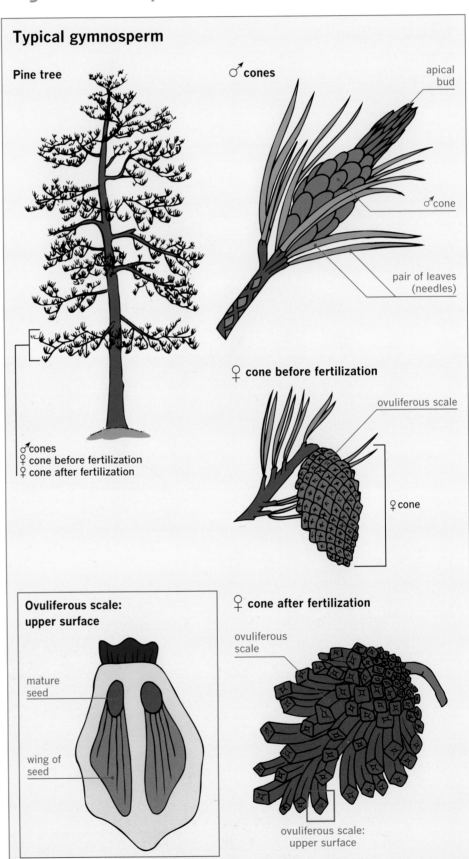

Typical gymnosperm

Pine tree

♂ cones

apical bud

♂ cone

pair of leaves (needles)

♂ cones
♀ cone before fertilization
♀ cone after fertilization

♀ cone before fertilization

ovuliferous scale

♀ cone

Ovuliferous scale: upper surface

mature seed

wing of seed

♀ cone after fertilization

ovuliferous scale

ovuliferous scale: upper surface

Kingdom Plantae: Angiospermae

Key words

anther	pistil
carpel	pollen
gamete	stamen
ovary	stigma
ovule	style

Typical angiosperm

Plant body

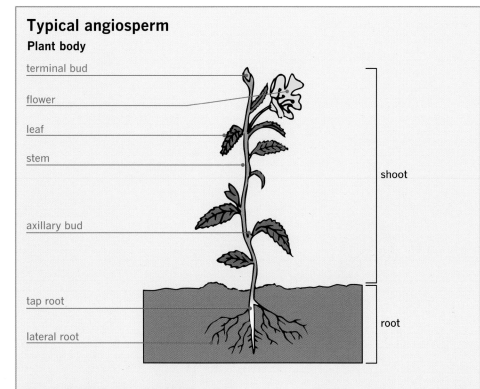

terminal bud
flower
leaf
stem
axillary bud
tap root
lateral root
shoot
root

Vertical section through flower

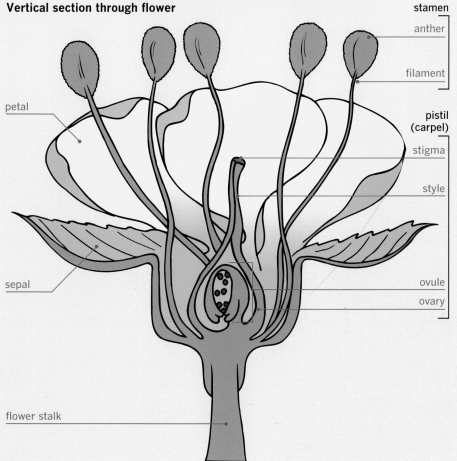

stamen
anther
filament
petal
pistil (carpel)
stigma
style
sepal
ovule
ovary
flower stalk

Flowering plants

- Angiospermae are plants that produce true seeds and fruits from flowers.
- Angiosperms are the most successful group of plants: they can survive a much wider range of environments than other groups.
- Almost all human food comes from angiosperm species, with the grass family, including wheat, corn, rice, and barley, contributing the largest proportion.

Adult form

- Angiosperms are a very wide group and range from tall woody trees to small floating water plants with almost no stem. However, they all have flowers that produce seeds.
- Angiosperms generally have a central stem bearing side branches with leaves that tend to be smaller than the large fronds of ferns, and flatter and wider than the needles of pines. Roots tend to be well developed, and water-conducting tissues in angiosperms are more advanced than in any other plant group.

Reproduction

- Reproduction depends on flowers, which contain the sex organs of the angiosperm. The *stamen*, the male portion of the flower, produces and stores *pollen*, microspores containing male *gametes*. The stamen consists of *anthers* (containing two pollen sacs) posted on stalks called filaments. The *pistil* or *carpel*, the female reproductive organ of the flower, consists of: the *stigma*, the *style*, the *ovary*, and the ovule.
- The male gamete tends to leave the flower when it is produced, while the female gametes are retained in the ovule for the whole of their life cycle. Angiosperms also produce fruits that aid in the dispersal of seeds.

Key words

diploid	sporophyte
gametophyte	zygote
haploid	
meiosis	
mitosis	

Flowers

● The Angiospermae are the only group of plants with fully-developed flowers. They also produce specialized structures to support dispersal and germination of the seeds produced.

The sporophyte generation

● As with all plants there are *sporophyte* and *gametophyte* generations. In angiosperms, the sporophyte generation is the visible plant and it is *diploid*; i.e. When mature, the *sporophyte* generation produces *haploid* gametes by *meiosis*. The gametes fuse during fertilization and the diploid number is then restored.

● The male gametes (the pollen grains) are produced by meiosis in anthers (b, c). These are released at maturity (d) and pass to the stigma of the ovule. The ovule contains the female gamete.

The gametophyte generation

● Angiosperms are unique in that they undergo double fertilization. Following pollination, the pollen grain germinates on the stigma of a flower of the same species, and the pollen tube grows down through the style to an ovule in the ovary (e). Two sperm nuclei enter the embryo sac. One fuses with the egg nucleus, leading to the formation of a *zygote*, while the other fuses with the two polar nuclei in the center to produce an endosperm nucleus (f). *Mitosis* then leads to the formation of the embryo and cotyledons.

● Another pollen grain nucleus fuses with other nuclei in the egg sac to form a storage tissue called endosperm (g).

● The seed is diploid and produces the larger sporophyte generation (h).

Kingdom Plantae: Angiospermae: life cycle

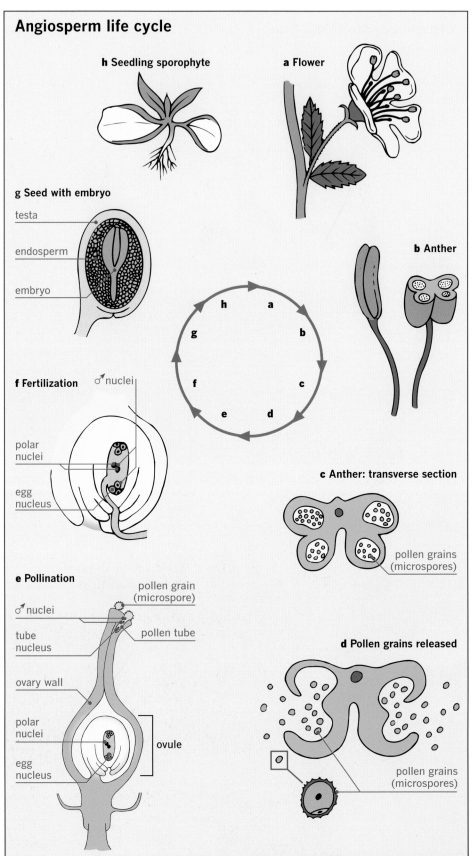

Angiosperm life cycle

h Seedling sporophyte

a Flower

g Seed with embryo

testa

endosperm

embryo

b Anther

f Fertilization

♂ nuclei

polar nuclei

egg nucleus

c Anther: transverse section

pollen grains (microspores)

e Pollination

pollen grain (microspore)

♂ nuclei

tube nucleus

pollen tube

ovary wall

polar nuclei

egg nucleus

ovule

d Pollen grains released

pollen grains (microspores)

Kingdom Animalia: classification

Tree diagram of Animalia

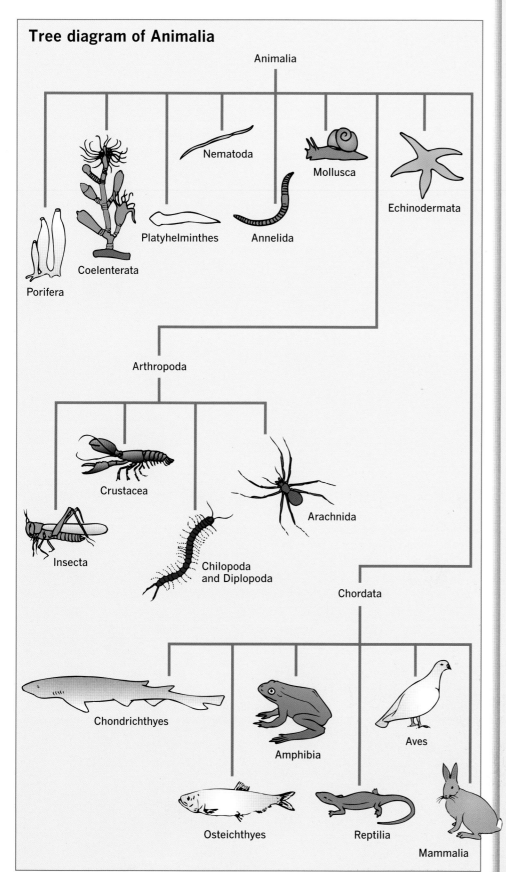

Animalia

Nematoda

Mollusca

Echinodermata

Coelenterata

Platyhelminthes

Annelida

Porifera

Arthropoda

Crustacea

Arachnida

Insecta

Chilopoda and Diplopoda

Chordata

Chondrichthyes

Amphibia

Aves

Osteichthyes

Reptilia

Mammalia

Key words

abdomen
exoskeleton
invertebrate
thorax
vertebrate

Backbone

- Animals are classified at the first level by the presence of a backbone: those with backbones are called *vertebrates* those without are *invertebrates*.
- Most of the lower animals are invertebrates and include a range of soft-bodied animals ranging from plantlike Porifera and worms through through "spiny-skinned" Echinodermata to Arthropoda.

The Arthropoda

- The arthropods do not possess bones but do have a hard structure surrounding their bodies called an *exoskeleton*. The most successful group of arthropods are the insects, which have three pairs of jointed legs and a segmented body divided into three parts: head, *thorax*, and *abdomen*.

The vertebrates

- Almost all large animals are vertebrates and have a well-developed backbone and a complex nervous system. Vertebrates are also called Chordata.
- The most primitive chordates are the cartilaginous fish (the Chondrichthyes), which do not possess true bone but rely on tough cartilage. The most well-known species in this group are the various types of shark.
- Mammals are the most successful group and are warm-blooded, possess fur, give birth to live young, and feed them on milk produced by the mammary glands.

Key words

cilium
gamete
life cycle
osculum
substrate

Invertebrates

- The Porifera or sponges are a primitive group of invertebrates. In many ways they look like plants in that they cannot move themselves and spend most of their *life cycle* attached to a firm *substrate*. There is some differentiation within the body, although they do not show the range of cell types present in higher animals

Body structure

- The outer surfaces of Porifera are covered with thin, flattened cells called pinacocytes. Porocytes (cells with pores) located all over the body allow water into the sponge. Because their bodies are hollow, their structure is supported by a soft network of fibers called spongin and/or by hard particles called spicule, which protect the animal. Between the outer body and the spongocoel (the central cavity) is a gelatinous layer called the mesohyal.
- Within the sponge, choanocytes, cells fringed with *cilia*, force water through the spongocoel, bringing in nutrients and removing waste. Ameobocytes take food to other cells. Water leaves the sponge through a large pore, usually at the top of the body, called the *osculum*. The mechanism is very efficient, with some sponges processing 20,000 times their own volume of water in 24 hours.

Reproduction

- Sponges reproduce sexually and asexually. Male *gametes* are released into the inner space and pass out through the osculum. These sperm are collected by other sponges, and female gametes are fertilized internally. Sponges can also reproduce asexually through the production of buds.

Kingdom Animalia: Porifera

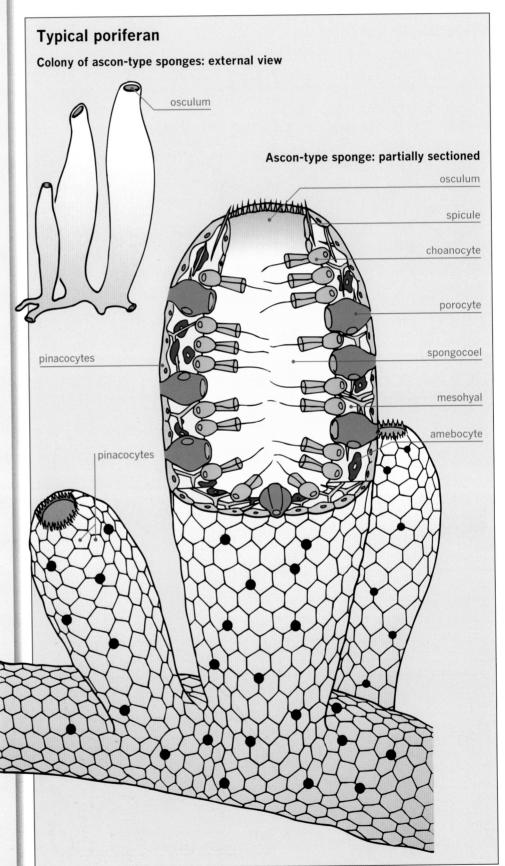

Typical poriferan

Colony of ascon-type sponges: external view

osculum

pinacocytes

pinacocytes

Ascon-type sponge: partially sectioned

osculum

spicule

choanocyte

porocyte

spongocoel

mesohyal

amebocyte

Kingdom Animalia: Cnidaria

Colonial polyps

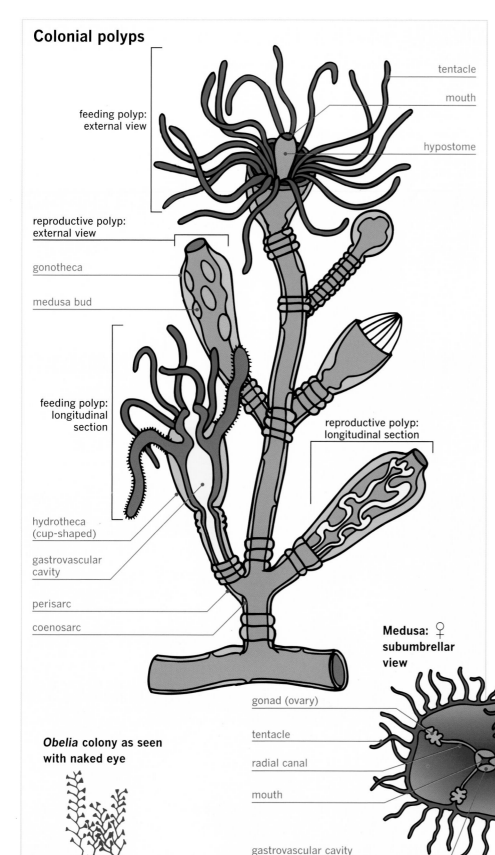

tentacle

mouth

hypostome

feeding polyp:
external view

reproductive polyp:
external view

gonotheca

medusa bud

feeding polyp:
longitudinal
section

reproductive polyp:
longitudinal section

hydrotheca
(cup-shaped)

gastrovascular
cavity

perisarc

coenosarc

***Obelia* colony as seen
with naked eye**

**Medusa: ♀
subumbrellar
view**

gonad (ovary)

tentacle

radial canal

mouth

gastrovascular cavity

Invertebrates

- Cnidaria are invertebrates that can be divided into two major groups: the *colonial polyps* that live their lives attached to a *substrate*, and the free-floating medusa-like forms that drift around in the oceans.

Body structure

- Colonial polyps are enclosed in a transparent, chitinous *exoskeleton* called the perisarc. Inside is living tissue, collectively called the coenosarc.
- Colonial polyps have a body made up of branched tubular structures specialized for feeding or reproduction.
- The feeding polyp, the hydranth, is enclosed in a thin chitinous cup called the hydrotheca. The mouth is located at the opening of the gastric column atop a low mount called the hypostome. It is surrounded by a ring of *tentacles* used to entangle and inject poison into small prey. Food is pushed into the gastrovascular cavity, where it is partially digested and distributed to all parts of the body.
- The reproductive polyp consists of an elongated cylinder called a gonotheca enclosing a blastostyle, a column that bears small medusa buds produced asexually. These eventually develop into medusae, which when mature break free and swim out the aperture of the gonotheca into the sea.
- *Obelia* Medusa, shown bottom left, begins life as a polyp. The polyps, in turn produce medusae, or jellyfish, which reproduce sexually and, in turn, produce polyps.

Invertebrates

● The Platyhelminthes or flatworms are a group of invertebrate worms that include two significant *parasites* of humans: liver flukes and tapeworms. They show extensive differentiation of cell types and have relatively complex bodies with a well-developed nervous system, including sense organs that respond to certain chemicals and light.

Body structure

● The flatworms or turbellarians have flattened bodies that allow diffusion of oxygen into every cell in the body. Carbon dioxide diffuses easily the other way. Consequently, they do not have a functional circulatory system.

● The *gut* in flatworms is often highly divided and reaches into the majority of the body. Again, this is required since they have no circulatory system to distribute food materials easily. The mouth of the gut also functions as the anus, and waste materials are passed out of it even as fresh foods are being drawn in.

● Flatworms are *hermaphrodite*—they have both male and female sex organs—and the parasitic forms like tapeworms and liver flukes have highly specialized life cycles, sometimes involving two hosts and the production of thousands of eggs from a single worm.

Kingdom Animalia: Platyhelminthes

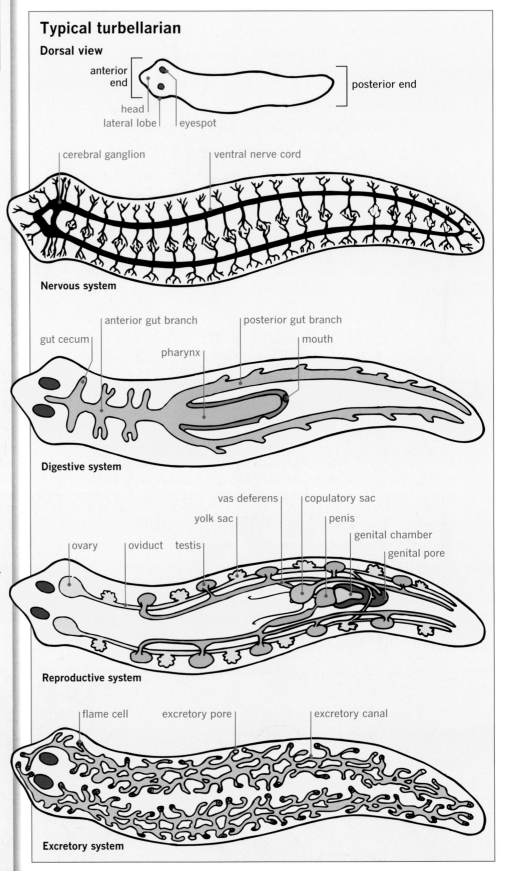

Typical turbellarian

Dorsal view

anterior end — head — lateral lobe — eyespot — posterior end

Nervous system

cerebral ganglion — ventral nerve cord

Digestive system

gut cecum — anterior gut branch — posterior gut branch — pharynx — mouth

Reproductive system

ovary — oviduct — testis — yolk sac — vas deferens — copulatory sac — penis — genital chamber — genital pore

Excretory system

flame cell — excretory pore — excretory canal

Kingdom Animalia: Platyhelminthes: tapeworm

Key words

feces
gut
hermaphrodite
host
parasite

The intestinal tapeworm

- The tapeworm is a *parasite* that lives inside the human *gut*. It enters the gut when meat containing its larvae is eaten. An ingested larva attaches itself to the gut wall by a sucker and hooks on its head. The body, which can reach up to 20 feet (6 m) in length, then dangles down into the gut space, absorbing food materials and releasing wastes.
- Most of the body of the tapeworm is devoted to reproduction as almost all of the other essential physiological processes are carried out by its *host*. Tapeworms are *hermaphrodite*.

Life in the primary host

- Humans are the primary hosts for tapeworms. The worm consists of a long series of segments called proglottids, which grow from the head (a). The segments are both male and female, and fertilization is internal. As the proglottid ages, it fills with fertilized eggs and is eventually shed from the end of the worm. It passes out of the body in the *feces* (b) and can get into a secondary host if it eats this contaminated feces (c).

Life in the secondary host

- In the secondary host (pigs, cows, and fish act as secondary hosts for different types of tapeworm), the tapeworm eggs hatch into larvae, which burrow into the host's muscles and form cysts (d–e).
- If meat from an infected animal is not cooked properly before it is eaten, the cysts can reach the intestine and develop into a new tapeworm (f).

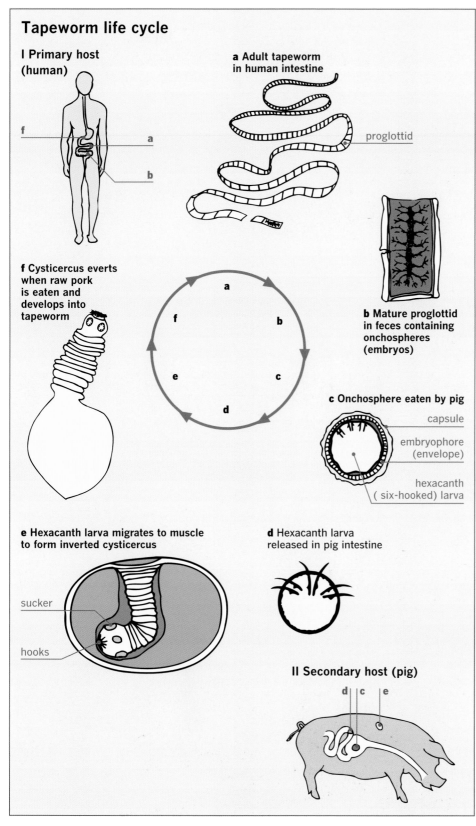

Tapeworm life cycle

I Primary host (human)

a Adult tapeworm in human intestine

proglottid

f Cysticercus everts when raw pork is eaten and develops into tapeworm

b Mature proglottid in feces containing onchospheres (embryos)

c Onchosphere eaten by pig

capsule

embryophore (envelope)

hexacanth (six-hooked) larva

e Hexacanth larva migrates to muscle to form inverted cysticercus

sucker

hooks

d Hexacanth larva released in pig intestine

II Secondary host (pig)

© Diagram Visual Information Ltd.

Key words

cyst
feces
gut
host
life cycle

Liver flukes

- Liver flukes infect a number of species including sheep, cattle, and humans. They have a complicated *life cycle* involving two *hosts* and can damage both hosts to some extent. They do not, in fact, live in the liver of the primary host but in the bile ducts.

Flukes in sheep

- A fluke enters the primary host when food containing a liver fluke larva (metacercaria) is eaten (i). The metacercaria develops in the *gut* to form a small worm that burrows through the intestine wall into the abdominal cavity. Here it migrates to the liver and burrows through it to reach the bile duct (a). It is this burrowing through the liver that damages the host.
- The adult flukes live in the bile duct leading from the liver to the gut. They produce eggs here and these pass into the gut and are expelled in *feces* (b).

Disaccharides

- The eggs hatch in water (c) to form a ciliated miracidium. This larval form can infect the secondary host, a species of water snail (d).
- Inside the snail, the miracidium becomes a sporocyst, which changes into a redia (e). The redia then produces a very small tadpole shaped cercaria, which leaves the snail and goes onto grass (f–h). There it forms a shell (is encysted) (i) and waits to be eaten (j). The stomach acids in the animal eating the contaminated food dissolve the *cyst*, and the liver fluke moves to the bile ducts and restarts the cycle.

Kingdom Animalia: Platyhelminthes: liver fluke

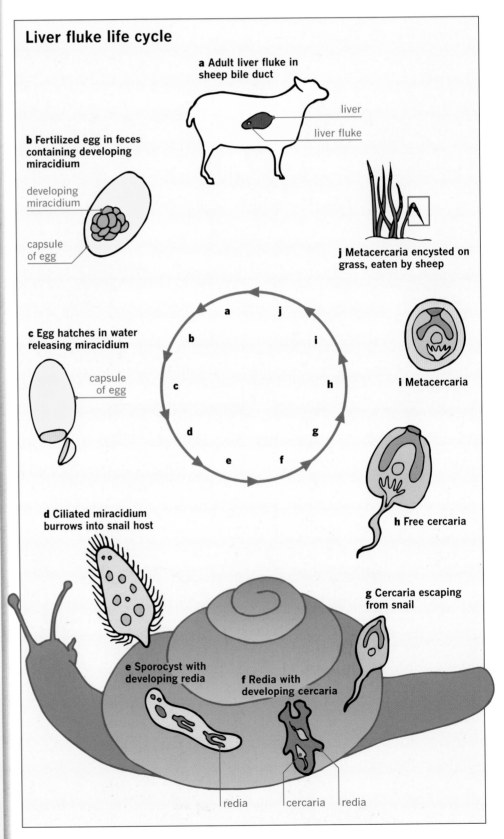

Liver fluke life cycle

a Adult liver fluke in sheep bile duct

liver
liver fluke

b Fertilized egg in feces containing developing miracidium

developing miracidium

capsule of egg

j Metacercaria encysted on grass, eaten by sheep

i Metacercaria

c Egg hatches in water releasing miracidium

capsule of egg

h Free cercaria

d Ciliated miracidium burrows into snail host

g Cercaria escaping from snail

e Sporocyst with developing redia

f Redia with developing cercaria

redia   cercaria   redia

Kingdom Animalia: Nematoda

Key words

buccal cavity
gut
hermaphrodite

Typical nematode

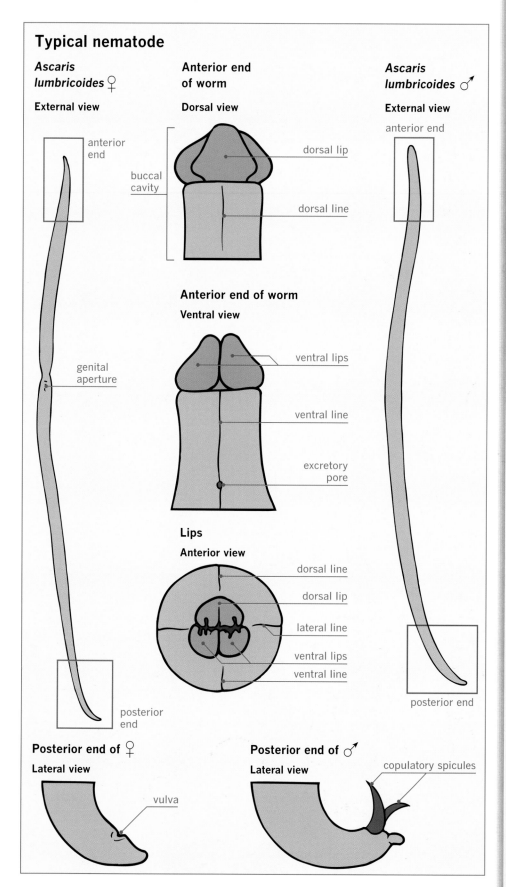

***Ascaris lumbricoides* ♀**

External view

anterior end

genital aperture

posterior end

Anterior end of worm

Dorsal view

dorsal lip

buccal cavity

dorsal line

Anterior end of worm

Ventral view

ventral lips

ventral line

excretory pore

Lips

Anterior view

dorsal line

dorsal lip

lateral line

ventral lips

ventral line

***Ascaris lumbricoides* ♂**

External view

anterior end

posterior end

Posterior end of ♀

Lateral view

vulva

Posterior end of ♂

Lateral view

copulatory spicules

Distribution
- Nematodes are the most numerous multicellular organisms on Earth, with over 20,000 different species known. A handful of soil will typically contain many thousands of the worms.

Nematode structure
- Nematode bodies typically have 1,000 cells, with a large proportion of these in the reproductive system.
- A *gut* reaches from the mouth at the anterior end to the anus at the posterior end. The mouth often has adaptations to aid the nematode in its diet. Some species have a sharp tubular structure that can penetrate cells and suck out the contents. Nematodes that feed on living prey have teeth-like structures. Nematodes that feed on bacteria can suck fluids into the *buccal cavity*, a triangular or cylindrical tube where digestion begins.

Reproduction
- Nematodes reproduce sexually and have male and female forms as well as *hermaphrodite* ones. Where the species is hermaphrodite, the worm is male first and then develops female organs.
- Male nematodes have copulary spicules used to hold the female during reproduction. The male nematode usually has a single testis that produces ameboid spermatozoa, which are released into the female vulva to give internal fertilization. The female form is usually larger than the male and has one or two ovaries. Eggs are laid that hatch to form new worms.

Key words

alveolus
feces
intestine
larva

Ascaris lumbricoides

● *Ascaris lumbricoides* or roundworms infect humans and pigs. The species can pass between humans and pigs in a manner similar to that of tapeworms but with the added complication that in humans the worm also passes through the lungs.

Reproduction and life cycle

● Adult females in the *intestine* produce eggs that pass out in the *feces*. A typical female can produce up to 200,000 eggs every day.

● The eggs can be ingested with contaminated food or water and form the first stage *larvae*. These burrow through the intestinal wall into the bloodstream and pass through the liver to the lungs. In the blood vessels of the lungs, they develop into the next stage and move into the *alveoli*.

● The larvae in the lungs are coughed up and pass down into the stomach and then to the small intestine. It is in the small intestine that they complete development to become sexually mature adults.

Kingdom Animalia: Nematoda: life cycle

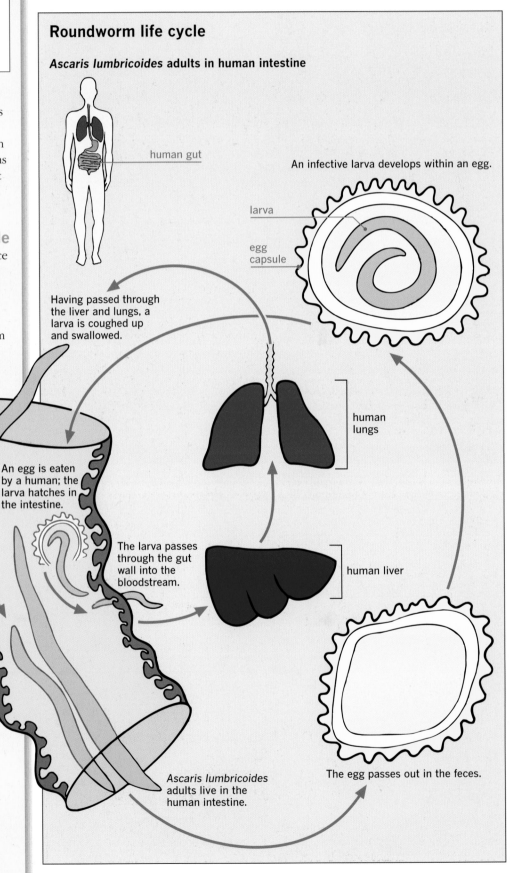

Roundworm life cycle

Ascaris lumbricoides adults in human intestine

human gut

An infective larva develops within an egg.

larva

egg capsule

Having passed through the liver and lungs, a larva is coughed up and swallowed.

An egg is eaten by a human; the larva hatches in the intestine.

The larva passes through the gut wall into the bloodstream.

human lungs

human liver

Ascaris lumbricoides adults live in the human intestine.

The egg passes out in the feces.

Kingdom Animalia: Annelida

Key words

hermaphrodite
segment

Earthworm

Lateral view

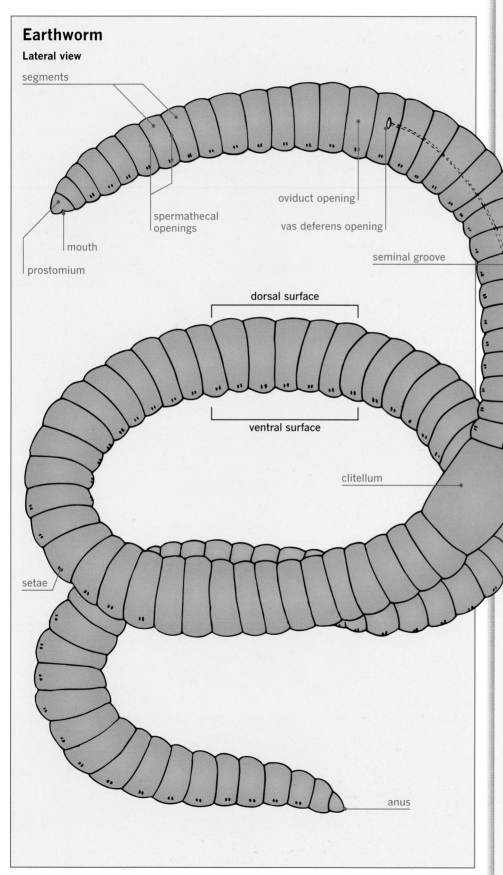

- segments
- spermathecal openings
- mouth
- prostomium
- oviduct opening
- vas deferens opening
- seminal groove
- dorsal surface
- ventral surface
- clitellum
- setae
- anus

Earthworms

- The 2,700 earthworm species are members of the annelida.

Body structure

- Earthworms have a segmented body, with each *segment* bearing the same fundamental structures.
- Visible external structures include the setae, tiny bristles that allow the worm to grip surfaces to help with movement.
- Earthworms have no eyes, but they do have light-sensitive cells on their outer skin that help them detect light levels.
- Earthworms eat by pulling food into their mouth using their prostomium.

Reproduction

- Earthworms are *hermaphrodite* but cannot fertilize their own eggs. Sperm travels from the opening of the vas deferens along the seminal groove to the clitellum.
- When two earthworms copulate, they lie side by side and head to tail so that the clitellum segments in each are opposite the segments containing the sexual organs of the other. Each exchange sperm, which is stored in internal sacs called spermathecae. The clitellum then secretes a slime tube, the cocoon, around each animal.
- The earthworm then wiggles out of the tube headfirst. While the tube passes from the clitellum to the prostomium, it passes over the oviduct, which deposits eggs into the cocoon, and then the spermathecal opening, which release the stored sperm.
- Once the worm is out of the cocoon, it seals to form an incubator.

© Diagram Visual Information Ltd.

Key words

gill
gut
hermaphrodite

Mollusks

- There are over 150,000 species of mollusks, and all have a muscular foot for locomotion and a mantle that covers the top of the animal. Many mollusks also have a hard shell made of calcium carbonate. The space between the mantle and this shell often houses *gills*, which can extract oxygen from water.

Clam body structure

- Clams are a good example of mollusks with two hard shells, called valves, that protect the soft body. The largest clams are the giant clams, which can reach sizes of four feet (1.22 m) across. Most clams are only a few inches long.
- Strong muscles, called the adductor muscles, open and close the clam. When it is open, the foot protrudes from between the valves and allows the clam to partially bury itself in the sand on the seabed or riverbed.
- Clams are filter feeders and take in water through two holes called siphons. Food particles can then be extracted and digested in the clam's *gut*. The gut is complete, running from mouth to anus. Flow is one-way.
- Clams reproduce sexually and are not *hermaphrodite*.
- Clams have a developed circulatory system to pass oxygen and food around their bodies.

Kingdom Animalia: Mollusca

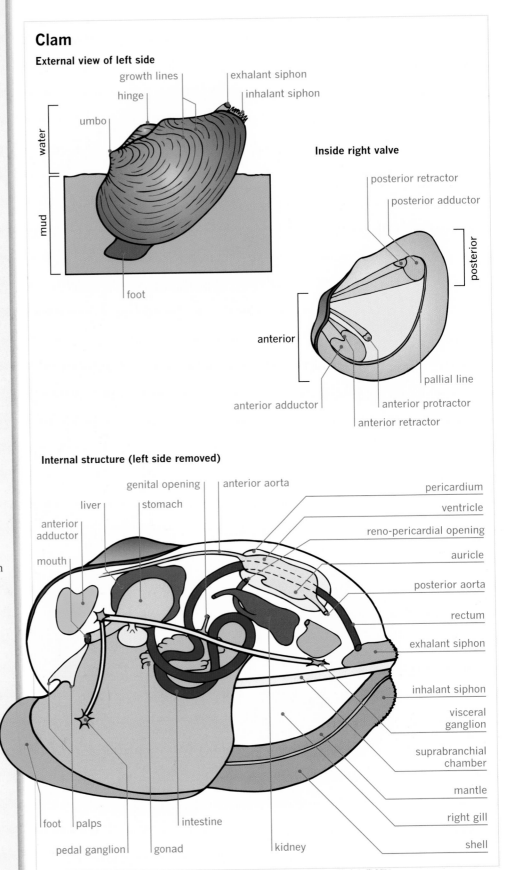

Clam

External view of left side

water · mud · umbo · hinge · growth lines · exhalant siphon · inhalant siphon · foot

Inside right valve

posterior retractor · posterior adductor · posterior · anterior · pallial line · anterior adductor · anterior protractor · anterior retractor

Internal structure (left side removed)

genital opening · anterior aorta · liver · stomach · anterior adductor · mouth · pericardium · ventricle · reno-pericardial opening · auricle · posterior aorta · rectum · exhalant siphon · inhalant siphon · visceral ganglion · suprabranchial chamber · mantle · right gill · shell · foot · palps · pedal ganglion · gonad · intestine · kidney

Kingdom Animalia: Mollusca: Gastropoda

Key words	
gaseous exchange	substrate
gill	
hermaphrodite	
tentacle	

Snail body structure

- Snails belong to the class Gastropoda, which is the largest group in the Mollusca, with up to 75,000 species.
- Snails have a single coiled shell with a space between the inside of the shell and the mantle that allows for *gaseous exchange*. Snails do not have *gills*, so the mantle acts as a simple lung.
- Snails have developed eyes and *tentacles* and are much more active than some of the other mollusks. Their head is well-developed and has a brain capable of handling a significant level of sensory input.
- Snails have an organ called a radula. This is an area of the body that is toughened and equipped with teethlike projections made of a tough, fibrous material called chitin. Snails use their radula to dislodge food from *substrates*. The radula can break up food, making it easier for the snail to swallow and digest it.
- Snails reproduce sexually, lay eggs, and are not *hermaphrodite*.

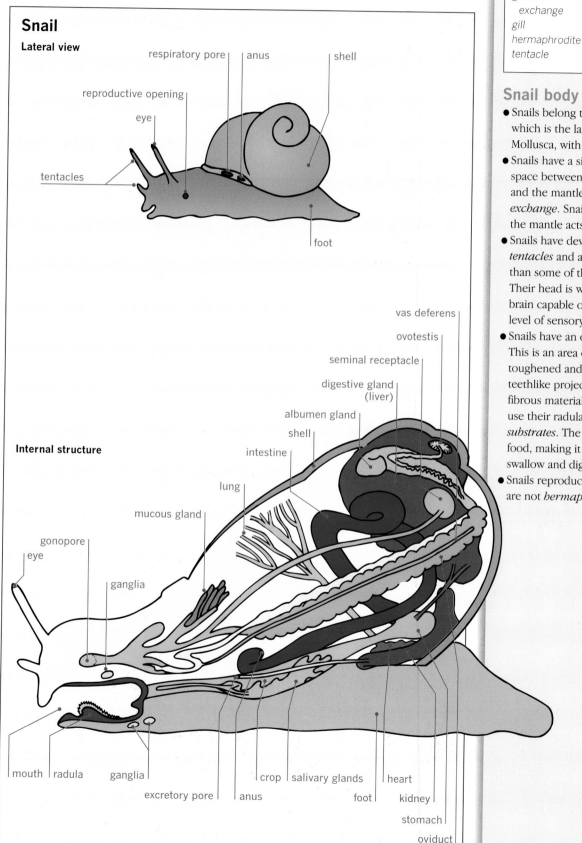

Snail

Lateral view

respiratory pore · anus · shell · reproductive opening · eye · tentacles · foot

Internal structure

vas deferens · ovotestis · seminal receptacle · digestive gland (liver) · albumen gland · shell · intestine · lung · mucous gland · gonopore · eye · ganglia · mouth · radula · ganglia · excretory pore · anus · crop · salivary glands · foot · heart · kidney · stomach · oviduct

Key words

abdomen
exoskeleton
spiracle
thorax

The insects

- In terms of numbers, the insects are the most successful group on the planet. There are both more individual insects and more species of insects than all the species of all other Animalia groups combined.

Insect body structure

- Insect bodies have three regions: the head, *thorax*, and *abdomen*. They have six jointed legs and many have pairs of wings. The whole of the body is covered by a tough *exoskeleton* made of a tough, fibrous material called chitin.
- The head is well supplied with sense organs, including compound eyes that are capable of forming accurate images. The antennae can detect vibrations, and some insects have extremely sensitive chemical detectors that can smell things over huge distances.
- Insects do not possess lungs. Gaseous exchange takes place through holes in the exoskeleton called *spiracles*. These communicate with a network of tubes running throughout the insect body. Insects have no circulatory system and this, combined with the absence of lungs, means that they cannot grow beyond a certain size or they will be unable to get oxygen to the innermost parts of their bodies.
- Some insects (ants, bees) have complex social structures with intricate behavior patterns. These sorts of insects often live in large communities with a single queen, producing most of the young.

Kingdom Animalia: Insecta

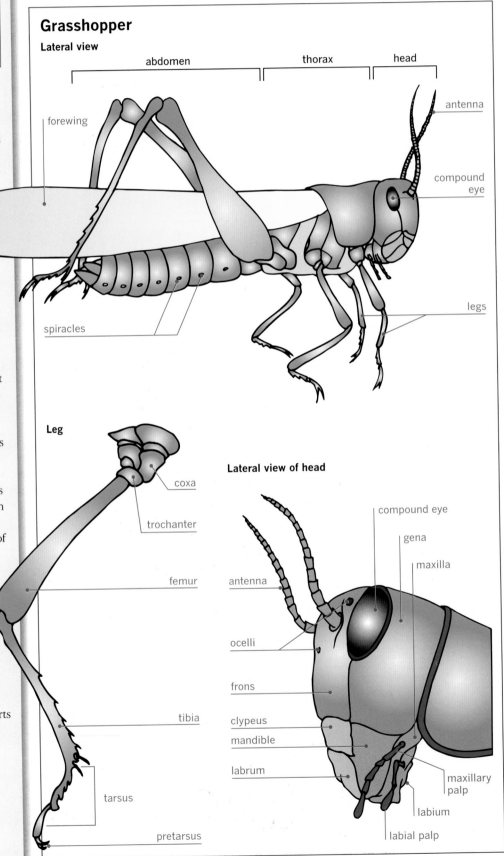

Grasshopper

Lateral view

abdomen · thorax · head

forewing

antenna

compound eye

legs

spiracles

Leg

coxa

trochanter

femur

tibia

tarsus

pretarsus

Lateral view of head

compound eye

gena

maxilla

antenna

ocelli

frons

clypeus

mandible

labrum

maxillary palp

labium

labial palp

Kingdom Animalia: Crustacea

Key words

abdomen
exoskeleton
segment
thorax

Crayfish

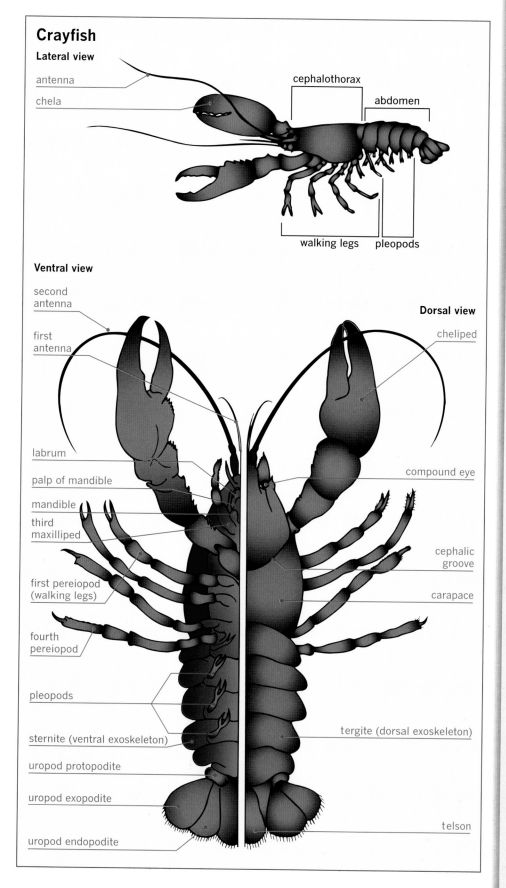

Lateral view

antenna

chela

cephalothorax

abdomen

walking legs   pleopods

Ventral view

second antenna

first antenna

Dorsal view

cheliped

labrum

palp of mandible

mandible

third maxilliped

first pereiopod (walking legs)

fourth pereiopod

pleopods

sternite (ventral exoskeleton)

uropod protopodite

uropod exopodite

uropod endopodite

compound eye

cephalic groove

carapace

tergite (dorsal exoskeleton)

telson

The Crustacea

- The Crustacea are a mainly marine group including crabs, lobsters, crayfish, and woodlice. Woodlice are terrestrial but need to live in cool damp places to avoid drying out.

Crustacean body structure

- Crustaceans have highly segmented bodies, although in some of the more advanced species the *segments* have fused together into larger blocks. The overall body plan follows standard arthropod structure with head, *thorax*, and *abdomen*, although the head and thorax are fused into a region called the cephalothorax.
- The head is well supplied with sense organs, including two pairs of antennae. In many crayfish and lobster species, a pair of front legs has been highly modified into pincers (chelipeds).
- The marine crustaceans like lobsters and crayfish grow in size by molting their *exoskeleton*, growing rapidly, and then reforming a tough exoskeleton. This can occur a number of times during an animal's life. The molting and redevelopment of the exoskeleton imposes a significant cost on the animal in terms of calcium, and this is recovered from the old exoskeleton before it is shed.
- Crustaceans can lay eggs containing either larvae (small shrimps, lobsters, and crabs) or fully formed, but small, adult forms (crayfish).

Key words

herbivore
maxilliped
predator
segment

The Chilopoda

- The Chilopoda are commonly known as centipedes. There are roughly 3,000 species of centipedes, ranging from about 1 inch (3 cm) in length to 10 inches (26 cm) for some tropical species.
- Centipedes have a single pair of legs on each *segment*, with the front-most ones being modified into claws equipped with poison glands. These front legs are called *maxillipeds* and allow the centipedes to be effective *predators*.
- Eyes are simple rather than compound.
- The upper and lower surfaces of the trunk segments are armored with thickened plates called tergal plates and are joined by a flexible membrane.
- The last division of the body, the telson, is not considered a true segment because it lacks legs.
- Centipedes live mainly in soil and humus and under stones and rocks.

The Diplopoda

- The Diplopoda, commonly known as millipedes, have two pairs of legs on each body segment. The average millipede species (of which there are 10,000) will have between 100 and 300 legs in total, although the *Illacme plenipes* species has 750 legs. Millipede length ranges from 0.08 to 12 inches (2–300 mm) with most species between 2 and 6 inches (50–150 mm).
- Most millipedes are detritivores or *herbivores*. They eat decaying organic matter and plants.
- Eyes tend to be simple.
- Milipedes are nocturnal and avoid becoming prey to the more aggressive centipedes by producing an irritating substance from glands in the thorax. This substance is released when they feel threatened.

Kingdom Animalia: Chilopoda and Diplopoda

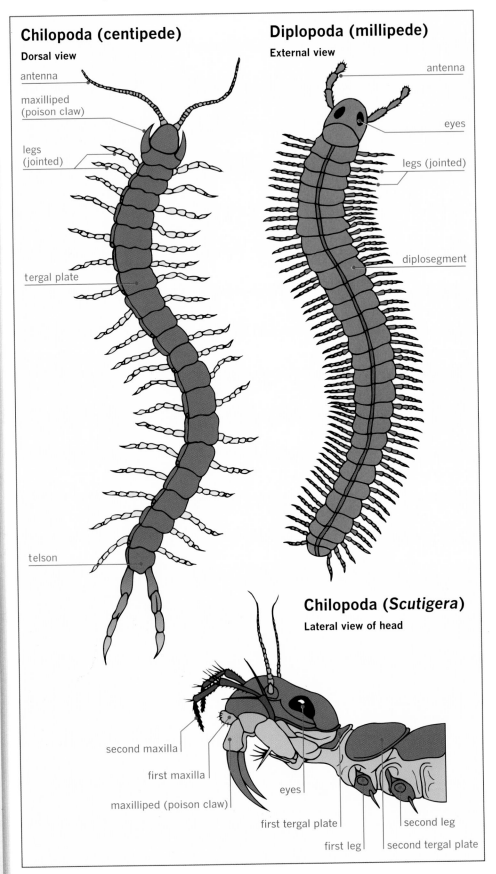

Chilopoda (centipede)

Dorsal view

- antenna
- maxilliped (poison claw)
- legs (jointed)
- tergal plate
- telson

Diplopoda (millipede)

External view

- antenna
- eyes
- legs (jointed)
- diplosegment

Chilopoda (*Scutigera*)

Lateral view of head

- second maxilla
- first maxilla
- maxilliped (poison claw)
- eyes
- first tergal plate
- first leg
- second leg
- second tergal plate

Kingdom Animalia: Arachnida

Key words

abdomen
exoskeleton
pedipalp
segment
spiracle

Spider

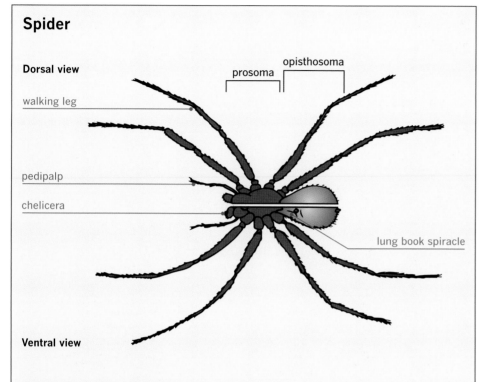

Dorsal view

prosoma opisthosoma

walking leg

pedipalp

chelicera

lung book spiracle

Ventral view

Scorpion (*Pandinus*)

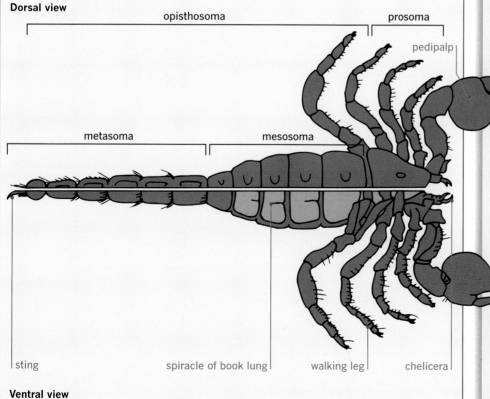

Dorsal view

opisthosoma prosoma

pedipalp

metasoma mesosoma

sting spiracle of book lung walking leg chelicera

Ventral view

The Arachnida

- The Arachnida has over 6,000 species, including all spiders and scorpions.

Spiders

- Spiders are *segmented*, but their segments are fused into two main parts—the prosoma at the front and the opisthosoma at the rear.
- Arachnids do not have true lungs. Instead, respiration occurs through rudimentary book lungs, which are a series of plates. Air bathes the outer surface of the plates, and blood circulates within them, facilitating the exchange of gases.
- Spiders have eight walking legs that arise from the prosoma. A pair of segmented legs, called pedipalps, at the front of the animal are used to grab and hold prey. The chelicera are used for holding, piercing, and injecting poisons that paralyze the prey.

Scorpions

- Scoprions are large arachnids that live in desert areas. They have a strong exoskeleton and an elongated body.
- The scorpion body is divided into two main segments: prosoma (head) and the opisthosoma (abdomen). The abdomen consists of the mesosoma—containing its book lungs, digestive tract, and sexual organs—and the metasoma or tail, which bears the telson (stinger). The movable tail is curled over the back so that the venomous stinger is in position to strike prey.
- Like spiders, scorpions use their pedipalps (claws) to grasp prey and defend against predators. Jawlike chelicera crush the prey and bring food to the mouth.

Key words

gamete

The Echinodermata

- The Echinodermata include over 6,000 species, all of which live in marine environments. The phylum includes the sea urchins and starfishes, but not fish, because echinoderms possess neither gills nor vertebrae.
- Echinoderms are radially symmetrical, which means that their body consists of legs or rays radiating out from a central hub, like a bicycle wheel.

Starfish body structure

- The central area of the starfish contains the stomach and intestines, though these are continuous with tubes that run out along each of the rays. Starfish can take food into their gut but often eat by everting the stomach onto the prey and digesting it outside the starfish body. They can eat bivalves like mollusks by prying apart the shells slightly and then inserting their stomach into the gap. After digestion is completed, the mollusk is just an empty shell.
- Starfish move using many tiny feet on the lower surface of the body. These structures, called tube feet, have suckers on the end that can hold tight to prey.
- Starfish have limited powers of regeneration and can grow back an arm that has been removed given sufficient time and good conditions. In some species, a severed ray can develop into a complete new starfish.
- Starfish commonly reproduce by a process called free-spawning. They release their *gametes* into the water, where they are fertilized by gametes from the opposite sex.

Kingdom Animalia: Echinodermata

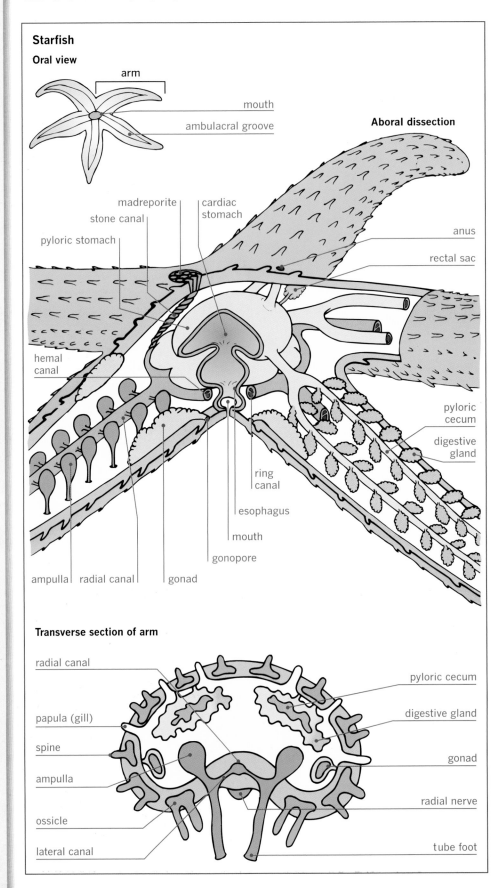

Starfish

Oral view

arm

mouth

ambulacral groove

Aboral dissection

madreporite

cardiac stomach

stone canal

pyloric stomach

anus

rectal sac

hemal canal

pyloric cecum

digestive gland

ring canal

esophagus

mouth

gonopore

ampulla   radial canal   gonad

Transverse section of arm

radial canal

pyloric cecum

papula (gill)

digestive gland

spine

gonad

ampulla

radial nerve

ossicle

lateral canal

tube foot

Kingdom Animalia: Chondrichthyes

Key words

calcification
gill
lateral line

Dogfish

Lateral view

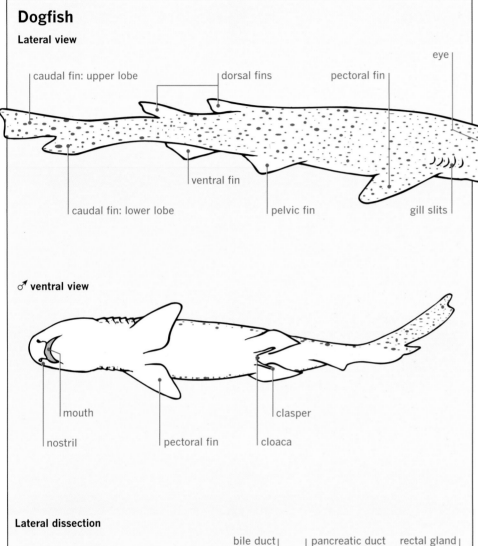

caudal fin: upper lobe

dorsal fins

pectoral fin

eye

ventral fin

caudal fin: lower lobe

pelvic fin

gill slits

♂ ventral view

mouth

nostril

pectoral fin

clasper

cloaca

Lateral dissection

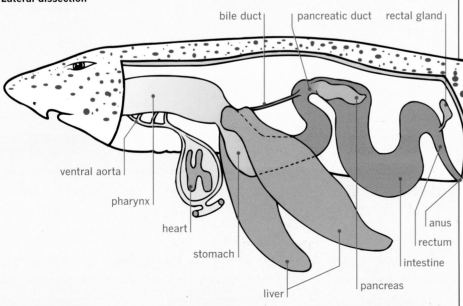

bile duct

pancreatic duct

rectal gland

ventral aorta

pharynx

heart

stomach

liver

pancreas

anus

rectum

intestine

Cartilaginous fish

- The Chondrichthyes is a class of vertebrates that includes sharks, skates, and rays and has about 1,000 living species. None of these species has any real bone, so the group is sometimes known as the cartilaginous fish. Only the teeth in sharks show *calcification* to make a bonelike material, but even here the calcium is laid down in a different pattern than true bone.
- Cartilaginous fish have a long fossil history stretching back 450 million years, and are regarded as more primitive than the bony fish.

Sharks and dogfish

- These animals share the same basic body pattern and are extremely well streamlined. They are both predators, feeding on mollusks and other fish.
- Sharks are ferocious hunters and have a series of sense organs running down their bodies called a *lateral line*. This line can detect minute changes in pressure caused by the presence of fish in the immediate area. Sharks also have a very good sense of smell and so can detect chemicals in the seawater at very low concentrations. Their eyesight is, however, poor.
- Sharks do not pump water over their gills, Instead, they must move forward at all times to maintain respiration. The gills are found on vertical arches that form the walls of the external gill slits. When water passes over the gills, capillaries in the gills absorb oxygen from the water. Shark nets kill sharks by preventing them from moving, which effectively drowns them.

© Diagram Visual Information Ltd.

Kingdom Animalia: Osteichthyes

Bony fish

- The Osteichthyes have skeletons made of bone and are sometimes called the bony fish. They are a more variable class than the cartilaginous fish and consist of 29,000 species spread across marine and fresh water.
- Bony fish have the good sense of smell and *lateral lines* of cartilaginous fish but also possess good eyesight.

Gaseous exchange

- Bony fish have a flaplike structure called an operculum that covers the *gills* on either side of the body. By moving this operculum the fish is able to draw water across its *gaseous exchange* membranes (the gills) even when the fish is stationary in the water.
- Bony fish also have structures called swim bladders, which allow them to control their buoyancy. Again, this helps the fish remain stationary in water. In some fish, oxygen can be extracted from the air in the swim bladder so that it acts as a very primitive lung.

Fins and skin

- Bony fish have paired fins that help in movement through the water—both in terms of creating a propulsive force and stabilizing the fish's movement. The fins are strengthened by flexible skeletal rays and do not contain muscle.
- The skin of bony fish is covered with overlapping scales.

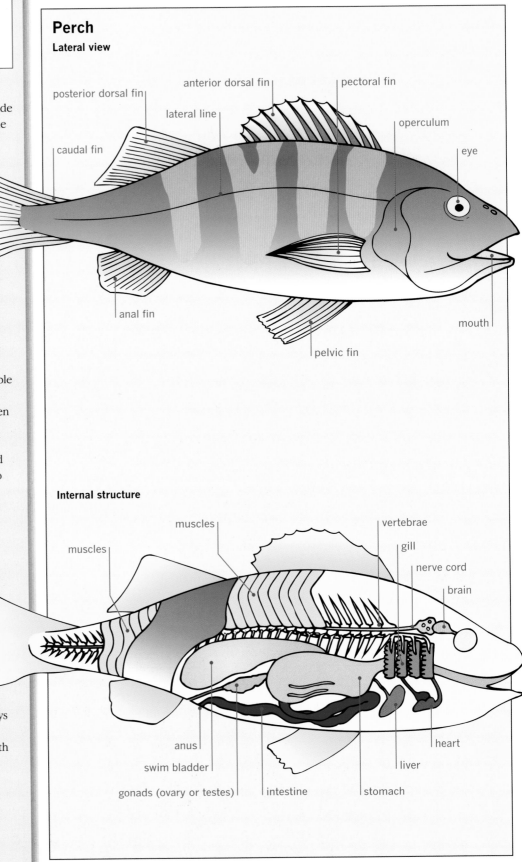

Perch
Lateral view

posterior dorsal fin · anterior dorsal fin · pectoral fin · lateral line · operculum · caudal fin · eye · anal fin · mouth · pelvic fin

Internal structure

muscles · muscles · vertebrae · gill · nerve cord · brain · anus · heart · swim bladder · liver · gonads (ovary or testes) · intestine · stomach

Kingdom Animalia: Amphibia

Key words

cloaca
gaseous
  exchange
gill
metamorphosis

Frog

External view

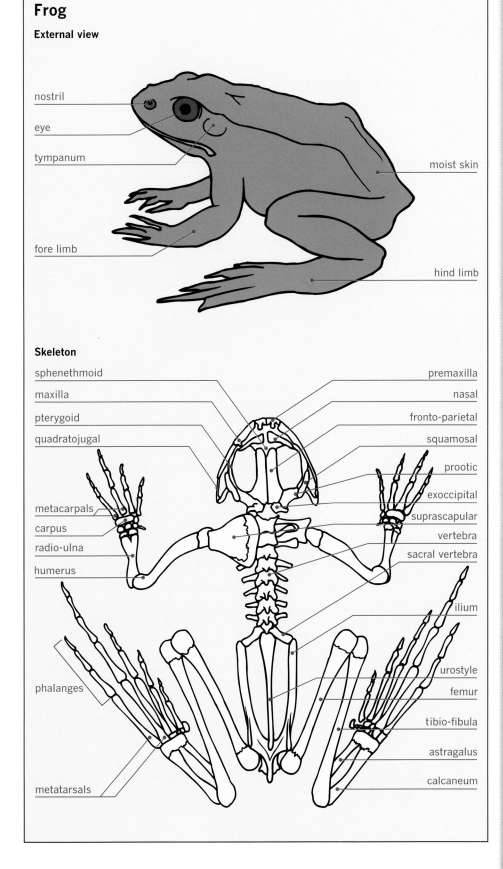

nostril

eye

tympanum

moist skin

fore limb

hind limb

Skeleton

sphenethmoid

maxilla

pterygoid

quadratojugal

premaxilla

nasal

fronto-parietal

squamosal

prootic

exoccipital

metacarpals

suprascapular

carpus

vertebra

radio-ulna

sacral vertebra

humerus

ilium

urostyle

phalanges

femur

tibio-fibula

astragalus

calcaneum

metatarsals

The Amphibia

- The class Amphibia includes over 5,000 species divided into three main groups: the frogs and toads, the newts and salamanders, and the caecilians, which are limbless amphibians that look more like snakes.
- The oldest amphibian fossils are about 360 million years old.
- Amphibians spend part of their lives in water and part on land.

Gaseous exchange

- When amphibians hatch from eggs, they have *gills* for *gaseous exchange* rather like fish. In tadpoles (the juvenile stage for frogs and toads), these gills are external. As the tadpoles age, they lose their gills, the tail shortens, and they develop legs and simple lungs. The *metamorphosis* is complete when the tadpole leaves the water as an adult frog.
- Adult frogs carry out most of their gaseous exchange through their skin, which is kept permanently moist for this purpose. Residual lungs are present but probably make a limited contribution to gaseous exchange. Close contact with the environment may explain the recent decline in amphibian species numbers across the globe, as pollutants build up in the environment.

Reproduction

- Amphibians fertilize their eggs in a variety of ways. Most frogs and toads employ external fertilization. Male salamanders deposit a packet of sperm onto the ground, and the female then pulls it into her *cloaca* where fertilization occurs internally. Caecilians and tailed frogs use internal fertilization just like reptiles, birds, and mammals.

Kingdom Animalia: Reptilia

Key words

amnion	lung
egg	
fetus	
gaseous	
exchange	

The Reptilia

- The class Reptilia includes over 7,000 species divided into two very large groups: the snakes and the lizards, and smaller numbers of turtles and crocodiles.
- Reptiles are found in a wide range of environments, from marine and freshwater to dry deserts.

Life in dry areas

- Reptiles can survive in drier areas than amphibians because their eggs are surrounded by an extra membrane called the *amnion*. This membrane helps to reduce water loss from the developing *egg* and *fetus*.
- Reptiles have *lungs* for *gaseous exchange* throughout their lives. Their heart and circulatory systems are well-developed, with minimal mixing of oxygenated and deoxygenated blood in the heart, although the separation of the two is not complete as it is in mammals and birds.
- Reptiles do not generate enough heat to maintain their body temperature. Instead, their body temperature varies. Certain behavior does help to moderate the effect of external temperature, e.g., some lizards move into sunlight on cold mornings to absorb more heat.
- Most reptiles display elaborate courtship rituals.
- Reptile fertilization is internal: the male's sperm fertilizes the female's eggs inside the female's body.

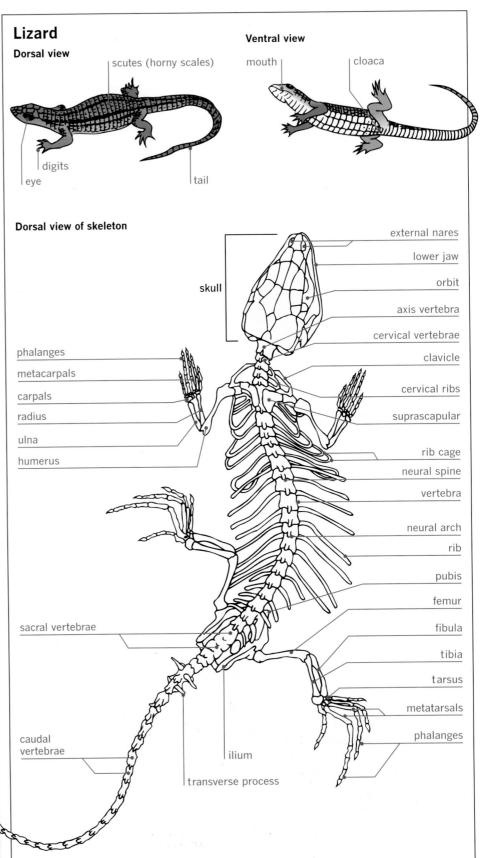

Lizard

Dorsal view

scutes (horny scales)

eye

digits

tail

Ventral view

mouth

cloaca

Dorsal view of skeleton

skull

phalanges

metacarpals

carpals

radius

ulna

humerus

sacral vertebrae

caudal vertebrae

ilium

transverse process

external nares

lower jaw

orbit

axis vertebra

cervical vertebrae

clavicle

cervical ribs

suprascapular

rib cage

neural spine

vertebra

neural arch

rib

pubis

femur

fibula

tibia

tarsus

metatarsals

phalanges

Kingdom Animalia: Aves

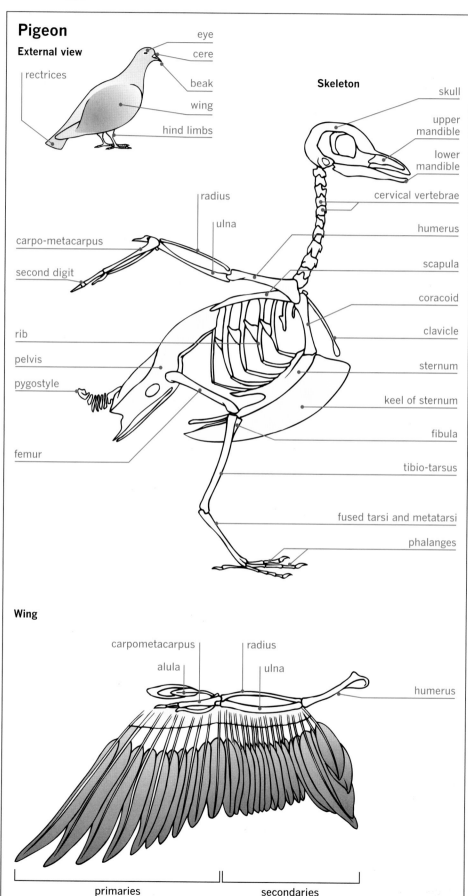

Pigeon

External view

- rectrices
- eye
- cere
- beak
- wing
- hind limbs

Skeleton

- skull
- upper mandible
- lower mandible
- cervical vertebrae
- radius
- ulna
- humerus
- carpo-metacarpus
- scapula
- second digit
- coracoid
- clavicle
- rib
- pelvis
- sternum
- pygostyle
- keel of sternum
- fibula
- femur
- tibio-tarsus
- fused tarsi and metatarsi
- phalanges

Wing

- carpometacarpus
- radius
- alula
- ulna
- humerus

primaries | secondaries

The Aves
- The class Aves, or birds, includes about 10,000 species, and the group is present in almost every environment and across every continent.
- Birds are characterized by the adapatations needed for the strenuous muscle activity required for flight.

Wings
- A bird's wing is composed of three limb bones: the humerus, ulna, and radius.
- The primary feathers, attached to the carpometacarpus, propel the bird through the air. They are the largest of the flight feathers and are the farthest away from the body. The secondary flight feathers run along the ulna of the wing and sustain the bird in the air, giving it lift.
- A group of feathers attached to the alula reduce turbulence and drag, and also assist with steering.

Warm blooded
- Flight requires a rapid *metabolism*, and birds maintain their body temperature above the environmental temperature.
- Avian circulatory systems are well developed, with complete separation of oxygenated and deoxygenated blood in a *double circulation* system. This increases the rate at which oxygen can be supplied to the powerful flight muscles.

Reproduction
- Fertilization in birds is internal.
- Development of the young occurs outside the body in hard-shelled eggs. There is often significant parental behavior to protect the eggs and raise the young.

Key words

fetus
mammary glands
placenta

The Mammalia

- Although mammals contain only about 5,000 species in total, the class is often regarded as the most successful animal group because of the sophistication of its members, and their relatively late arrival in evolutionary terms.
- Mammals are divided two main groups: the marsupials, who give birth to live but very undeveloped young, and placentals, who give birth to well-developed young.

Hair

- All mammals have hair or fur on their bodies. Even marine mammals like whales and walruses have some hair.
- Hair is important in: heat insulation (all mammals are warm-blooded); protection against sunlight; sensitivity (as in whiskers); and for identification, e.g., males and females of the same species may have different hair color.

Reproductive advantages

- Mammals have entirely internal fertilization, with the penis of the male being inserted into the vagina of the female. Development of the *fetus* is also internal due to the presence of the *placenta*, an organ that allows materials to be exchanged between the mother and the fetus.
- After birth the young are fed on milk produced by *mammary glands*. In some species extensive parental behavior also helps to protect and raise the young.

Kingdom Animalia: Mammalia

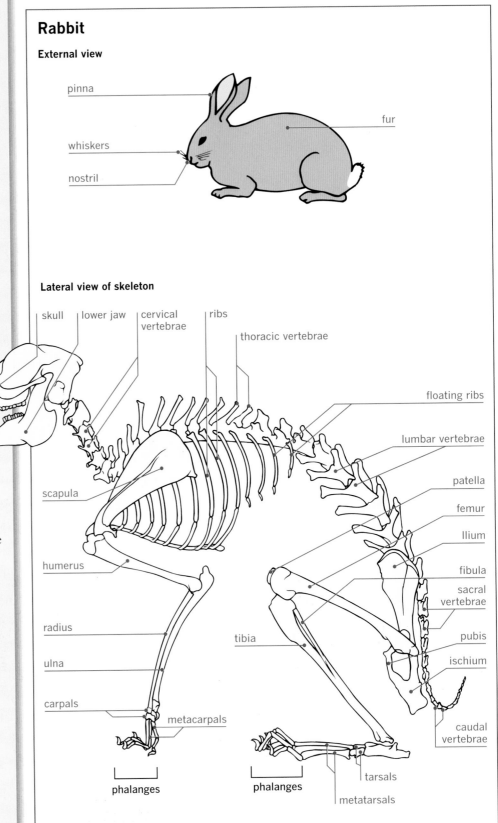

Rabbit

External view

- pinna
- whiskers
- nostril
- fur

Lateral view of skeleton

- skull
- lower jaw
- cervical vertebrae
- ribs
- thoracic vertebrae
- floating ribs
- lumbar vertebrae
- scapula
- patella
- femur
- Ilium
- humerus
- fibula
- sacral vertebrae
- radius
- tibia
- pubis
- ulna
- ischium
- carpals
- metacarpals
- caudal vertebrae
- phalanges
- phalanges
- tarsals
- metatarsals

Nutrition: types

Tree diagram of nutrition types

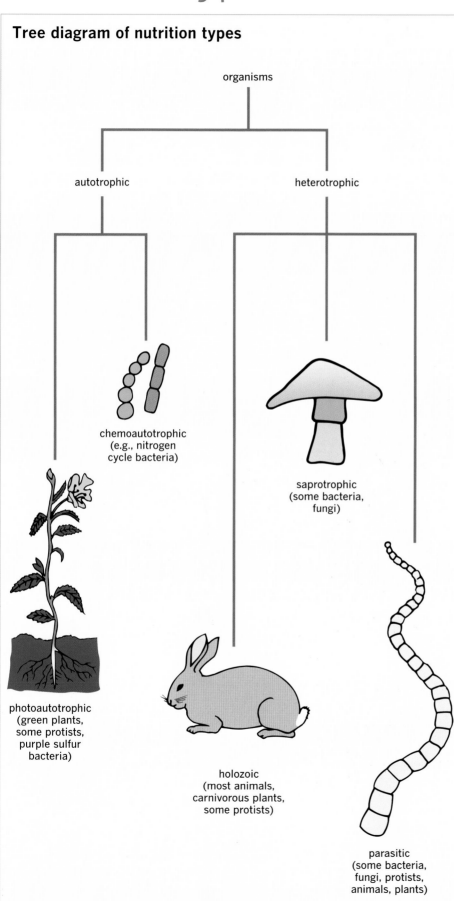

organisms

autotrophic

heterotrophic

chemoautotrophic
(e.g., nitrogen
cycle bacteria)

saprotrophic
(some bacteria,
fungi)

photoautotrophic
(green plants,
some protists,
purple sulfur
bacteria)

holozoic
(most animals,
carnivorous plants,
some protists)

parasitic
(some bacteria,
fungi, protists,
animals, plants)

Key words

organic matter
parasite

Organic matter

● Biologists regard *organic matter* as material that has been produced by living organisms.
● Inorganic matter is regarded as simple materials like water, mineral salts, and carbon dioxide. The vast majority of material in the world is inorganic. To convert simple inorganic matter into more complex organic matter requires an input of energy.

Autotrophic nutrition

● Autotrophic organisms are able to produce organic matter from simple inorganic materials. They consequently create their own food—but require a source of energy to do this.
● Photoautotrophs harvest energy from light to produce organic matter.
● Chemoautotrophs use energy from inorganic reactions in the environment to drive the creation of organic matter.

Heterotrophic nutrition

● Heterotrophic nutritrion is typical of animals. These organisms eat organic matter in other organisms—either alive (as hunters) or dead (as scavengers).
● Saprotrophic organisms are the decay organisms. They digest dead materials using enzymes that they secrete externally. Fungi and many bacteria are saprotrophes.
● *Parasites* (biotrophs) feed on living organisms without killing them.

Key words

absorption	pseudopodium
exocytosis	vacuole
gut	
lysosome	
organelle	

Ameba feeding

- Amebas are examples of Protista that feed by engulfing their prey in extensions of the body called pseudopodia. Amebas will eat bacteria and small algae.

Ingestion

- *Pseudopodia* extend from the ameba to surround the prey. These pseudopodia join up to completely engulf the prey and form a food *vacuole*, which then passes into the cell body.
- Once inside the cell, *lysosomes*, membrane-bound *organelles* containing digestive enzymes, join with the vacuole membrane and empty their contents into the vacuole.
- Powerful enzymes break down the food in much the same way as occurs in mammalian *guts*. Interestingly, the vacuole contents are at first acid, then neutral, and then faintly alkaline—mirroring the sequence in the guts of higher animals.

Absorption and exocytosis

- The digested materials pass into the cell body of the ameba by diffusion and selective *absorption*.
- In a process known as *exocytosis*, indigestible remains are passed to the outside world when the food vacuole fuses with the cell membrane.

Nutrition: Protista

Feeding and intracellular digestion in *Amoeba proteus*

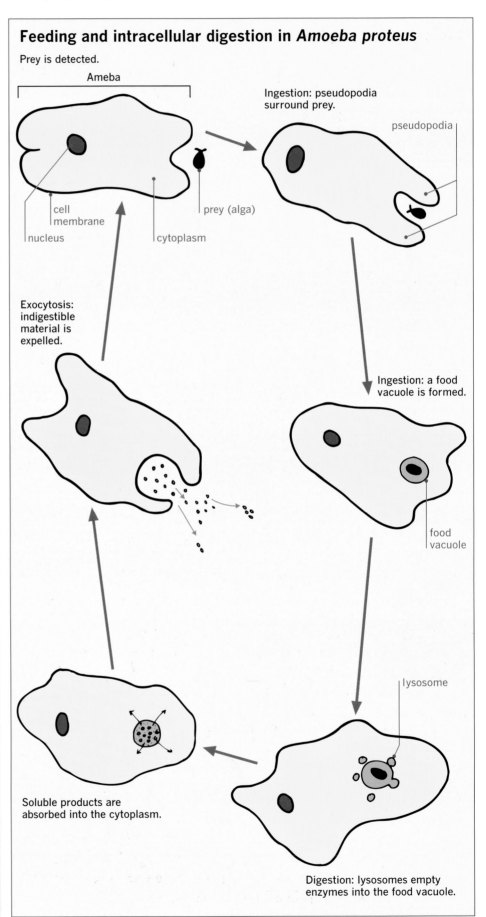

Prey is detected.

Ameba

cell membrane

nucleus

cytoplasm

prey (alga)

Ingestion: pseudopodia surround prey.

pseudopodia

Ingestion: a food vacuole is formed.

food vacuole

Exocytosis: indigestible material is expelled.

Soluble products are absorbed into the cytoplasm.

lysosome

Digestion: lysosomes empty enzymes into the food vacuole.

Nutrition: leaf structure

Typical flowering plant (dicotyledon)

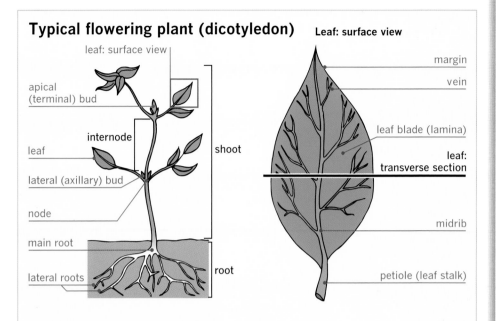

Leaf: surface view

- leaf: surface view
- apical (terminal) bud
- internode
- leaf
- lateral (axillary) bud
- node
- main root
- lateral roots
- shoot
- root
- margin
- vein
- leaf blade (lamina)
- leaf: transverse section
- midrib
- petiole (leaf stalk)

Leaf: transverse section (low power)

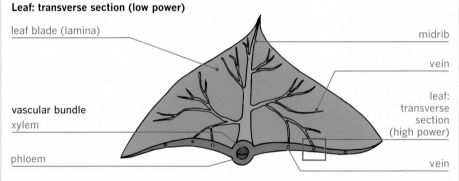

- leaf blade (lamina)
- vascular bundle
- xylem
- phloem
- midrib
- vein
- leaf: transverse section (high power)
- vein

Leaf: transverse section (high power)

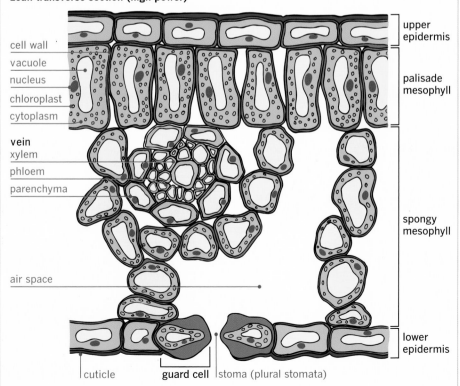

- cell wall
- vacuole
- nucleus
- chloroplast
- cytoplasm
- vein
  - xylem
  - phloem
  - parenchyma
- air space
- upper epidermis
- palisade mesophyll
- spongy mesophyll
- lower epidermis
- cuticle
- guard cell
- stoma (plural stomata)

Photosynthesis

- Leaves are structures that carry out *photosynthesis* in green plants.
- In order to do this they need to be able to collect sunlight, water, and carbon dioxide, and get rid of waste oxygen.

Harvesting light

- The larger the surface area, the more light that can be collected.
- The upper surface of the leaf tends to receive more light than the lower surface. Plants concentrate their most effective photosynthetic cells near the upper surface for this reason.

Carbon dioxide supply

- Only 0.03 percent of the atmosphere is carbon dioxide. Plants need to process large volumes of air to gather enough carbon dioxide for photosynthesis. Holes in the lower surface of the leaf (called *stomata*) allow air to enter the leaf and get directly to the active photosynthetic tissues.
- Waste oxygen can also leave through the stomata.

Water supply

- Photosynthesis requires a supply of water. This is provided through the *veins* of the leaf. A constant supply of water is also required to replace the water lost by *transpiration* through the stomata.
- Veins also carry the products of photosynthesis to the rest of the plant.

Key words

diffusion
guard cell
osmosis
stoma

Diffusion

- *Diffusion* is the random movement of particles from areas of high concentration to areas of low concentration. It requires no energy input from a living organism.
- Gases diffuse in and out of leaves via leaf pores (*stomata*).

Stomatal structure

- Stomata are made of pairs of cells called *guard cells* that are joined at the ends. The cell walls of guard cells are not equally thick all around the cell—the thickest parts are the walls immediately adjacent to the next cell in a pair. The cell walls here are also separated by a small space called the stoma or pore.

Stomatal functioning

- Stomata can increase the size of their opening. This occurs when the guard cells take in water by *osmosis* and swell. The unequal thickness of the cell walls leads to the cells bulging outward in the area farthest away from the thick walls. Forces in the cell walls then push the thickened cell walls away from each other—and so the pore widens. Deflating the guard cells closes the pore again.
- Stomata tend to open during daylight hours when the plant needs carbon dioxide for photosynthesis. During times of drought, the stomata will close to conserve water.

Nutrition: stomata

Stomata

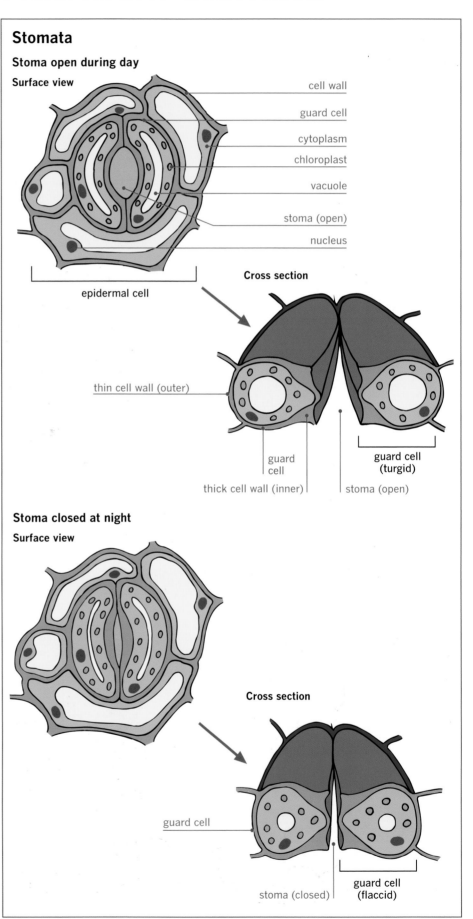

Stoma open during day

Surface view

- cell wall
- guard cell
- cytoplasm
- chloroplast
- vacuole
- stoma (open)
- nucleus

epidermal cell

Cross section

thin cell wall (outer)

guard cell

thick cell wall (inner)

guard cell (turgid)

stoma (open)

Stoma closed at night

Surface view

Cross section

guard cell

stoma (closed)

guard cell (flaccid)

Transport: stem structure

Stems

Generalized plant

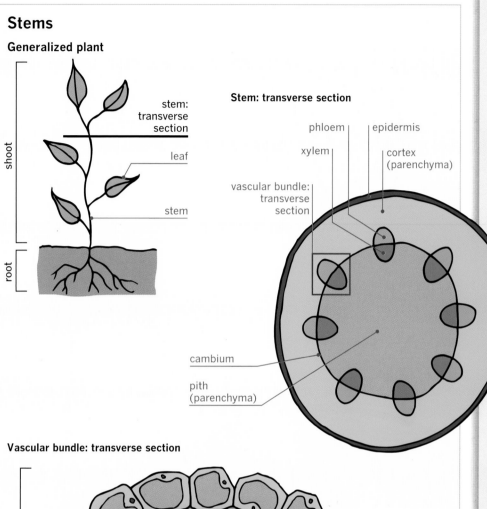

Stem: transverse section

- phloem
- xylem
- epidermis
- cortex (parenchyma)
- vascular bundle: transverse section
- cambium
- pith (parenchyma)
- shoot
- stem: transverse section
- leaf
- stem
- root

Vascular bundle: transverse section

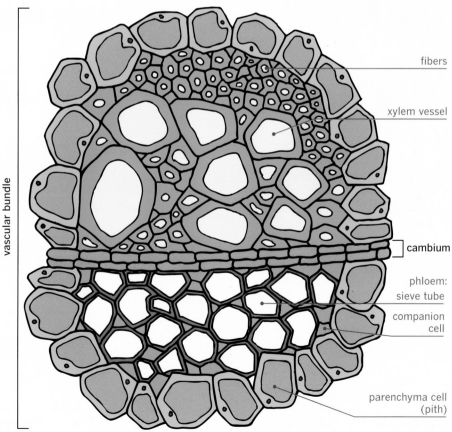

- vascular bundle
- fibers
- xylem vessel
- cambium
- phloem: sieve tube
- companion cell
- parenchyma cell (pith)

Materials

- Plants have two separate transport systems: *xylem*, which moves water and mineral salts from the roots to the leaves, and *phloem*, which moves sugars and organic materials from the leaves to all other parts of the plant.
- Both of these transport systems use tubes of conducting cells. These are found in the *vascular bundles* separated by the *cambium*, which divides to produce new xylem and phloem.
- Parenchyma cells beneath the *epidermis* constitute the cortex, the outer portion of the stem, and are used for storing food. Parenchyma cells in the center of the stem form the pith, the soft spongelike core of the stem.

Xylem

- Xylem tissue consists of long columns of cells stacked one on top of the other. These cells are dead at maturity and have lost their end walls. A xylem vessel looks like a hollow tube made up of many cylindrical sections.
- Xylem cell walls are thickened with *lignin*, which gives them strength and also makes them waterproof (see page 132). Perforations allow water to enter and leave the vessels.

Phloem

- Phloem tissue has two cell types: sieve tube elements and companion cells.
- Sieve tube elements are arranged in columns as they are in xylem, but their end walls are still present, though perforated with many holes. The cell contents of the elements are also highly modified to form a slime plug with no visible *organelles*.
- Companion cells support and nourish sieve tube elements in the phloem.

Transport: woody stem

Key words

cambium
lignin
phloem
photosynthesis
xylem

The need for light

- Food is manufactured in the leaves and green stems of plants by *photosynthesis*. Photosynthesis requires a constant energy input in the form of light. Plants that are shaded make less food.
- Plants with tall stems are less likely to be shaded than plants with short stems. However, the stem needs to be strengthened to prevent it collapsing: reinforcement produces rigid woody stems that can support the leaves in the light.

Lignin

- The strengthening of stems is provided by a complex carbohydrate called *lignin*, which lines the walls of *xylem* vessels.
- Xylem vessels are produced by the division of *cambium* cells, which form a continuous cylinder separating the *phloem* on the outside and *xylem* on the inside.
- Lignin is waterproof, so the xylem vessels are supplied with perforations that allow water to pass into and out of the xylem vessels.

Annual rings

- More vessels are produced during the active growing seasons (spring and summer).
- These periods of growth produce annual rings, which can be seen in a transverse section of the main trunk. Counting the number of annual rings provides an estimate of the age of the tree.

Woody stems

Generalized tree

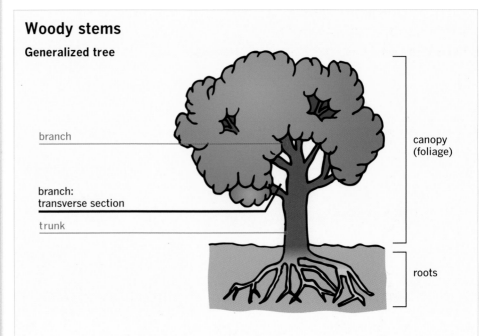

branch

branch:
transverse section

trunk

canopy
(foliage)

roots

Branch: transverse section

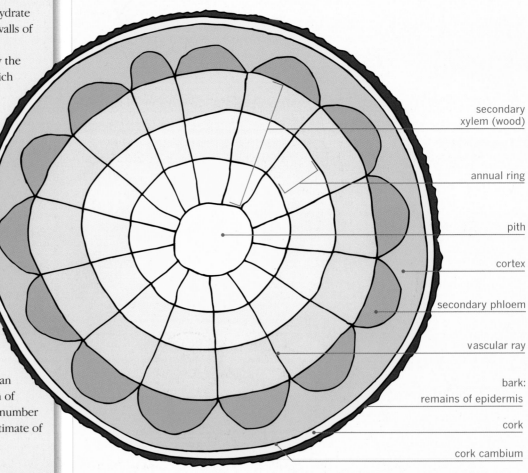

secondary
xylem (wood)

annual ring

pith

cortex

secondary phloem

vascular ray

bark:
remains of epidermis

cork

cork cambium

Transport: root structure

Dicotyledon root structure

Generalized plant

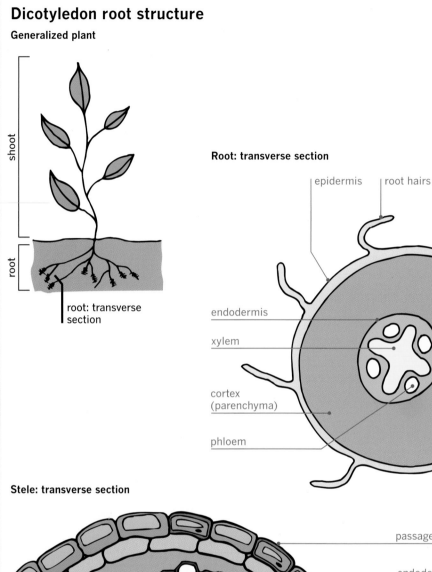

shoot

root

root: transverse section

Root: transverse section

epidermis

root hairs

endodermis

xylem

stele

cortex (parenchyma)

phloem

Stele: transverse section

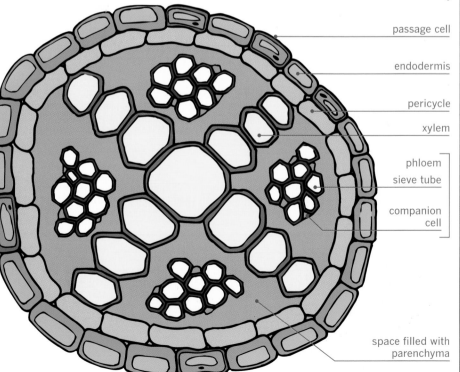

passage cell

endodermis

pericycle

xylem

phloem
sieve tube

companion cell

space filled with parenchyma

Key words

endodermis   xylem
epidermis
phloem
root hair
suberin

Roots and stems

- The root is the part of the stem that is adapted to conditions underground.
- It has the same basic tissues as the stem (*xylem* and *phloem*) but arranged in slightly different configurations.

Epidermis and cortex

- The *epidermis* of a root is supplied with many *root hairs*. These are concentrated near the growing tips of the root and are concerned with absorption of water and minerals from the soil.
- Immediately inside the epidermis is a region of the root called the cortex. This is made up of parenchyma cells, and water and minerals from the soil can flow easily between these cells.

The stele

- A continuous cylinder of cells called the *endodermis* surrounds the inner part of the root, the stele. Endodermal cells have a waterproofing substance called *suberin* in their cell walls, which blocks movement of water from the cortex between the cells. Water now has to pass through the cells rather than between them: this gives the plant a degree of control over water and mineral salt movement into the stele.
- The pericycle conducts water and nutrients inward to the xylem and phloem.
- The stele is the central core containing the xylem and phloem tissues. This is usually arranged in a cross shape with xylem in the middle. As the root ages the structure changes to the bundles more typical of the stem.

Key words

active process
osmosis
transpiration
xylem

Xylem tissues

- Water movement in plants is largely through *xylem* vessels.
- Xylem vessels are made of elements stacked on top of each other. The end walls have been lost, effectively leaving empty cylinders reaching from the root to the leaves.

Absorption of water and salts

- Water is absorbed through the root by *osmosis*. Mineral salts are similarly transported in solution and pass up the plant through the xylem.
- Some minerals are also absorbed by *active processes* requiring an energy input by the plant.

Transpiration suction

- Water is constantly evaporating from the aerial parts of the plant. This process is called *transpiration* and occurs mainly through the leaves during daylight hours. In optimal conditions a typical herbaceous plant can transpire up to 40 times its own weight in water every day.
- Transpiration reduces water concentration in the leaves. This, in turn, creates a force on the water in the veins sucking water outward. The veins are continuous with the xylem vessels, so the force is transmitted through the water column all the way down to the roots. This force, called transpiration suction, pulls water up the plant. It requires no energy input from the plant.

Transport: water and minerals in plants

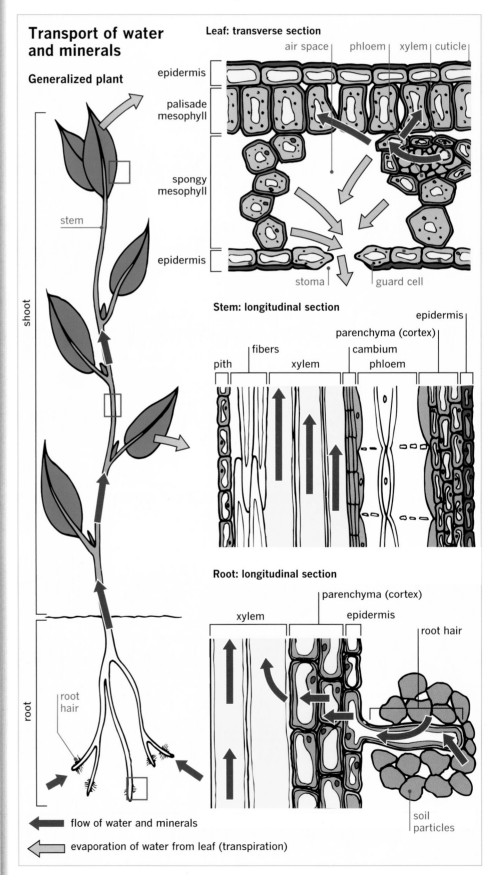

Transport of water and minerals

Generalized plant

stem

shoot

root

root hair

Leaf: transverse section

air space | phloem | xylem | cuticle

epidermis

palisade mesophyll

spongy mesophyll

epidermis

stoma | guard cell

Stem: longitudinal section

epidermis

parenchyma (cortex)

fibers | cambium

pith | xylem | phloem

Root: longitudinal section

parenchyma (cortex)

xylem | epidermis

root hair

soil particles

→ flow of water and minerals

→ evaporation of water from leaf (transpiration)

Transport: food in plants

Transport of food

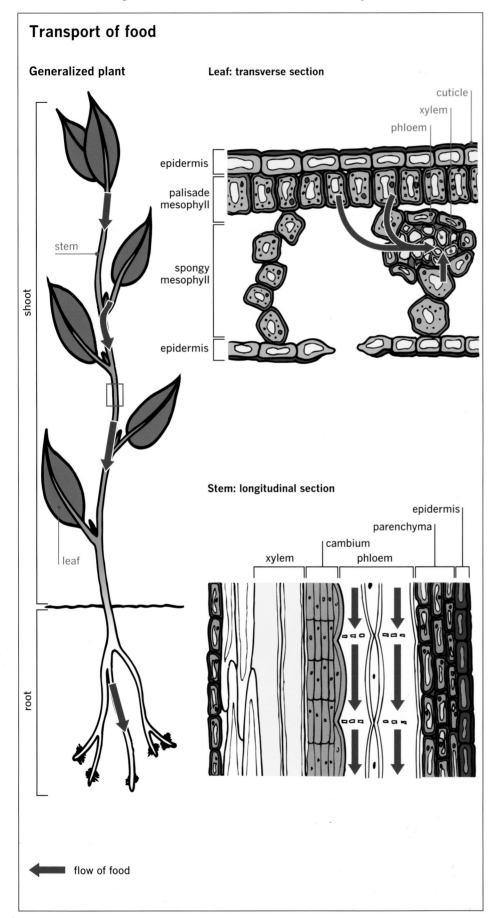

Generalized plant

Leaf: transverse section

cuticle
xylem
phloem

epidermis

palisade mesophyll

stem

spongy mesophyll

shoot

epidermis

leaf

root

Stem: longitudinal section

epidermis
parenchyma
cambium
phloem
xylem

flow of food

Key words

active transport   *xylem*
glucose
phloem
photosynthesis
vascular bundle

Sources and sinks

- Food is manufactured in the leaves and green stems of plants by *photosynthesis*. These areas are called the sources.
- Food is used in all parts of the plant. Some areas are particularly adapted to store food, for example tubers in potatoes and many fruits in flowering plants. These areas are called sinks.

Leaves and stems

- Leaves create *glucose* from carbon dioxide and water using light as an energy source. Glucose is difficult to transport through plants because it requires large amounts of water. Leaves convert this glucose into another sugar called sucrose, which is easier to move.
- Veins in the leaf contain *vascular bundles* that contain two types of conducting vessels: *xylem* and *phloem*.
- Phloem transports sugars away from the leaf.
- Xylem conducts water and dissolved minerals from the roots to the stem and leaves.

Roots and fruits

- Vascular bundles in the leaf connect with similar structures in the roots. Each sieve tube, a part of the phloem, is continuous with those in the roots. Sugar is loaded in and passes down by *active transport*. In the roots the sugar is taken out of the phloem tubes and converted to starch for storage, or is used to keep the root alive.
- Fruits and flowers require sugar because they do not carry out photosynthesis.

Transport: frog

Circulatory system

- Frogs have a well-developed circulatory system with blood that is held within tubes that penetrate the whole body.
- Frog blood is supplied with a form of *hemoglobin* that reacts reversibly with oxygen to collect oxygen from the exchange surfaces and deliver it to the cells of the body.

Circulatory system plan

- The circulatory system of the frog has *arteries* that carry blood away from the heart and *veins* that carry it back.
- Arteries and veins are named after the organ they take blood to (in arteries) or away from (in veins).
- Organs have a single artery and vein although it may subdivide into smaller vessels before it enters the organ. Inside the organ the vessels subdivide further to form *capillaries* that are ultimately one blood cell wide. No cell in the body is further than 0.004 inch (0.1 mm) from a blood capillary. Materials are exchanged with the blood at this point.

Frog heart

- The heart pushes fluid around the vessels to maintain a constant supply of fresh oxygenated blood.
- With a single *ventricle*, the frog heart is less developed than mammalian hearts.

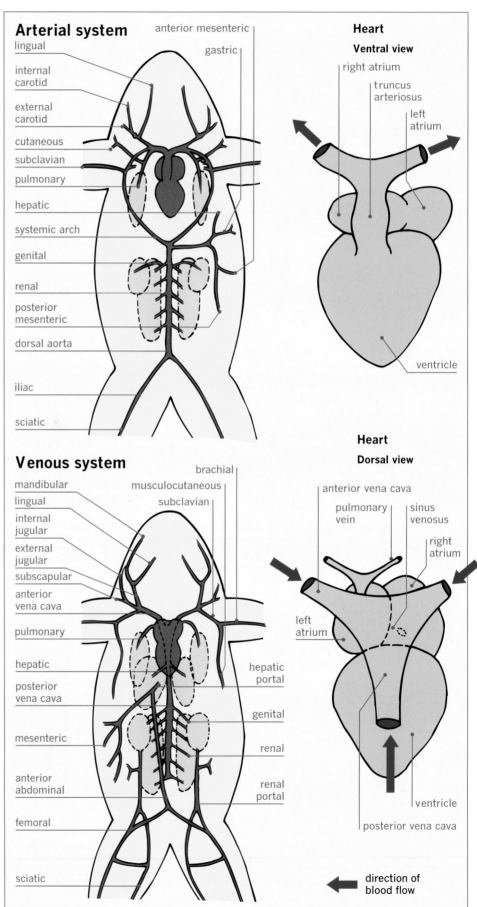

Arterial system

- anterior mesenteric
- lingual
- gastric
- internal carotid
- external carotid
- cutaneous
- subclavian
- pulmonary
- hepatic
- systemic arch
- genital
- renal
- posterior mesenteric
- dorsal aorta
- iliac
- sciatic

Venous system

- mandibular
- brachial
- musculocutaneous
- lingual
- subclavian
- internal jugular
- external jugular
- subscapular
- anterior vena cava
- pulmonary
- hepatic
- hepatic portal
- posterior vena cava
- genital
- mesenteric
- renal
- anterior abdominal
- renal portal
- femoral
- sciatic

Heart
Ventral view

- right atrium
- truncus arteriosus
- left atrium
- ventricle

Heart
Dorsal view

- anterior vena cava
- pulmonary vein
- sinus venosus
- right atrium
- left atrium
- ventricle
- posterior vena cava

direction of blood flow

Respiration: plants

Key words
diffusion
lenticel
photosynthesis
respiration
root hair

Respiration in plants

Leaf: transverse section

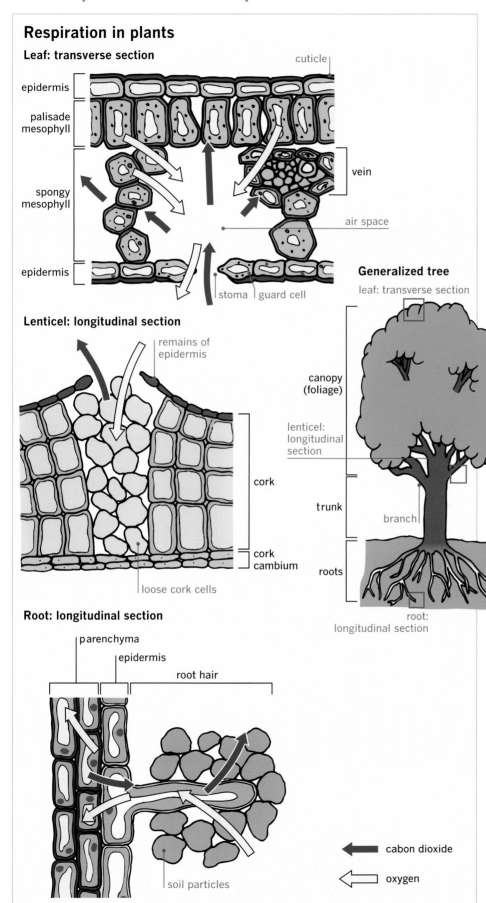

cuticle

epidermis

palisade mesophyll

spongy mesophyll

epidermis

vein

air space

stoma   guard cell

Lenticel: longitudinal section

remains of epidermis

cork

cork cambium

loose cork cells

Generalized tree
leaf: transverse section

canopy (foliage)

lenticel: longitudinal section

trunk

branch

roots

root: longitudinal section

Root: longitudinal section

parenchyma

epidermis

root hair

soil particles

→ cabon dioxide

⇨ oxygen

Respiration in plants

- Plants carry out *respiration* at all times of the day and night.
- During daylight hours, the plant obtains all the oxygen it needs as a by-product of *photosynthesis*. The leaves are thus net exporters of oxygen.
- During the night, or when photosynthesis is halted for some other reason, plants take in oxygen for respiration by *diffusion* through the leaves.

Woody stems

- Woody stems do not carry out photosynthesis, so they need to obtain oxygen directly from the atmosphere.
- The bark of trees prevents the passage of oxygen, so plants have structures called *lenticels*, which are breaks in the bark covering. Oxygen can diffuse into the stem through these. Once inside the plant, the gas moves in solution between the cells by diffusion.
- Lenticels have cells that are less tightly packed than most cells in the stems to provide an increased surface area for the exchange of oxygen with the atmosphere.

Roots

- Since roots do not receive light, they cannot carry out photosynthesis, so are always net importers of oxygen.
- The gas diffuses into the root through *root hairs*, which penetrate air spaces in the soil.

Respiration: gas exchange across body surfaces

Key words

concentration
  gradient
diffusion
gaseous
  exchange

Oxygen source

- Oxygen is available in the environment either as a gas or dissolved in water.
- The point at which oxygen passes into the body of an animal is called the respiratory surface. It must be kept moist.

Animals without circulatory systems

- In animals without specialized circulatory systems, such as amebas and *Hydras*, oxygen dissolves in the moisture on the surface of the body and passes by *diffusion* to adjacent cells. Carbon dioxide passes the other way.
- Since respiration uses up oxygen and produces carbon dioxide, a *concentration gradient* in the gases ensures transport in the correct direction. An increase in activity increases the gradient, leading to a faster rate of diffusion.
- However, since diffusion cannot rapidly move materials over large distances, a size limitation is imposed on simpler animals. To reduce this limitation, a number of these animals have flattened body shapes to increase the surface available for *gaseous exchange* and reduce the distance the oxygen needs to diffuse inside the body e.g., flatworms.

Animals with circulatory systems

- The earthworm has a simple circulatory system that transports oxygen absorbed through the skin deeper into the body.
- Carbon dioxide produced inside the body is moved by the same mechanism in the opposite direction. This allows the earthworm to have a rounder body shape than the more primitive flatworms.

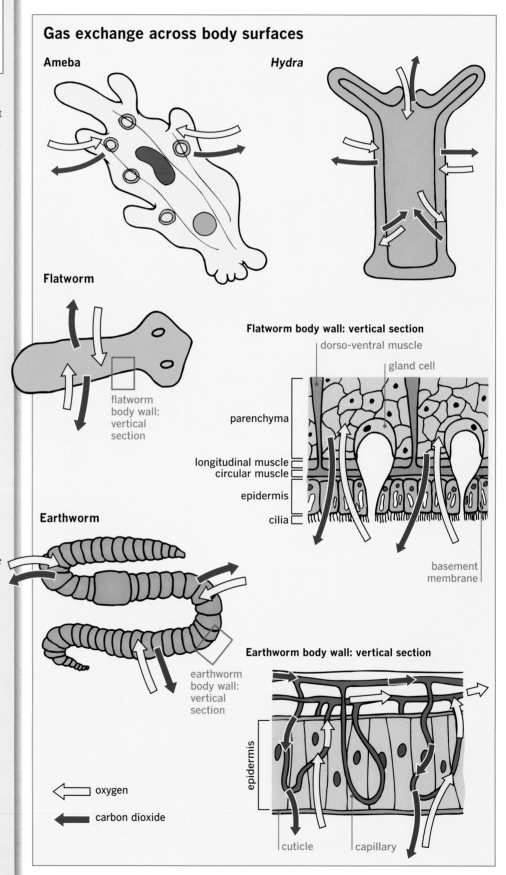

Gas exchange across body surfaces

Ameba

Hydra

Flatworm

flatworm body wall: vertical section

Flatworm body wall: vertical section

dorso-ventral muscle

gland cell

parenchyma

longitudinal muscle
circular muscle

epidermis

cilia

basement membrane

Earthworm

earthworm body wall: vertical section

Earthworm body wall: vertical section

epidermis

cuticle

capillary

⇦ oxygen

⬅ carbon dioxide

Respiration: respiratory surfaces in animals

Key words

gill
lung
tracheole

Surfaces for gaseous exchange in a range of animals

Entire body surface (*Hydra*, earthworm)

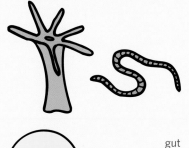

gut

body surface

Flattened body (flatworm)

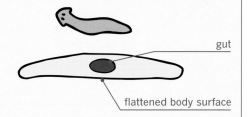

gut

flattened body surface

Tracheal system (grasshopper)

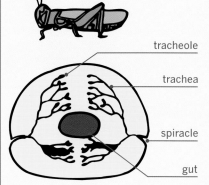

tracheole

trachea

spiracle

gut

External gills (young tadpole)

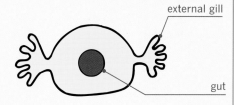

external gill

gut

Internal gills (fish)

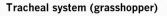

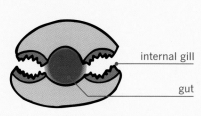

internal gill

gut

Lungs (human)

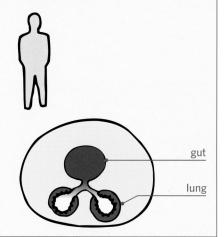

gut

lung

Mass flow

- In the simplest animals, the respiratory surface is the whole of the external body surface. In animals with *gills* or *lungs*, the surface is contained within the body.
- The oxygenating medium must be actively pumped across this surface to provide constant fresh supplies. This is an example of mass flow.

Gills

- Gills are organs with extensive folded membranes supplied with blood vessels.
- In internal gills, a mass flow mechanism maintains a flow of the oxygenating medium: the water containing the dissolved oxygen.
- Internal gills are less susceptible to mechanical damage than external gills.

Tracheoles

- Insects have thin tubes called *tracheoles* to carry air deep into the body.
- Insects have very limited mass flow systems. This prevents growth of insects above a certain size.

Lungs

- Lungs have a very large surface area inside the body, and a system of muscles and tubes maintains the flow of air across these surfaces.

© Diagram Visual Information Ltd.

Key words

concentration
  gradient
gill

Oxygen source

- Oxygen is available to fish dissolved in water.
- The oxygen that forms part of water molecules cannot be used by fish.

Mass flow

- Fish have two mass flow systems: one to force oxygenated water across the respiratory surface and one to carry oxygenated blood around the body.
- Water is taken in through the mouth and pumped over the *gill* surfaces. The flow is one-way, with water leaving through the operculum, a flap of tissue covering the exits from the gills behind the head of the fish.

Gill structure

- Gills are made of a series of arches that are supplied with a stack of flattened structures called gill filaments.
- The gill filaments are well-supplied with blood through an afferent vessel (a vessel carrying blood toward the heart). Blood passes along the filaments and into gill plates that are held perpendicular to the filament. It is in the gill plates that gaseous exchange occurs.
- Blood flows through the plate in the opposite direction to the water. This countercurrent multiplier system means that the freshest water meets the most oxygenated blood. The oxygen *concentration gradient* is maintained further back because, although some of the oxygen has been removed from the water, it is now passing over the least oxygenated blood.

Respiration: fish

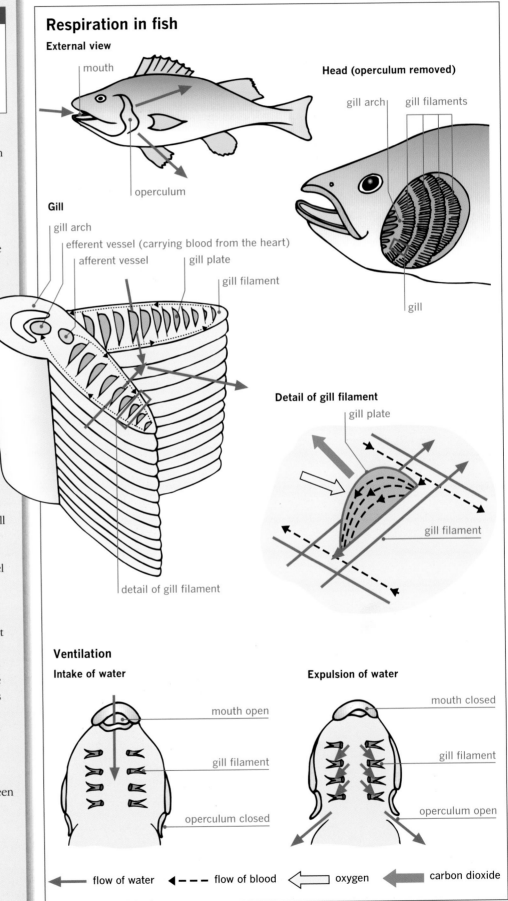

Respiration in fish

External view

mouth

operculum

Head (operculum removed)

gill arch   gill filaments

gill

Gill

gill arch

efferent vessel (carrying blood from the heart)

afferent vessel   gill plate

gill filament

detail of gill filament

Detail of gill filament

gill plate

gill filament

Ventilation

Intake of water

mouth open

gill filament

operculum closed

Expulsion of water

mouth closed

gill filament

operculum open

⟵ flow of water   ◀--- flow of blood   ⇐ oxygen   ⟵ carbon dioxide

Respiration: frog

Respiration in frogs

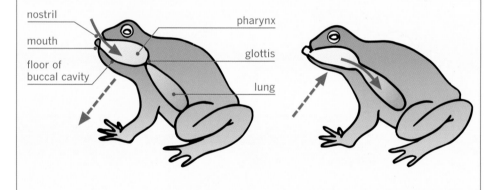

Labels: pharynx, nostril, glottis, mouth, floor of buccal cavity, lung, skin

Ventilation of lungs

Inhalation

Labels: nostril, mouth, floor of buccal cavity, pharynx, glottis, lung

Exhalation

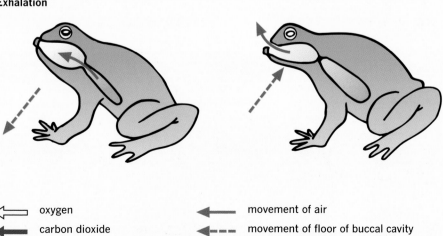

⇦ oxygen   ← movement of air

⬅ carbon dioxide   ⇠- - movement of floor of buccal cavity

Key words

buccal cavity   lung
gaseous
  exchange
gill
life cycle

Sites of gaseous exchange

- In common with all amphibians, frogs spend part of their *life cycle* in water and part on land. This requires a complex mixture of mechanisms for *gaseous exchange* that develop and change throughout the lifetime of the creature.
- The adult frog uses *lungs* and the surface of its whole body for gaseous exchange. The larval stage (tadpoles) uses external *gills*.

Ventilation

- Moving air into and out of the lungs is called ventilation. Ventilation ensures a constant supply of fresh oxygen and allows the removal of carbon dioxide-rich air. However, it also leads to the loss of moisture in exhaled air.
- The floor of the *buccal cavity* (the mouth or oral cavity) can be dropped in the frog to create a zone of low pressure. This sucks air in, and if the entrance to the lungs is closed this must come from the outside through the nostril.
- Closing the nostril and raising the floor of the buccal cavity creates a rise in pressure. If the tube to the lungs is opened at the same time, air is forced into the lungs where gaseous exchange can take place. This allows inhalation.
- Exhalation occurs when the procedures are reversed.

Key words

central nervous
 system
spinal cord

Nerve nets

- The simplest nervous systems are nets with no central control.
- For example, animals like *Hydra* have a nervous system that is spread across the entire body with no distinct head area.

Heads

- As animals developed the ability to move in a particular direction, they began to develop heads. This is the front end of the organism and tends to have the highest concentration of sense organs to gather information about the environments into which the animal is moving.
- Processing this sensory information requires a large amount of nervous tissue, so the nerve tissue close to these organs began to swell in size. This was the beginning of a brain.

Central nervous systems

- At the same time as the heads were developing, animals were also developing backbones and spinal cords. Vertebrates have a well-developed *spinal cord* that can carry information to and from the brain. The brain and spinal cord together are called the *central nervous system*.
- Invertebrates like the grasshopper tended to develop smaller brains called ganglia, which were distributed throughout the body, rather than a brain and spinal cord arrangement. Even in these cases, however, the most important ganglion was in the head near the sense organs.

Coordination: nervous systems

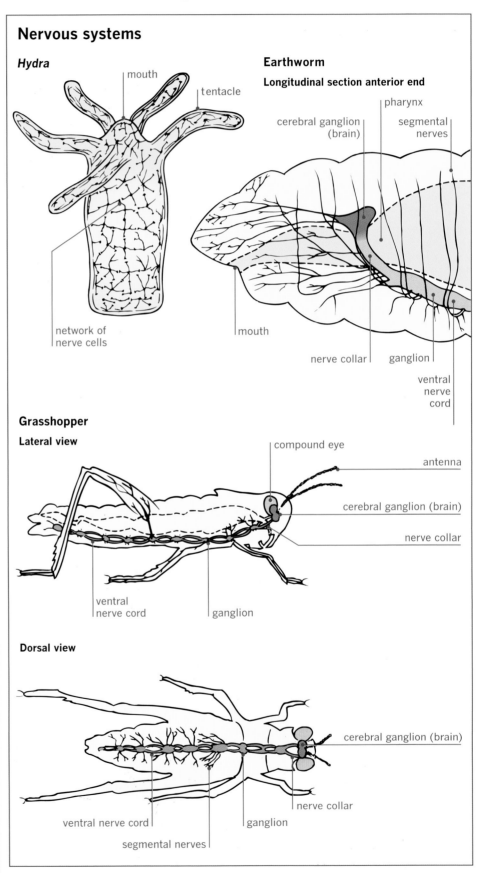

Nervous systems

Hydra

mouth

tentacle

network of nerve cells

Earthworm

Longitudinal section anterior end

cerebral ganglion (brain)

pharynx

segmental nerves

mouth

nerve collar

ganglion

ventral nerve cord

Grasshopper

Lateral view

compound eye

antenna

cerebral ganglion (brain)

nerve collar

ventral nerve cord

ganglion

Dorsal view

cerebral ganglion (brain)

nerve collar

ventral nerve cord

ganglion

segmental nerves

Excretion and osmoregulation: Protista

Key words

contractile	osmosis
vacuole	
diffusion	
metabolism	
osmoregulation	

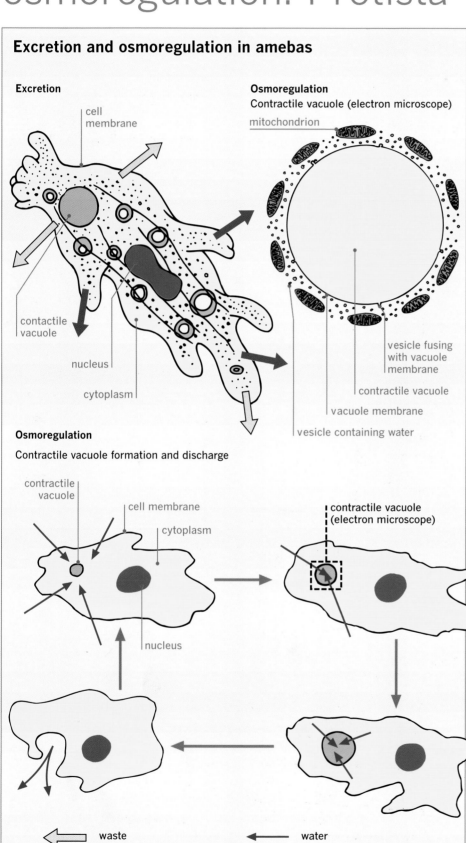

Excretion and osmoregulation in amebas

Excretion

cell membrane

contactile vacuole

nucleus

cytoplasm

Osmoregulation
Contractile vacuole (electron microscope)

mitochondrion

vesicle fusing with vacuole membrane

contractile vacuole

vacuole membrane

vesicle containing water

Osmoregulation
Contractile vacuole formation and discharge

contractile vacuole

cell membrane

cytoplasm

nucleus

contractile vacuole (electron microscope)

waste

water

carbon dioxide

Excretion and osmoregulation

- Excretion is the removal of the waste products of *metabolism* from the organism.
- *Osmoregulation* is the maintenance of the correct water potential within a cell. Thus, osmoregulation is not primarily concerned with the products of metabolism.

Excretion

- Waste products of metabolism in Protista diffuse through the cell membrane. Since the protists are unicellular organisms, *diffusion* is rapid enough to clear away all unwanted chemicals, and no specialized excretory structures are required.

Osmoregulation

- Water constantly enters protists like ameba due to *osmosis*. If this water were not removed, the cell would swell and could burst. Even before this occurred, the cell contents would be diluted to such an extent that essential metabolic processes could be disrupted.
- The ameba collects water in the cell by an active process and pumps it into a sac called a *contractile vacuole*. This swells as it gains water and when full migrates to the edge of the cell, fuses with the cell membrane, and releases the water into the environment.

Locomotion: earthworm

Key words

muscle
segment

Pushing and pulling

- Earthworms move through the soil by alternately contracting and relaxing sets of *muscles*. This makes the earthworm stretch or contract body *segments*, which are pushed or pulled through the soil.

Setae

- Setae are small hair-like projections from the surface of the earthworm's body.
- They can be extended or retracted by muscles. When extended, they effectively anchor that part of the earthworm in place.

Movement

- An earthworm at rest tends to be short and fat, with its circular muscles relaxed.
- To move, the earthworm extends setae at the back of its body and contracts circular muscles in the segments at the front. The contracting muscles squeeze on the body contents, raising the pressure, and the segments elongate.
- The earthworm then extends setae from the frontmost segments and retracts them in the rear segments. Circular muscles in the front relax, and longitudinal muscles contract. The rear segments elongate or are pulled slightly forward.
- Step by step the front segments contract and fatten while the rear segments are first elongated and then dragged forward.

Locomotion in earthworms

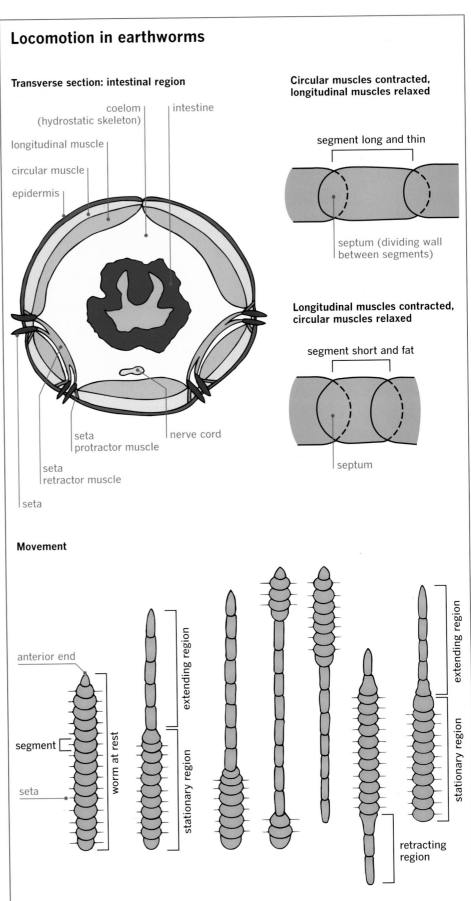

Transverse section: intestinal region

coelom (hydrostatic skeleton)
intestine
longitudinal muscle
circular muscle
epidermis
seta protractor muscle
nerve cord
seta retractor muscle
seta

Circular muscles contracted, longitudinal muscles relaxed

segment long and thin
septum (dividing wall between segments)

Longitudinal muscles contracted, circular muscles relaxed

segment short and fat
septum

Movement

anterior end
segment
seta
worm at rest
extending region
stationary region
extending region
retracting region
stationary region

Locomotion: grasshopper

Locomotion in grasshoppers

External view

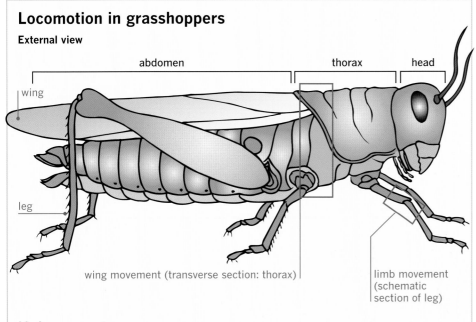

wing movement (transverse section: thorax)

limb movement (schematic section of leg)

Limb movement

Schematic section of leg
Extended　　　　　　　　　　**Flexed**

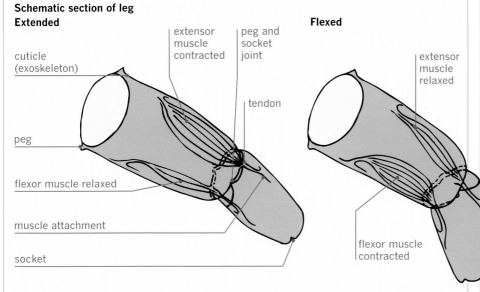

Wing movement

Transverse section: thorax
Downstroke　　　　　　　　**Upstroke**

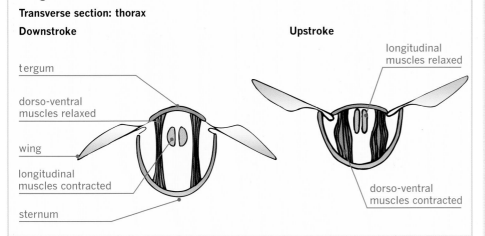

Key words

antagonistic pair
exoskeleton
muscle

Exoskeleton

- Grasshoppers, as with all insects, have a rigid *exoskeleton* covering their body.
- *Muscles* are attached to the inside of the skeleton.
- Joints in the exoskeleton allow the limbs to bend.

Joints

- The rigid exoskeleton cannot bend, and joints can only operate in one plane. The joints are connected by a peg and socket arrangement. This means that in order to allow a wider range of movement limbs are broken up into a number of sections with the joint between each section allowing movement in a different plane.
- Muscles work in *antagonistic pairs* as in mammals, with flexors bending limbs and extensors straightening them.

Wing movement

- The muscles that move the wings up and down are attached to the exoskeleton. Muscles running from the top of the body to the bottom contract to pull the wings up. The elasticity of the exoskeleton and muscles running along the length of the body help to pull the wings down.
- Since the muscles moving the wings are held inside the body, the wings can be very light in weight. This makes them easier to move and allows them to be larger, creating more downdraft, which helps the grasshopper to fly.

Key words

bacteriophage
bacterium
nucleic acid
virus

Obligate parasites

- All *viruses* are obligate parasites, which means they cannot reproduce outside a living host.

Bacteriophages

- *Bacteriophages* are a group of viruses that infect and kill bacterial cells.
- Bacteriophages typically have a head to their body that contains a length of *nucleic acid*. The head is connected to a tail consisting of a sheath that can contract and a base piece with fibers that can attach to bacterial cell walls.
- Particular bacteriophages attack specific bacteria.

Lytic life cycle

- Lysis is the rupture and destruction of a cell.
- A bacteriophage attaches itself to the outside of a susceptible *bacterium* with its base plate. The tail then contracts and pierces the surface of the bacterium.
- Nucleic acid from the bacteriophage passes into the bacterium. Here it starts to replicate while the normal bacterial DNA is switched off.
- Over a period of time, the bacterial cell is full of bacteriophage DNA. Protein coats for the virus are then manufactured by the bacterium following instructions stored in the viral DNA.
- The viral DNA is inserted into the viral protein coats, and the bacterial cell bursts to release the completed bacteriophages.

Reproduction: viruses

Reproduction in viruses

Bacteriophage structure

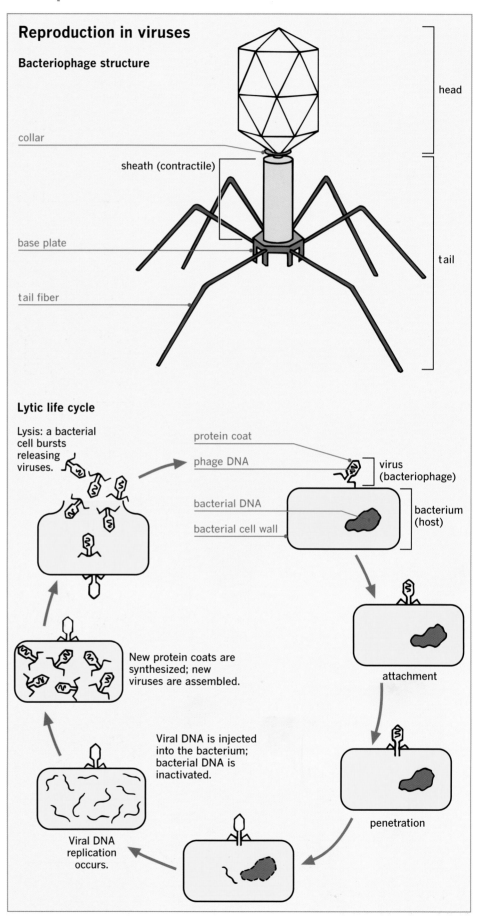

Lytic life cycle

Reproduction: butterfly

© Diagram Visual Information Ltd.

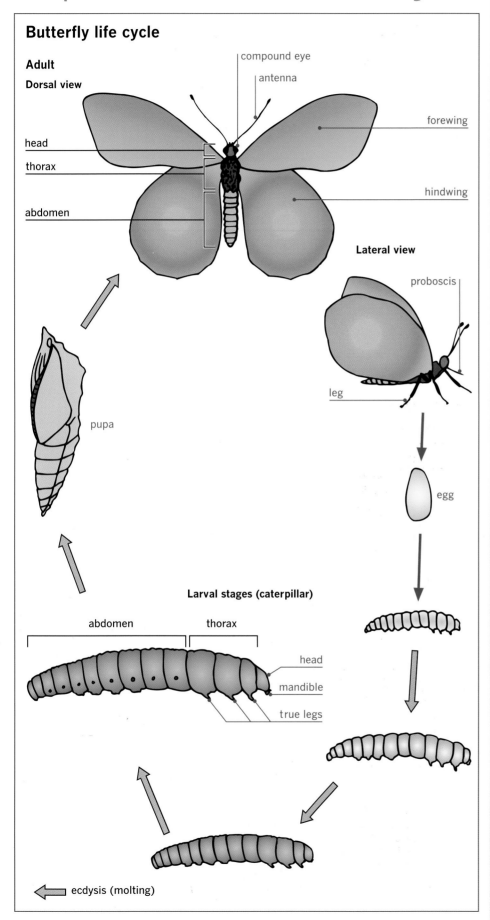

Butterfly life cycle

Adult
Dorsal view

compound eye

antenna

forewing

head

thorax

abdomen

hindwing

Lateral view

proboscis

leg

pupa

egg

Larval stages (caterpillar)

abdomen

thorax

head

mandible

true legs

ecdysis (molting)

Complete life cycle

- Butterflies undergo a complete *metamorphosis* during the four stages of their *life cycle*: egg, *larva*, *pupa*, butterfly. The female lays eggs, which first develop into larva called caterpillars. This juvenile form has no wings and uses its mandible to feed on leaves. As the larva grows, it molts (sheds its external skeleton) multiple times. When the larva reaches a certain minimum weight, it transforms into a pupa. After it emerges from the pupal stage, it is a winged butterfly, which feeds on nectar from flowers.
- Although the adult and larval stages look very different, they possess the same basic body parts common to all insects: head, *thorax*, and *abdomen*.

Survival rates

- Adult butterflies lay eggs. To increase the chances of successful hatching and larval growth, the eggs are typically laid in areas where food will be plentiful, e.g., on the underside of leaves.
- Larvae that survive the first few days have to eat large amounts of plant food to amass enough energy for the next stage of development. Many larvae are lost to *predators* at this stage.
- Pupae are also susceptible to selection pressures. They rely on camouflage to avoid predators.
- The hatched butterfly is a prime source of food to many insect-eating birds. Only a minority will survive long enough to produce eggs and start the cycle again. For all of these reasons, butterflies produce large numbers of eggs.

Key words

cloaca
fertilization
gamete
life cycle
metamorphosis

Complete life cycle

- Frogs undergo a complete *metamorphosis* during their *life cycle*. Their juvenile form is a tadpole that has no lungs or legs and lives entirely in water. The adult frog has lungs and legs and can survive out of water for extended periods.
- The change from tadpole to frog is a continuous process—there is no pupal stage as there is in metamorphosing insects.
- Tadpoles live for three to four months, with the exact time depending on certain environmental conditions. Adult frogs can survive the winter and live for many years, provided the temperature does not drop too low.

Fertilization and development

- *Fertilization* in frogs is primarily internal with mating pairs of frogs exchanging *gametes* by bringing their cloacas close together. The *cloaca* is an opening that connects the bladder and the reproductive systems with the outside world.
- Mating frogs do not just mate in pairs. If sufficient numbers of compatible males and females are available in an area, they will mate in larger groups, implying that some fertilization takes place externally.
- The eggs are covered in an outer shell of protective jelly, which swells in contact with water. The female lays her eggs in a sheltered pond or creek. The eggs hatch into tadpoles, which gradually develop into froglets—resembling adults but retaining a vestigial tail—and then mature frogs.
- Tadpole development is strongly affected by temperature and oxygen availability. The presence of meat or a source of iodine encourages early change into a frog and produces very small adults.

Reproduction: frog

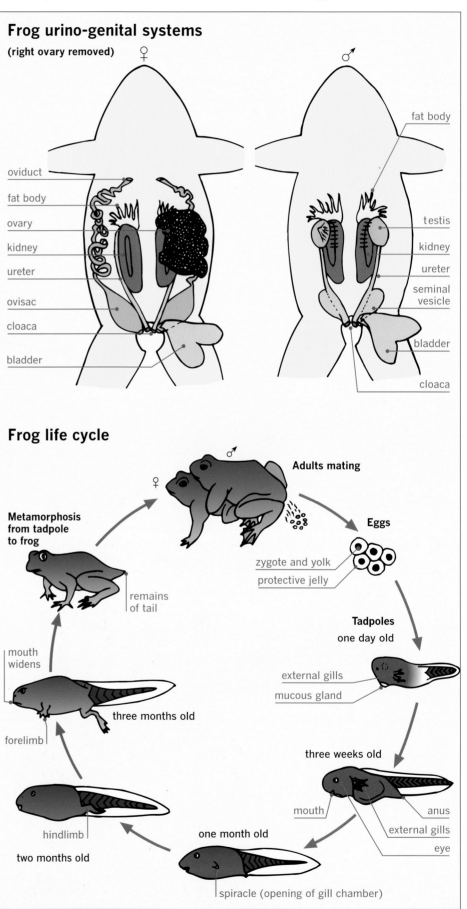

Frog urino-genital systems

(right ovary removed) ♀   ♂

oviduct
fat body
ovary
kidney
ureter
ovisac
cloaca
bladder

fat body
testis
kidney
ureter
seminal vesicle
bladder
cloaca

Frog life cycle

Adults mating

Metamorphosis from tadpole to frog

Eggs

zygote and yolk
protective jelly

remains of tail

Tadpoles
one day old

external gills
mucous gland

mouth widens

three months old

forelimb

three weeks old

mouth
anus
external gills
eye

hindlimb

two months old

one month old

spiracle (opening of gill chamber)

Growth and development: plants: monocotyledons

Key words

cotyledon
endosperm
germination
monocotyledon
photosynthesis

Monocotyledons

- *Cotyledons* are swollen leaves that act as a source of energy while the seed is germinating. During the first stages of *germination*, *photosynthesis* cannot occur, so only stored food is available to the plant for development.

- *Monocotyledons* like corn have a single cotyledon (unlike the bean family and many other vegetables which are dicotyledonous and have two) with a large supply of *endosperm*—specialized storage tissue that nourishes the embryo.

Germination

- Germination is a multistage process that mobilizes the stored food reserves of the seed and prepares the plant for the active production of food by photosynthesis.

- The root is the first structure to develop to allow the intake of water. This develops from the radicle, the root of the embryo plant. The radicle is protected by a sheath called the coleorhiza. As water is absorbed, the coleoptile can develop.

- The coleoptile is a photosynthetically active organ rather like a sheath protecting the growing stem or plumule. It pushes above the ground and the stem grows out of it. Adventitious roots then grow from the stem.

- Prop roots develop to support the stem, and the first true leaves are then produced from the stem.

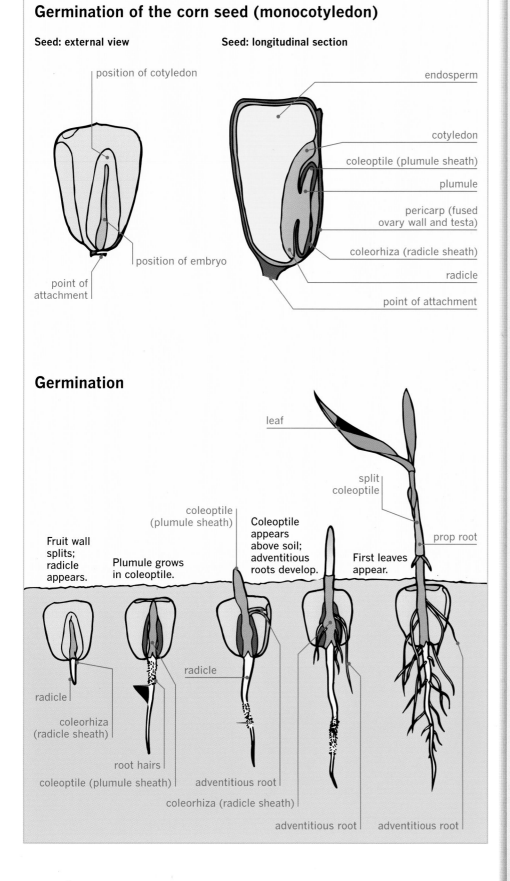

Germination of the corn seed (monocotyledon)

Seed: external view

- position of cotyledon
- point of attachment
- position of embryo

Seed: longitudinal section

- endosperm
- cotyledon
- coleoptile (plumule sheath)
- plumule
- pericarp (fused ovary wall and testa)
- coleorhiza (radicle sheath)
- radicle
- point of attachment

Germination

- Fruit wall splits; radicle appears.
- Plumule grows in coleoptile.
- Coleoptile appears above soil; adventitious roots develop.
- First leaves appear.

- leaf
- split coleoptile
- prop root
- coleoptile (plumule sheath)
- radicle
- radicle
- coleorhiza (radicle sheath)
- root hairs
- coleoptile (plumule sheath)
- adventitious root
- coleorhiza (radicle sheath)
- adventitious root
- adventitious root

Key words

cotyledon
dicotyledon
germination
photosynthesis

Dicotyledons

- *Dicotyledons* are plants that have two *cotyledons*, leaf-like parts of the embryo that act as is a food reservoir while the seed is *germinating*. During the first stages of germination, *photosynthesis* cannot occur, so the plant must use stored food for development.
- Within each seed are the cotyledons, the radicle (the root of the embryo), and the plumule (the embryonic leaves of the plant). The complete seed is covered by the testa (seed coat) which protects the seed against mechanical damage.

Germination

- The radicle is the first structure to develop to allow the intake of water. The hypocotyls, the part of the seedling stem below the cotyledons and above the radicle, emerges from the testa and pushes its way up through the soil. It is bent in an arch as it grows. Once the hypocotyl arch emerges from the soil, it straightens out in response to light. The cotyledons spread apart, and the epicotyl forms a young stem.
- The germination process differs among plants. Plants like peas experience hypogeal germination—the cotyledons remain below ground as the plumule develops. Plants like beans experience epigeal germination—the growth of the hypocotyl raises the cotyledons above ground. The cotyledons often then become *photosynthetically* active and form the first leaves of the new plant.

Growth and development: plants: dicotyledons

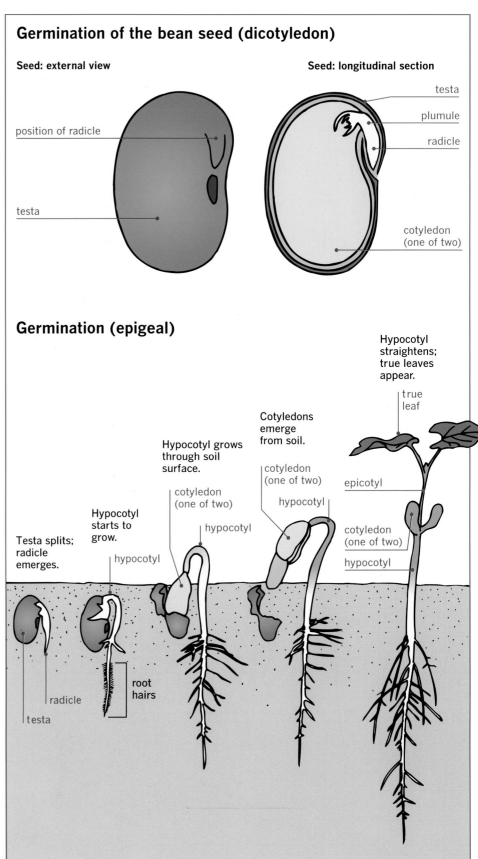

Germination of the bean seed (dicotyledon)

Seed: external view

Seed: longitudinal section

position of radicle

testa

testa

plumule

radicle

cotyledon (one of two)

Germination (epigeal)

Hypocotyl straightens; true leaves appear.

true leaf

Cotyledons emerge from soil.

cotyledon (one of two)

hypocotyl

epicotyl

Hypocotyl grows through soil surface.

cotyledon (one of two)

hypocotyl

cotyledon (one of two)

hypocotyl

Hypocotyl starts to grow.

hypocotyl

Testa splits; radicle emerges.

radicle

root hairs

testa

Growth and development: plants: tropisms

Key words

auxin
tropism

Tropisms

- *Tropisms* are directional growth responses to environmental stimuli. So hydrotropism is directional growth related to water. Phototropism is related to light.
- Roots are positively hydrotropic, which means they grow toward sources of water. They are negatively phototropic and grow away from sources of light.
- Stems are positively phototropic and negatively hydrotropic.

Mechanism of tropisms

- Tropisms are growth responses. The hormone *auxin* has an effect on the growth and development of cells. In the stem, an increase in the level of auxin increases growth of cells by allowing them to enlarge more easily.
- In the root, auxin increases lead to a reduction in cell growth.
- Light tends to inhibit the production of auxin. So, if a shoot is illuminated from one side, the side in the dark will grow more rapidly, and the shoot will bend toward the light.
- Auxin is only produced by the growing tip of the plant. If this is removed, growth ceases. If the tip is covered by a light-proof cap, the stem does not exhibit phototropism. The auxin diffuses downward through the stem and can be collected in an agar block. The block then has the ability to act as a source of auxin to a decapitated stem and so produce growth.

Growth responses to light (phototropism) of oat coleoptile

Exposed to light from all directions

The plant grows upward.

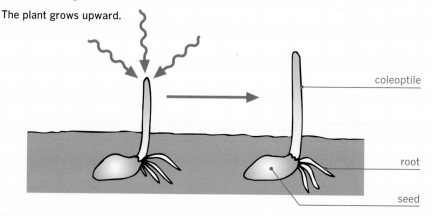

coleoptile

root

seed

Exposed to light from one direction

The plant grows toward light (positive phototropism).   The tip is removed: no growth.

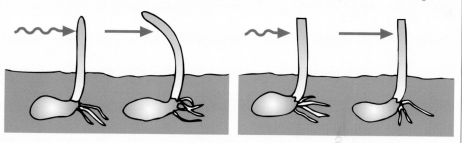

Tip is covered by lightproof cap: grows upward.   Zone of elongation covered by lightproof collar: grows toward light.

lightproof cap

lightproof collar

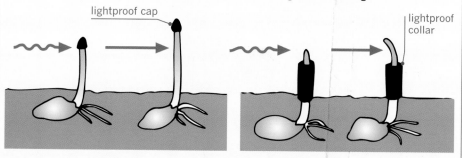

Tip is removed and placed on agar block. The block is replaced on the right side of another decapitated coleoptile. Auxin diffuses into zone of elongation, causing growth to the left.

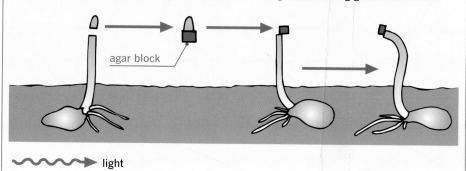

agar block

〰〰〰➤ light

Key words

absorption
assimilation
digestion
gut

Digestion to assimilation

- Food particles need to be broken down into smaller molecules before they can pass into the bloodstream. *Digestion* is the process of breaking large particles into smaller molecules. It involves both mechanical manipulation and chemical action.
- *Absorption* is the process that takes food molecules into the body. This takes place in the *gut*, mainly in the small intestine.
- *Assimilation* is the process of using absorbed materials to build new tissues. This occurs throughout the body.

Mechanical digestion

- Mechanical digestion is the breakdown of large lumps into smaller particles. This begins in the mouth.
- Teeth such as the incisors tear off lumps of food, while molars crush these lumps into smaller particles.
- Food leaving the mouth has been reduced to a small particle size to increase its surface area and so increase the rate of enzyme activity lower in the gut.

Chemical digestion

- Enzymes act on large, insoluble molecules to break them down into smaller, soluble molecules that pass through the gut wall into the bloodstream.
- The gut produces a series of enzymes to break down food molecules. The higher part of the gut is acidic, the lower part is neutral.

Nutrition: digestive system

Human digestive system

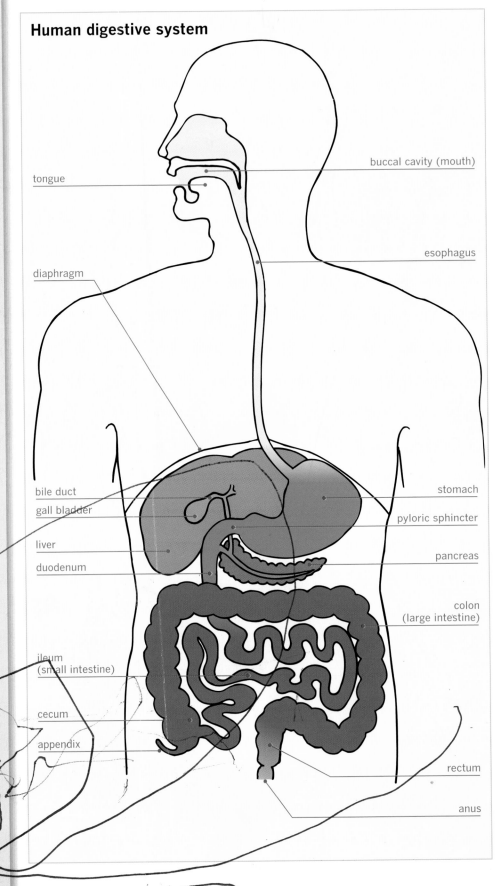

tongue
buccal cavity (mouth)
esophagus
diaphragm
bile duct
gall bladder
liver
duodenum
ileum (small intestine)
cecum
appendix
stomach
pyloric sphincter
pancreas
colon (large intestine)
rectum
anus

Nutrition: teeth

Human teeth

- From the age of about 6 years, the 20 deciduous ("baby") teeth of a child are gradually replaced by 32 permanent teeth.
- The third molars, or wisdom teeth, are usually the last to appear, generally in early adulthood.
- The chisel-shaped incisors are adapted for biting and cutting food, while the broader premolars and molars are responsible for grinding and chewing.
- Each tooth has a crown, covered in hard-wearing enamel to resist abrasion, and a root that is held in its own socket by cement and a fibrous lining.

Key words

canine
incisor
molar
premolar

Tooth types

- There are a number of different types of teeth. Each type has a particular function in the mechanical breakdown of food.
- *Incisors* at the front of the mouth cut food into smaller lumps.
- *Canines* tear off lumps of food. These are not particularly well developed in humans compared with other carnivores like tigers and dogs.
- *Premolars* and *molars* are large teeth at the back of the mouth with flattened top surfaces. These crush food lumps to reduce them to a fine particles.

Tooth structure

- The portion of the tooth below the gumline is the root. The part that rises above is called the crown.
- All teeth have the same internal structure, with a layer of hard enamel on the outside supported by softer dentine inside, packed around a central pulp cavity. Enamel is non-living material like hair and nails, dentine is living material.
- The pulp cavity contains a blood supply and a nerve.

Skull

Side view

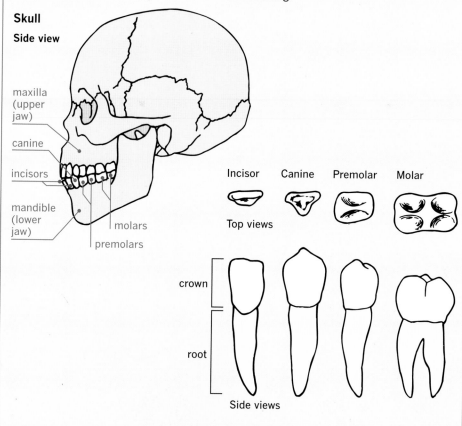

maxilla (upper jaw)

canine

incisors

mandible (lower jaw)

molars

premolars

Incisor Canine Premolar Molar

Top views

crown

root

Side views

Incisor

Vertical section

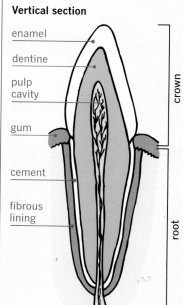

enamel

dentine

pulp cavity

gum

cement

fibrous lining

crown

root

Molar

Vertical section

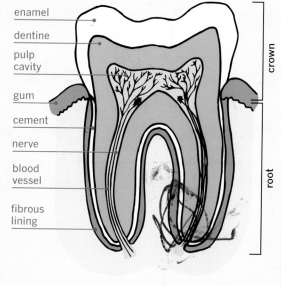

enamel

dentine

pulp cavity

gum

cement

nerve

blood vessel

fibrous lining

crown

root

Key words

bile	vein
chyme	insulin
enzyme	liver
gut	
hepatic portal	

Liver

- The *liver* is a complex organ that carries out a range of metabolic functions, not all of them concerning digestion. Blood from the *gut* drains into the liver through the *hepatic portal vein*, and all digested food chemicals pass through the liver for sorting before they pass on to the rest of the body.
- The liver also produces *bile*, which is an alkaline solution that helps with the digestion of fat. It is stored in the gall bladder and expelled into the duodenum when fatty food is present.

Stomach

- The stomach is a large muscular sac that acts as a storage vessel for food, passing it out through the pyloric sphincter to the duodenum. The muscles contract and relax to mix the food and stomach secretions into a slurry called *chyme*.
- It also starts protein digestion using an *enzyme* called pepsin. The stomach contents are strongly acidic, which helps pepsin to work and kills bacteria in the food.
- The stomach protects its wall from the acid and enzymes by secreting a layer of mucus that covers the inner surface.

Pancreas

- The pancreas produces a package of digestive enzymes. These pass to the gut in pancreatic juices along the pancreatic duct.
- Cells in the pancreas called islets of Langerhans also produce the hormone insulin, which regulates the level of sugar in the blood.

Nutrition: liver, stomach, and pancreas

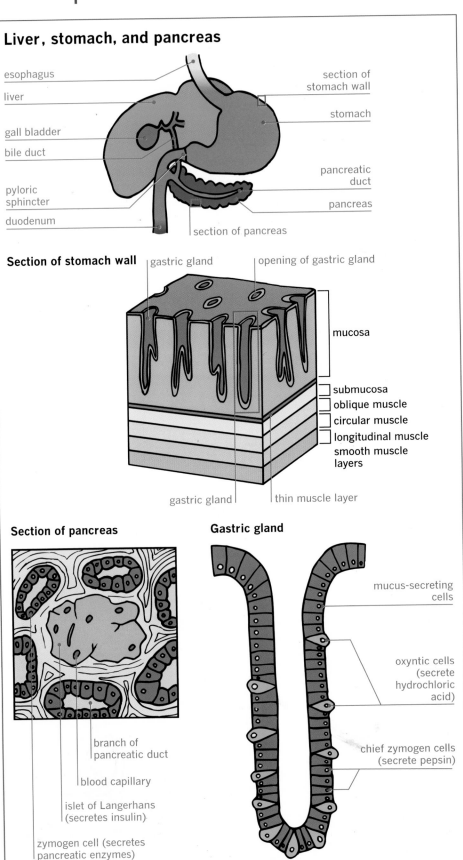

Liver, stomach, and pancreas

esophagus
liver
gall bladder
bile duct
pyloric sphincter
duodenum
section of stomach wall
stomach
pancreatic duct
pancreas
section of pancreas

Section of stomach wall

gastric gland
opening of gastric gland
mucosa
submucosa
oblique muscle
circular muscle
longitudinal muscle
smooth muscle layers
gastric gland
thin muscle layer

Section of pancreas

branch of pancreatic duct
blood capillary
islet of Langerhans (secretes insulin)
zymogen cell (secretes pancreatic enzymes)

Gastric gland

mucus-secreting cells
oxyntic cells (secrete hydrochloric acid)
chief zymogen cells (secrete pepsin)

Nutrition: small intestine

Key words

absorption	liver
gut	villus
hepatic portal vein	
lymphatic system	

Ileum

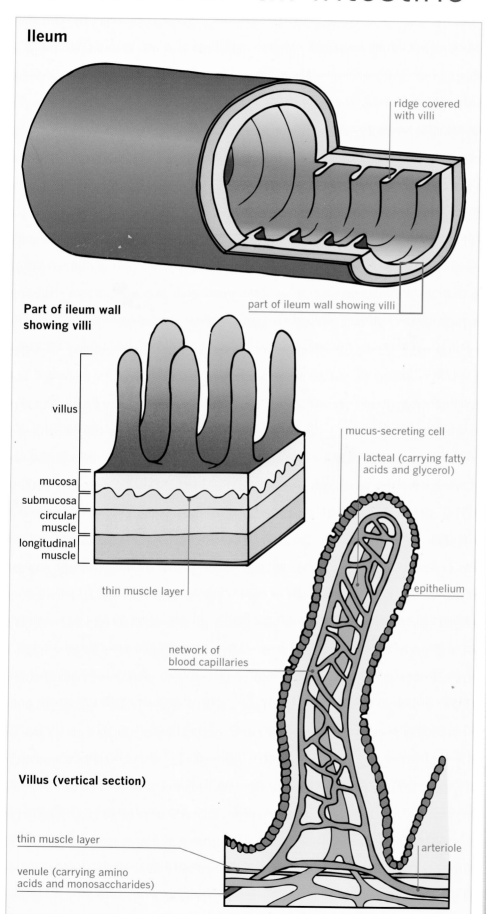

ridge covered with villi

part of ileum wall showing villi

Part of ileum wall showing villi

villus

mucosa

submucosa

circular muscle

longitudinal muscle

thin muscle layer

mucus-secreting cell

lacteal (carrying fatty acids and glycerol)

epithelium

network of blood capillaries

Villus (vertical section)

thin muscle layer

venule (carrying amino acids and monosaccharides)

arteriole

Morphology

- The small intestine, or ileum, is a long muscular tube running from the duodenum to the large intestine. In humans it is over 18 feet (6 m) in length.
- The inner surface has many ridges that increase the surface area. This is essential for the *absorption* of digested foods.
- The small intestine is well-supplied with blood vessels. These supply oxygen to the cells of the intestine, which are metabolically quite active, producing a constant stream of enzymes to digest food in the *gut*. Blood is drained away from the small intestine by the *hepatic portal vein*, which carries the food-rich blood to the *liver*.
- As with all of the gut, the ileum has two layers of muscle in its wall: one set running around the intestine (the circular muscles) and one set running the length of it (the longitudinal muscles).

Microscopic structure

- The inner wall of the ileum is covered with small fingerlike projections called *villi*. These further massively increase the surface area available for absorption.
- A villus has a network of capillaries in it, and dissolved food materials pass into this through the outer wall of the villus. A central space called the lacteal provides a transport route for fatty substances that do not dissolve easily in blood. The lacteals are filled with a fatty fluid and drain into the *lymphatic system*.

Key words

absorption
enzyme
gut

Sequence of processes

- Digestion is the breaking down of large, insoluble molecules into smaller, soluble molecules.
- The first part of digestion is the breaking down of large lumps of food into smaller particles. This is called mechanical digestion and is done by the teeth. The next stage is chemical digestion of large molecules by *enzymes*.

Enzymes

- Enzymes, such as amylase and pepsin, are complex proteins that speed up reactions in living organisms. They are used in digestive processes to break down large molecules.
- Enzymes are generally specific—they can only speed up a single reaction, and each step in a chain of reactions may need its own particular enzyme.
- Digestive enzymes are unusual in that they are often able to speed up a number of reactions among related chemicals. However, the range of chemicals a digestive enzyme can handle is still limited, so the gut produces a range of enzymes to cover all of the chemicals found in food.

Absorption

- *Absorption* is the passage of food chemicals into the body.
- This occurs mainly in the lower parts of the gut and is increased by the large surface area of the ileum (small intestine).

Nutrition: digestion and absorption

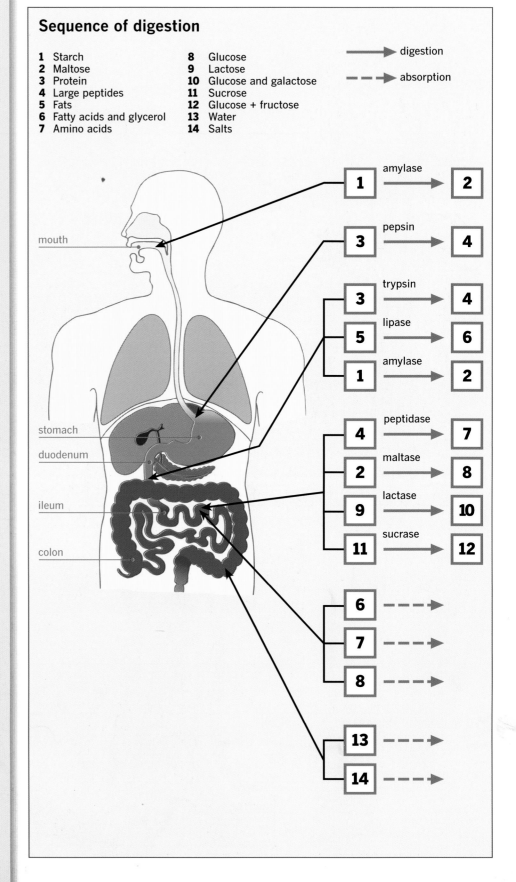

Sequence of digestion

1 Starch
2 Maltose
3 Protein
4 Large peptides
5 Fats
6 Fatty acids and glycerol
7 Amino acids
8 Glucose
9 Lactose
10 Glucose and galactose
11 Sucrose
12 Glucose + fructose
13 Water
14 Salts

→ digestion
--→ absorption

Transport: circulatory system map

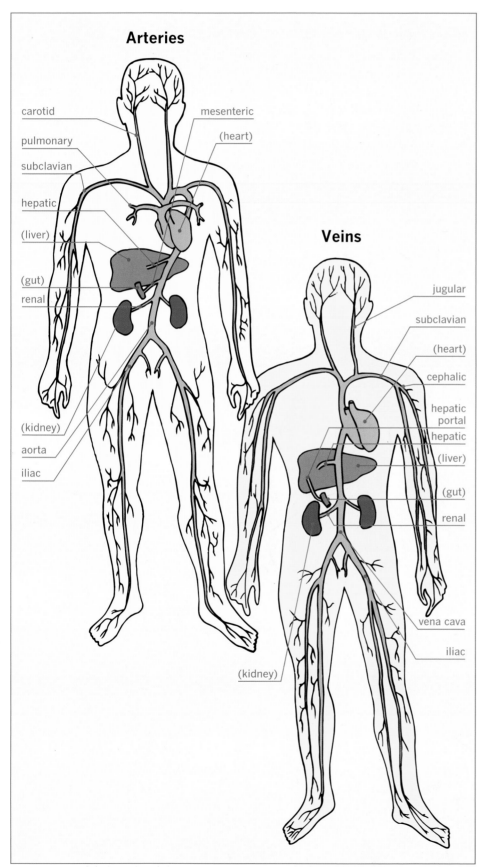

Arteries

carotid
pulmonary
subclavian
hepatic
(liver)
(gut)
renal
(kidney)
aorta
iliac

mesenteric
(heart)

Veins

jugular
subclavian
(heart)
cephalic
hepatic portal
hepatic
(liver)
(gut)
renal
vena cava
iliac
(kidney)

Key words

artery
capillary
double circulation
vein

A closed circulation

- Blood passes around the body in a closed circulatory system. This is different from circulation in many lower animals, where the cells are bathed in blood directly.
- The advantage of a closed system is that it can transport materials much more rapidly.
- The human circulatory system consists of a central pump (the heart) and three types of tubes (*arteries*, *capillaries*, and *veins*).

The heart

- The heart consists of two pumps. The right side pumps blood from the body to the lungs. The left side takes blood from the lungs and pumps it around the body. The left side is slightly larger and more muscular because it has a greater distance to push the blood.
- This system, known as *double circulation*, separates oxygenated and deoxygenated blood. This means that the blood must go through the lungs for every single circuit of the body.

Blood vessels

- Arteries carry blood away from the heart under high pressure.
- Blood from the arteries flows into capillaries, microscopic blood vessels that penetrate every organ in the body.
- Blood flows out of the capillaries and into veins to be carried back to the heart under low pressure.

Key words

aorta	liver
artery	vein
gut	
hepatic portal	
vein	

Two circulations

- The pulmonary circulation forms a complete circuit, taking deoxygenated blood from the heart to the lungs along the pulmonary *artery* and then returning oxygenated blood to the heart along the pulmonary *vein*.
- The main circulation in the body takes oxygenated blood from the heart, travelling through the *aorta*, and returns deoxygenated blood to the heart through the vena cava.

System plan

- Tall arteries arise ultimately from the aorta. The system is a series of parallel circuits so each organ has its own artery supplying oxygenated blood. Each organ also has a vein leading out that carries blood back to the heart.
- The one exception is the *liver*, which has two inputs: the hepatic artery, which provides oxygenated blood, and the *hepatic portal vein*, which carries blood to the liver from the *gut*. This means that the chemicals absorbed into the blood by the gut can be sorted and, possibly, changed before they pass on to the rest of the body. A substance absorbed in the gut thus has to go through the liver before it can reach any other cell in the body.
- The hepatic vein drains blood from the liver back to the heart.
- Arteries and veins are named after the organs they serve.

Transport: circulatory system scheme

Schematic representation of circulatory system

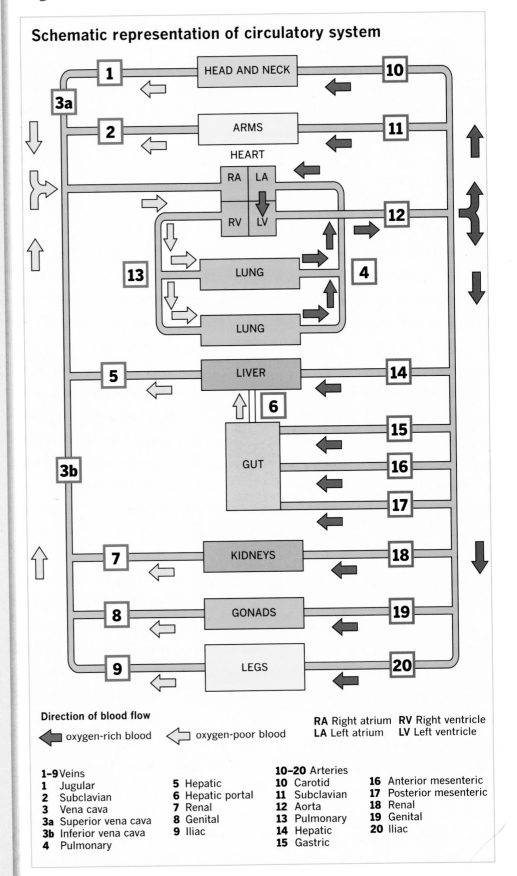

Direction of blood flow

⬅ oxygen-rich blood   ⬅ oxygen-poor blood

RA Right atrium **RV** Right ventricle
LA Left atrium **LV** Left ventricle

1–9 Veins
1 Jugular
2 Subclavian
3 Vena cava
3a Superior vena cava
3b Inferior vena cava
4 Pulmonary

5 Hepatic
6 Hepatic portal
7 Renal
8 Genital
9 Iliac

10–20 Arteries
10 Carotid
11 Subclavian
12 Aorta
13 Pulmonary
14 Hepatic
15 Gastric

16 Anterior mesenteric
17 Posterior mesenteric
18 Renal
19 Genital
20 Iliac

Transport: heart structure

Heart

External view (ventral)

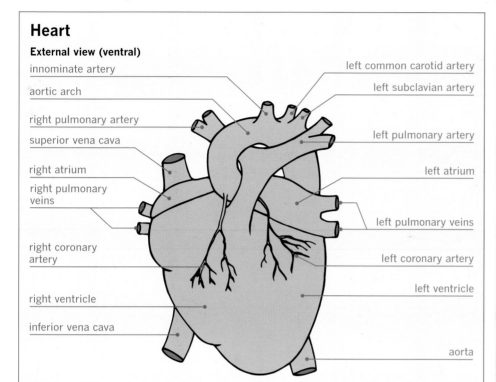

- innominate artery
- aortic arch
- right pulmonary artery
- superior vena cava
- right atrium
- right pulmonary veins
- right coronary artery
- right ventricle
- inferior vena cava

- left common carotid artery
- left subclavian artery
- left pulmonary artery
- left atrium
- left pulmonary veins
- left coronary artery
- left ventricle
- aorta

Section

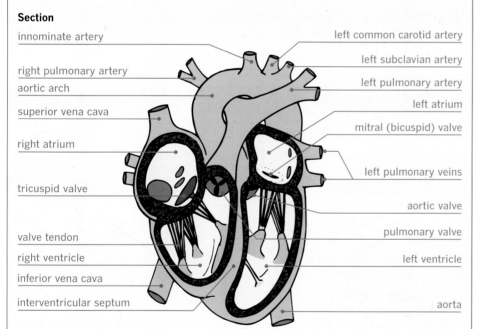

- innominate artery
- right pulmonary artery
- aortic arch
- superior vena cava
- right atrium
- tricuspid valve
- valve tendon
- right ventricle
- inferior vena cava
- interventricular septum

- left common carotid artery
- left subclavian artery
- left pulmonary artery
- left atrium
- mitral (bicuspid) valve
- left pulmonary veins
- aortic valve
- pulmonary valve
- left ventricle
- aorta

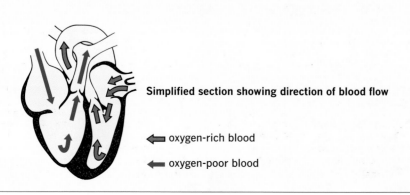

Simplified section showing direction of blood flow

⬅ oxygen-rich blood

⬅ oxygen-poor blood

Key words

thorax
ventricle

Two pumps

- The heart consists of two complete and functionally separate pumps held within a single muscle mass in the *thorax*.
- The right side receives blood from the body and pumps it to the lungs.
- The left side, which is slightly more muscular, collects blood from the lungs and pumps this around the whole body.

Right side

- Blood enters the right atrium from the vena cava at low pressure. The walls of the right atrium are fairly thin—if it were too muscular, the blood would not be able to push into the chamber.
- The atrium walls contract, and blood passes into the right *ventricle*.
- The walls of the ventricle are much more muscular and give the blood a push out along the pulmonary artery to the lungs. The tricuspid valve separating the atrium and ventricle prevents backflow into the atrium during the power stroke. The pulmonary valve at the entrance of the pulmonary artery prevents backflow into the ventricle when it is refilling with blood again from the atrium.

Left side

- The left side undergoes exactly the same sequence and has basically the same structural adaptations.
- The muscles of the heart are supplied with blood, and so oxygen, through the coronary artery, reaches both sides.

Key words

diastole
systole
ventricle

Diastole and systole

- The heartbeat is a complex series of events that splits into two main groups: *diastole*, where the heart muscle is relaxed, and *systole*, where the muscle actively contracts.

Filling of atria

- Blood from the body enters the heart at low pressure through the vena cava. The pressure is sufficient to inflate the atria, which have relatively thin walls.
- As the atria fill, the blood pushes its way through the atrioventricular valves in the *ventricles*.
- To complete the process the muscles in the atria contract, the passages to the veins are constricted, and blood is actively pumped into the ventricles. By the end of diastole, the blood is present in the ventricles.

Emptying of the ventricles

- When the ventricles are full of blood, the atrioventricular valves close. The muscles in the wall of the ventricle now contract, and blood is pushed through the aortic and pulmonary valves along the arteries. Tendons attached to the atrioventricular valves keep the atrioventricular valves closed during this process.
- The process begins again as the ventricles empty of blood and the muscles relax. Aortic and pulmonary valves prevent the backflow of blood from the arteries into the ventricles.

Transport: heartbeat

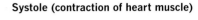

Pumping action of the heart

Diastole (relaxation of heart muscle)

Atria fill; atrioventricular (mitral and tricuspid) valves are closed.

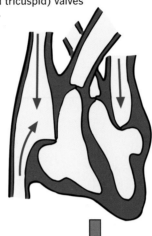

Atrioventricular valves are pushed open by rising atrial pressure; ventricles start to fill.

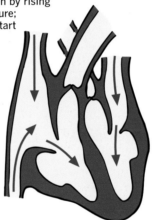

Ventricles continue to fill by suction from relaxed ventricular walls and atrial contraction.

Systole (contraction of heart muscle)

Ventricles continue to contract; rising pressure pushes open the aortic and pulmonary valves.

Ventricles contract and pressure increases; aortic and pulmonary valves remain closed.

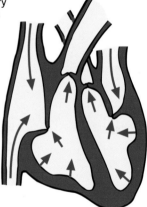

Ventricles become full and stretched; atrioventricular valves close.

Transport: regulation of heartbeat

Key words

medulla	sympathetic
oblongata	nervous system
parasympathetic	ventricle
nervous system	
sinoatrial node	

Heartbeat regulation

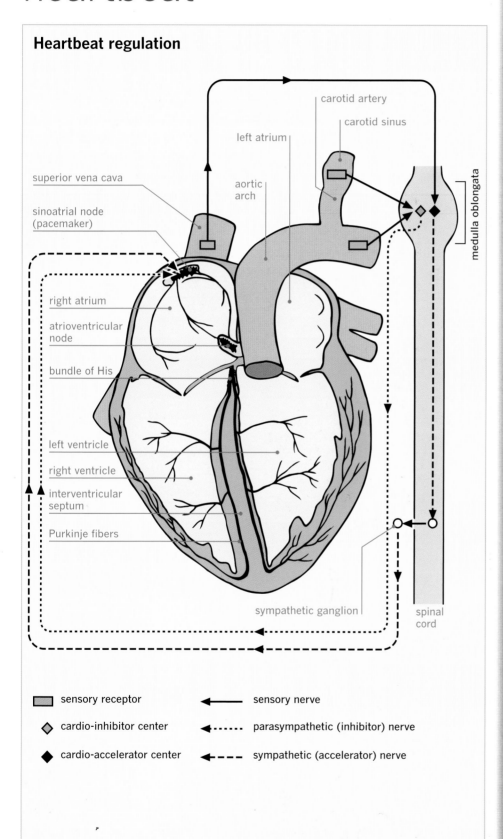

- superior vena cava
- sinoatrial node (pacemaker)
- carotid artery
- carotid sinus
- left atrium
- aortic arch
- medulla oblongata
- right atrium
- atrioventricular node
- bundle of His
- left ventricle
- right ventricle
- interventricular septum
- Purkinje fibers
- sympathetic ganglion
- spinal cord

☐ sensory receptor   ← sensory nerve

◇ cardio-inhibitor center   ←······ parasympathetic (inhibitor) nerve

◆ cardio-accelerator center   ←--- sympathetic (accelerator) nerve

Pacemaker region

- The muscles of the heart are unique in the body in that they can contract without direct nervous stimulation. This means that transplanted hearts, which have no connection to the patient's central nervous system, can still beat.
- The organization of the heartbeat depends on the *sinoatrial node*, called the pacemaker, located near the top of the heart in the right atrium.

Creating a beat

- Signals from the sinoatrial node cause the atria to contract. This pushes blood into the *ventricles*. By the time the ventricles have filled with blood, the impulse has reached the ventricular walls. The impulse passes along a bundle of specialized muscle fibers, known as the bundle of His, located between the two ventricles. Specialized nerve cells called Purkinje fibers distribute these signals.
- The ventricle walls now contract to push blood along the arteries. At this point the atrial walls are beginning to relax as the signal has passed on.

Regulating the heartbeat

- The sinoatrial node produces regular impulses.
- The number of these impulses (and therefore heartbeats) per minute can be changed by impulses delivered from the *medulla oblongata* by nerves of the *parasympathetic* (slowing down) and *sympathetic* (speeding up) *nervous systems*.

© Diagram Visual Information Ltd.

Key words

aorta	smooth muscle
artery	systole
capillary	vein
diastole	white blood cell
red blood	
corpuscle	

Arteries

- *Arteries* carry blood at high pressure away from the heart. They have the thickest walls of all blood vessels, with a layer of *smooth muscle* in them. This muscle can contract to constrict the blood vessels, raising the blood pressure even further.
- The arteries also contain elastic tissue that facilitates the flow of blood by stretching during *diastole* and contracting during *systole*. The *aorta* is particularly well supplied with elastic tissue.

Capillaries

- *Capillaries* are microscopic blood vessels that penetrate all active tissues. Their walls are one cell thick and allow the rapid exchange of materials.
- *White blood cells* can leave capillaries by squeezing between cells of the endothelium. *Red blood corpuscles* cannot leave capillaries unless the walls have been damaged. This leads to a bruise as the blood leaks into the tissues.

Veins

- *Veins* are large blood vessels carrying blood at low pressure back toward the heart. They have thinner walls than arteries, with less muscle.
- Valves prevent the backflow of blood in the veins.

Transport: blood vessels

Blood vessels
Cut open longitudinally

Artery
- fibrous (collagen) layer (tunica externa)
- smooth muscle and elastic fiber layer (tunica media)
- endothelial layer (tunica intima)

Vein
- fibrous (collagen) layer (tunica externa)
- smooth muscle and elastic fiber layer (tunica media)
- endothelial layer (tunica intima)
- valve flaps

Capillary
- endothelial cell

Transverse sections

Artery
- lumen
- endothelial layer (tunica intima)
- smooth muscle and elastic fiber layer (tunica media)
- fibrous (collagen) layer (tunica externa)

Vein
- lumen (inner space through which blood flows)
- endothelial layer (tunica intima)
- smooth muscle and elastic fiber layer (tunica media)
- fibrous (collagen) layer (tunica externa)

Capillary
- lumen
- endothelial cell

Transport: capillaries and tissues

Relationship between capillaries, lymphatic vessels, and tissue cells

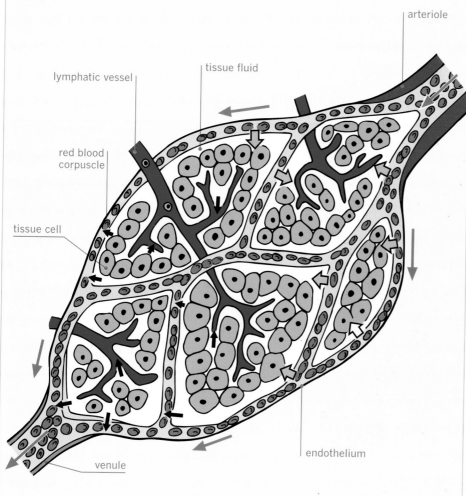

arteriole

tissue fluid

lymphatic vessel

red blood corpuscle

tissue cell

endothelium

venule

 blood flow

flow of tissue fluid rich in waste

flow of tissue fluid rich in oxygen and food

The capillary network
The networks of capillaries linking arteries and veins are known as capillary beds. Each capillary bed provides a link between many arterioles (tiny arteries) and venules (tiny veins).

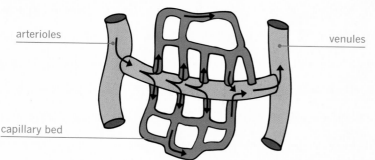

arterioles

venules

capillary bed

Key words

capillary
lymph vessel
red blood
   corpuscle
white blood cell

Size of capillaries
- *Capillaries* are microscopic blood vessels with an internal diameter typically large enough to let *red blood corpuscles* pass in single file.
- The total internal volume of the capillaries in the body is very large because of the very large numbers of capillaries in each organ. The total volume is up to ten times larger than the volume of blood in the system.

Exchange
- Capillary walls are one cell thick and allow rapid exchange of materials. Oxygen and food materials pass to the tissues, and wastes pass back into the blood.
- *White blood cells* can leave capillaries by squeezing between cells of the endothelium. Red blood corpuscles cannot leave capillaries unless the walls have been damaged.

Tissue fluid and lymph
- Blood entering a capillary bed is at a higher hydrostatic pressure than the fluid surrounding the cells of the tissue. This causes fluid to leak out of the capillaries and surround the cells. This is called tissue fluid.
- At the venous (venule) end of the capillary bed, fluid passes the other way, but some is always left in the tissues. This fluid is drained away by *lymph vessels* and is returned to the bloodstream as lymph fluid in other parts of the system.

Key words

lymph vessel
pathogen
white blood cell

Lymphatic fluid

- Lymphatic fluid is derived from tissue fluid that has been drained away from tissues by *lymph vessels*.
- Lymphatic fluid contains a range of chemicals and *white blood cells*. It effectively washes the cells and can carry *pathogens*, microorganisms that cause disease, from tissues toward the lymph nodes.

Vessels, nodes, and ducts

- Lymph vessels are vessels that carry lymphatic tissue toward lymph nodes and then to the bloodstream. In the tissues these vessels are microscopic, typically the size of capillaries, but as they join up they become larger, and the largest of them are visible to the naked eye.
- A lymph node is a knot of lymphatic tissue that is particularly well-supplied with phagocytic lymphocytes. These are able to filter pathogens from the lymph. Swollen lymph nodes are a characteristic sign of certain infections, as the lymphocytes multiply to combat the invading microorganisms.
- The thoracic duct, the largest lymphatic vessel, collects most of the lymph in the body (except that from the right arm and the right side of the chest, neck, and head, which is collected by the right lymphatic duct) and drains it into the blood stream at the junction of the left subclavian vein and left jugular vein.
- The lymphatic system also transports fats from the ileum (small intestine) to the blood.

Transport: lymphatic system

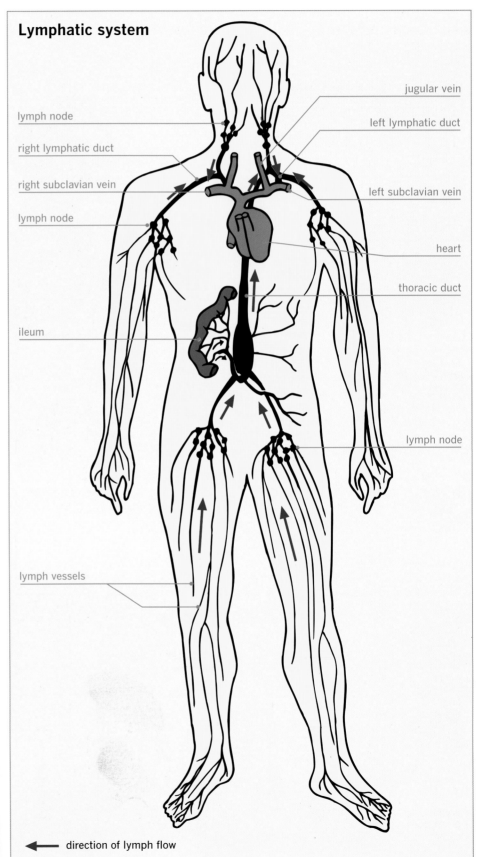

Lymphatic system

- jugular vein
- lymph node
- left lymphatic duct
- right lymphatic duct
- right subclavian vein
- left subclavian vein
- lymph node
- heart
- thoracic duct
- ileum
- lymph node
- lymph vessels

⟵ direction of lymph flow

Transport: blood composition

Key words

hemoglobin
liver
plasma
platelet
red blood
corpuscle

spleen
white blood cell

Functions of plasma

- Transports nutrients and waste products.
- Transports hormones and other signal substances.
- Contains plasma proteins, which are important in blood clotting and immunity.
- Regulates water and ionic content of cells and dampens (buffers) changes in pH to maintain a constant environment for tissue function.
- Regulates body temperature.

Functions of blood cells

The vast majority of the cells are erythrocytes (red blood corpuscles, which are responsible for transporting oxygen and carbon dioxide. There are several types of leukocytes (white blood cells), which help to defend the body against disease:
- granulocytes have a granular cytoplasm and engulf bacteria or attack parasites;
- lymphocytes produce antibodies and regulate the immune responses;
- monocytes can leave the blood to become tissue macrophages: cells capable of ingesting bacteria, cell debris, and cancer cells.

Platelets are bodies formed by the fragmentation of larger cells. They are vital for blood clotting at sites of injury.

Blood components separated by centrifugation

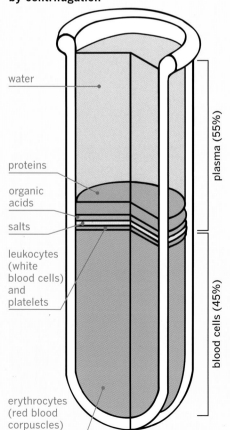

water

proteins

organic acids

salts

leukocytes (white blood cells) and platelets

erythrocytes (red blood corpuscles)

plasma (55%)

blood cells (45%)

Blood cells

Leukocytes:

Granulocyte

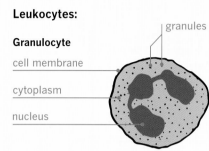

granules

cell membrane

cytoplasm

nucleus

Lymphocyte

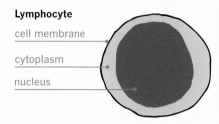

cell membrane

cytoplasm

nucleus

Monocyte

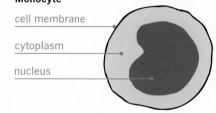

cell membrane

cytoplasm

nucleus

Platelets

cell membrane

cytoplasm

Red blood corpuscle (erythrocyte)

Surface view

Section

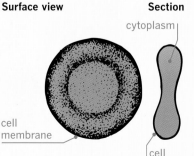

cytoplasm

cell membrane

cell membrane

Cellular components

- Roughly 45 percent of the volume of whole blood is made of cells, red and white.
- *Red blood corpuscles* are biconcave disks, packed with *hemoglobin*, that transport oxygen from the lungs to the tissues of the body. They have no nucleus when mature and last about 120 days. They are made in the red bone marrow of large bones and are destroyed at the end of their lives by cells in the *spleen* and *liver*.
- *White blood cells* include a number of different types, but all are involved in defense against disease. They are made in yellow bone marrow and lymph nodes. White blood cells are much less common than red blood corpuscles (typically 1 percent), though their numbers increase during infection.
- *Platelets* are subcellular components that circulate in the blood and are involved in clotting. They are manufactured in the bone marrow.

Plasma

- The liquid component of blood is called *plasma*. It contains a wide variety of chemicals in solution or suspension.
- Much of the carbon dioxide transported around the body is carried in solution in the plasma, although red blood corpuscles are involved in helping the gas to dissolve.

© Diagram Visual Information Ltd.

Key words

antibody
antigen
plasma
red blood
  corpuscle

Blood types

- There are many ways to classify blood, and a complete typology involves more than 20 different criteria.
- The first and most commonly cited blood group depends on the ABO system, which can place everyone into one of four groups: A, B, AB, and O.

Antigens and antibodies

- *Red blood corpuscles* have proteins on their cell surface called *antigens*. There are two types: A and B. Blood group A has antigen A on its cell surface, B has B, AB has both, and O has neither.
- Blood *plasma* contains *antibodies*, proteins the immune system uses to neutralize foreign objects, that react with these antigens. Blood group A has anti-B, B has anti-A, O has both anti-A and anti-B, while AB has neither.

Agglutination

- When antigen A reacts with anti-A, red blood cells clump together to form a clot. This reaction is called agglutination. For this reason, if recipients have anti-A in their plasma, they cannot receive blood from group A
- The antibodies in the donor can be ignored during transfusions—only the antibodies in the recipient are significant. This means AB (which has no antibodies) can receive blood from any group and is called the universal recipient. Blood group O is the universal donor because it has no antibodies.

Transport: blood types

Antibody/antigen composition of different blood types

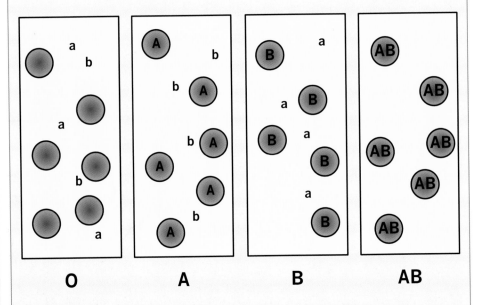

Reactions that occur when different blood groups are mixed

O is universal donor
AB is universal recipient
Agglutination occurs if the recipient's blood contains antibodies to the donor's antigens

Blood types (Donor)	O	A	B	AB
O	–	–	–	–
A	+	–	+	–
B	+	+	–	–
AB	+	+	+	–

Recipient (column header); *Donor* (row header)

- (gray circle) = red blood corpuscle with no antigens
- (A) = red blood corpuscle with A antigen
- (B) = red blood corpuscle with B antigen
- (AB) = red blood corpuscle with A and B antigens
- a = anti-A antibody in plasma
- b = anti-B antibody in plasma
- + = agglutination occurs
- – = agglutination does not occur

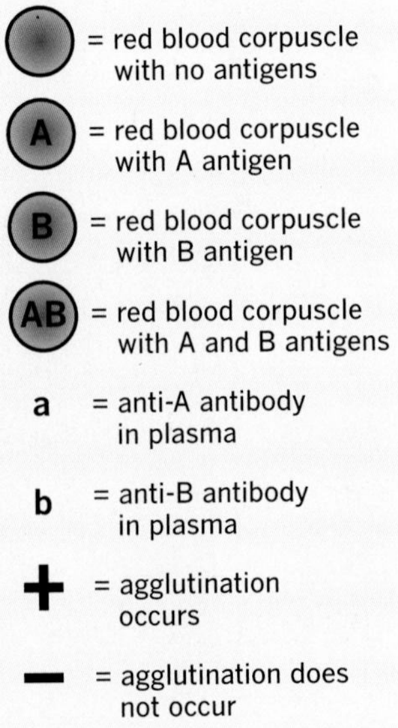

Respiration: respiratory system

Section of head and thorax

Right lung: section

Left lung: surface view

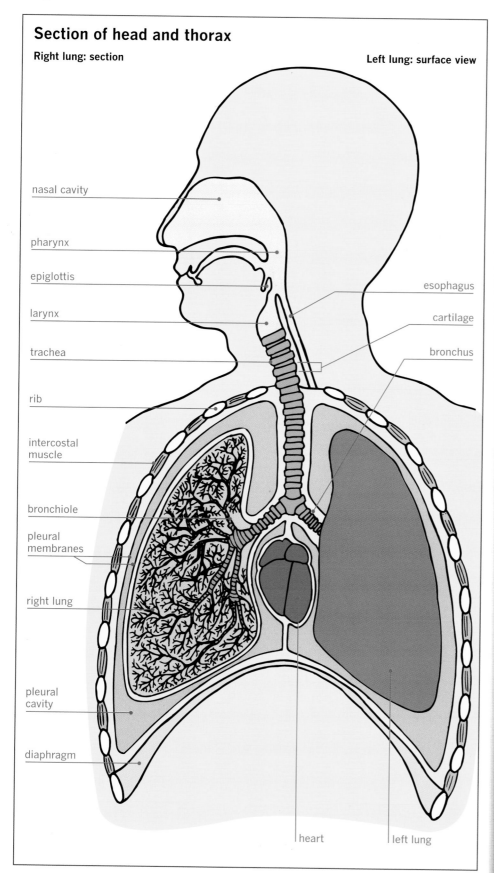

nasal cavity

pharynx

epiglottis

larynx

trachea

rib

intercostal muscle

bronchiole

pleural membranes

right lung

pleural cavity

diaphragm

esophagus

cartilage

bronchus

heart

left lung

Key words

alveolus
bronchiole
diaphragm
intercostal muscle
lung

Respiration and breathing

- The terms respiration and breathing are often used to mean the same thing—the moving of air into and out of lungs.
- However, respiration can also mean the chemical reactions going on in all cells that transfer energy from food and oxygen to drive cell processes.

System components

- The respiratory system consists of the nose, nasal cavity, pharynx, larynx, trachea, smaller conducting passageways (bronchi and *bronchioles*), and *alveoli*.
- The lungs are found in the thoracic region and are protected by the ribs. Immediately below the lungs is a sheet of muscle called the *diaphragm* that separates the lungs from the gut and liver.
- Muscles between the ribs—the *intercostals*—contract and relax to move air into and out of the lungs.
- The lungs are not attached to the ribs. They are separated by the pleural membrane, which produces a fluid to allow them to slide over the moving ribs during breathing.
- Hairs and mucus in the nose clean the air before it passes into the nasal cavity. Air travels down through the pharynx and is passed to the trachea.
- The trachea is a pipe strengthened with rings of cartilage to prevent it from collapsing. It divides into two bronchi, one for each lung. At the point where the trachea joins the esophagus is the epiglottis. This small flap of tissue closes the entrance to the lungs when food is swallowed.
- Inside the lungs, the bronchi divide to form smaller and smaller bronchioles, which eventually terminate in swollen air sacs called alveoli.

Key words

alveolus	thorax
bronchiole	
gaseous	
exchange	
lung	

Macrostructure

- The *lungs* are large air-filled spaces in the *thorax*. They are protected by the rib cage and connect to the outside world through the windpipe, or trachea.
- The lungs are connected to the trachea by the bronchi. The bronchi enter the lungs and branch out to form bronchial trees. The bronchi divide into smaller *bronchioles*, which terminate into *alveoli*.

Microstructure

- The alveoli are swollen sacs of tissue that have very thin walls and a very good blood supply. A branch of the pulmonary artery supplies deoxygenated blood to the network of capillaries covering the outside of the alveolus. A branch of the pulmonary vein drains oxygenated blood from these capillaries and returns it to the heart.
- *Gaseous exchange* occurs between the air in the alveolus and the blood in the capillaries. Oxygen passes into the blood, while carbon dioxide passes from the blood to the alveolar air.
- Muscular movements in the ribs and the diaphragm maintain a constant supply of fresh air to the alveoli.

Respiration: lungs

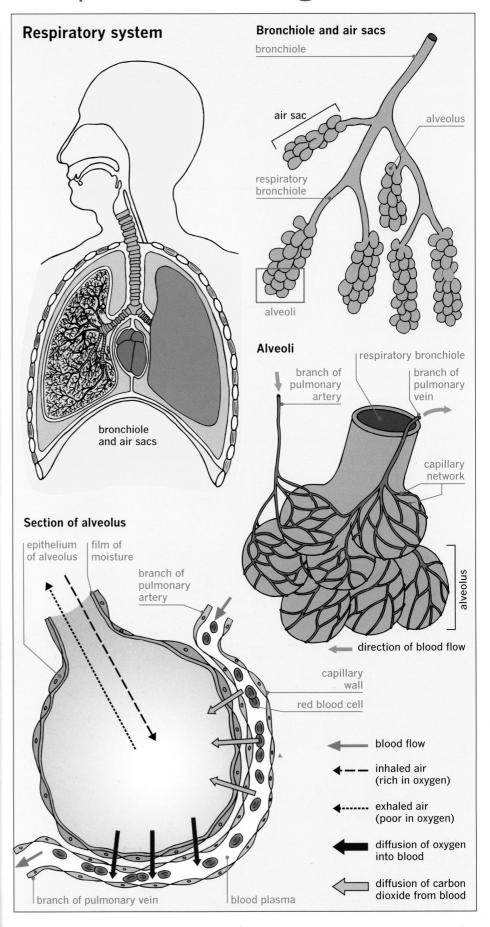

Respiratory system

bronchiole and air sacs

Bronchiole and air sacs

bronchiole

air sac

alveolus

respiratory bronchiole

alveoli

Alveoli

respiratory bronchiole

branch of pulmonary artery

branch of pulmonary vein

capillary network

alveolus

direction of blood flow

Section of alveolus

epithelium of alveolus

film of moisture

branch of pulmonary artery

capillary wall

red blood cell

branch of pulmonary vein

blood plasma

blood flow

inhaled air (rich in oxygen)

exhaled air (poor in oxygen)

diffusion of oxygen into blood

diffusion of carbon dioxide from blood

Respiration: breathing

Key words
abdomen
diaphragm
intercostal
lung

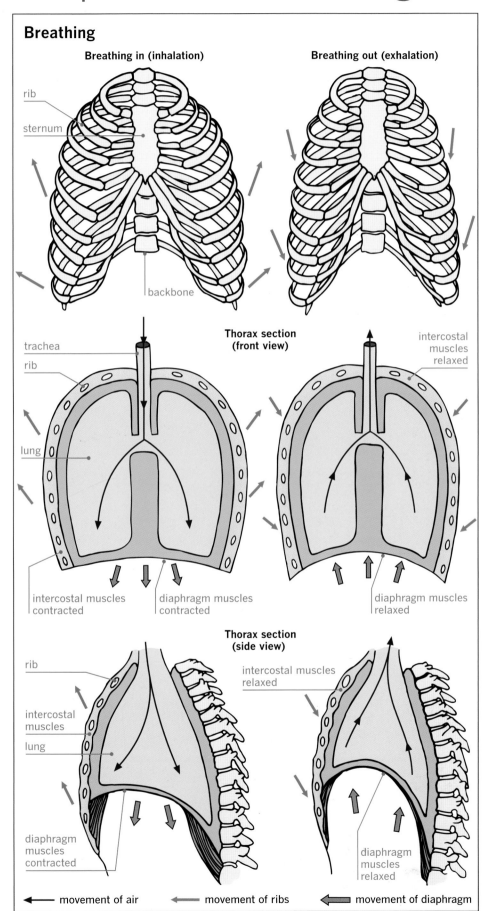

Breathing

Breathing in (inhalation)

rib
sternum

backbone

Breathing out (exhalation)

Thorax section (front view)

trachea
rib

lung

intercostal muscles relaxed

intercostal muscles contracted
diaphragm muscles contracted
diaphragm muscles relaxed

Thorax section (side view)

rib

intercostal muscles

lung

intercostal muscles relaxed

diaphragm muscles contracted
diaphragm muscles relaxed

◄─── movement of air ◄─── movement of ribs ◄═══ movement of diaphragm

Muscles involved

- For gentle breathing, the *diaphragm*, which separates the *lungs* from the *abdomen*, contracts and relaxes.
- During heavier breathing, muscles between the ribs—the *intercostals*—are also involved, and significantly increase the airflow.

Inhaling

- During gentle inhalation, the diaphragm contracts and falls away from the lungs. The lungs are pulled down, and air is drawn into them by suction. The diaphragm is not physically connected to the lungs—a vacuum between the surface of the lungs and the inside of the ribs pulls the lungs down while allowing them to move around.
- To increase inhalation, the external intercostals muscles contract. These pull the ribs upward and outward to increase the volume of the chest. This pulls air into the lungs.

Exhalation

- When muscles in the body wall contract, the liver and stomach push against the diaphragm. The relaxed diaphragm then pushes up into the chest space and squeezes air out of the lungs.
- To increase exhalation, the internal intercostals contract and pull the ribs downward and inward to push on the lungs.

© Diagram Visual Information Ltd.

Key words

bile	*urea*
feces	
gut	
metabolism	
spleen	

Excretion

- Excretion is the removal of waste and breakdown products of *metabolism* from the body.
- Since the roughage that forms most *feces* has never been inside the body (the *gut* space is regarded as outside of the body), most of it is not an excretory product.

Excretory products

- Carbon dioxide and water made by respiration.
- *Urea* made by the liver from excess amino acids or broken down protein molecules.
- Excess salts that were absorbed through the gut.
- *Bile* salts made by the *spleen* from old red blood cells.
- Assorted chemicals absorbed by the body or toxins that have been broken down by the liver.

Routes out of the body

- Carbon dioxide and a small amount of water leave in exhaled air.
- Urea passes out in solution as urine made by the kidneys. Urine also contains waste salts, other assorted waste products, and water.
- Sweat contains water, some salts, and urea, but is not a major route out of the body for these substances in normal circumstances.
- Bile pigments are passed into the gut and pass out in feces.

Excretion: excretory systems

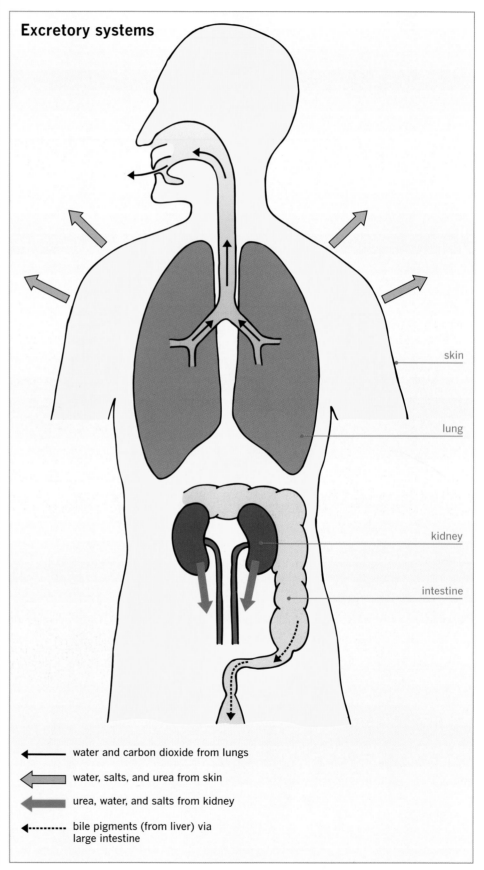

Excretory systems

skin

lung

kidney

intestine

⟵ water and carbon dioxide from lungs

⟸ water, salts, and urea from skin

⟹ urea, water, and salts from kidney

⇠ bile pigments (from liver) via large intestine

Excretion: urinary system

Urinary system

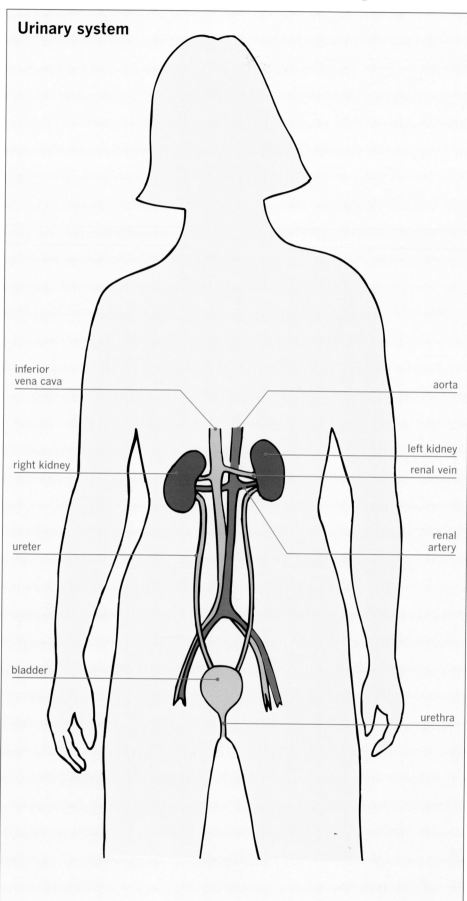

inferior vena cava

aorta

right kidney

left kidney

renal vein

ureter

renal artery

bladder

urethra

Key words

kidney
metabolism
osmoregulation
ureter

Excretion and osmoregulation

- Excretion is the removal of the breakdown products of *metabolism* and other waste from the body.
- *Osmoregulation* is the control of the water potential of fluids within the body.
- The *kidneys* are involved in both crucial processes.

The kidneys

- Human beings have two kidneys attached to the back of the abdominal cavity. Bony extensions of the spine protect these vital organs.
- *Ureters* connect the kidneys to the bladder. There are no valves in the ureters, so fluid drains downward by gravity. Backflow of urine to the kidneys is prevented by the constant production of fluid by the kidneys.
- Blood supply to the kidneys is through the renal artery, a branch of the aorta. This blood is at high pressure, which is essential for efficient kidney function. The renal vein, which opens into the vena cava, drains blood from the kidneys at low pressure.

Bladder and ureters

- The bladder acts as a storage organ, holding urine until it is convenient to release it to the outside world.
- The urine then flows along the urethra. A valve in the urethra prevents backflow of urine into the bladder.

Key words	
aorta	nephron
Bowman's capsule	ureter
glomerulus	
kidney	

Gross anatomy

- The human *kidney* is supplied with blood by a branch of the *aorta* called the renal artery and is drained of blood by a branch from the vena cava called the renal vein.
- Urine produced by the kidney is conducted by the *ureter* to the bladder for storage.

Cortex and medulla

- The outer part of the kidney is called the cortex. It surrounds the medulla, which includes in the middle a space connected to the ureter.
- The renal artery branches repeatedly in the kidney, delivering blood to the cortex.

Nephrons

- *Nephrons* are long tubules that start in the cortex with a small knot of capillaries called a *glomerulus*. The glomerulus is surrounded by a cup-shaped structure called the *Bowman's capsule*, which serves as a filter to remove organic wastes, excess inorganic salts, and water. Fluids from blood in the glomerulus are collected in the Bowman's capsule and further processed along the nephron to form urine.
- A proximal convoluted tubule receives the fluids from the renal corpuscle. The proximal tubule leads to a long tubular loop called the loop of Henle, which is concerned with absorbing water from the urine before it is released. The ascending limb of the loop of Henle returns the urine to the cortical region of the kidney where it enters the distal convoluted tubule. This tubule carries the urine to the collecting duct, which empties into the renal pelvis and then into the ureter and bladder.

Excretion: kidney structure

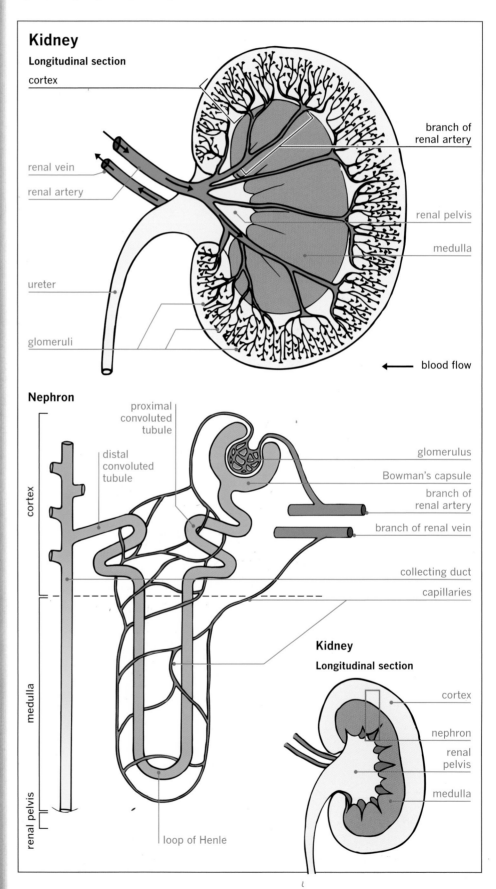

Kidney
Longitudinal section
- cortex
- renal vein
- renal artery
- ureter
- glomeruli
- branch of renal artery
- renal pelvis
- medulla
- ← blood flow

Nephron
- proximal convoluted tubule
- distal convoluted tubule
- cortex
- medulla
- renal pelvis
- loop of Henle
- glomerulus
- Bowman's capsule
- branch of renal artery
- branch of renal vein
- collecting duct
- capillaries

Kidney
Longitudinal section
- cortex
- nephron
- renal pelvis
- medulla

Excretion: kidney function

Key words

Bowman's capsule	nephron
concentration	selective
gradient	reabsorption
glomerulus	ultrafiltration
kidney	urea
	ureter

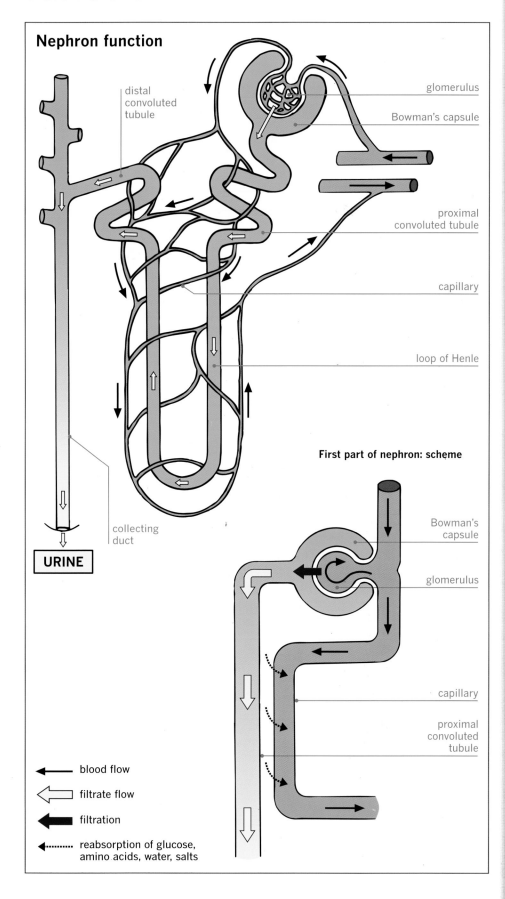

Nephron function

distal convoluted tubule

glomerulus

Bowman's capsule

proximal convoluted tubule

capillary

loop of Henle

collecting duct

URINE

First part of nephron: scheme

Bowman's capsule

glomerulus

capillary

proximal convoluted tubule

➡ blood flow

⬅ filtrate flow

➡ filtration

◄┄┄┄ reabsorption of glucose, amino acids, water, salts

Ultrafiltration

- The human *kidney* is supplied with blood by a branch of the aorta called the renal artery. This enters the kidney at high pressure, and plasma is forced out of the capillaries in the *glomerulus*. This process is called *ultrafiltration*.
- The glomerular filtrate that collects in the space of the *Bowman's capsule* contains a wide range of useful materials (salts, sugar, etc.) as well as waste products like *urea*.
- If this liquid were passed out as urine, the body would be losing valuable materials and a huge amount of water every day.

Selective reabsorption

- As the fluid passes along the nephron toward the collecting duct that will take it to the *ureters* and then to the bladder, useful materials are reabsorbed.
- Glucose and many salts are reabsorbed in the first part of the *nephron* called the proximal convoluted tubule. Glucose is actively reabsorbed. Many other substances diffuse back into the blood along a *concentration gradient*.
- The loop of Henle is important for reabsorbing water. Sodium ions are pumped into and out of the loop in a particular pattern to cause water to follow them by osmosis. This process can create a highly concentrated urine that can conserve water in times of stress. When water is plentiful, this process is modified, and mammals produce large volumes of dilute urine.

© Diagram Visual Information Ltd.

Key words

epidermis
keratin
Malpighian layer

Skin layers
- The skin is made up of three distinct layers: the *epidermis*, the dermis, and a layer of fat called subcutaneous fat.

Epidermis
- The epidermis is the outer layer of the skin and includes everything from the *Malpighian layer* outward.
- Mature epidermal cells are dead and are constantly lost from the surface. The Malpighian layer replaces these cells at the base of the epidermis so that there is a constant migration of cells from inside to outside. During this migration, the cells are filled with *keratin*, which helps to waterproof the skin.
- Melanocytes in the skin produce the pigment melanin in response to UV light. This darkens the skin and protects the delicate dermis from radiation.

Dermis
- The dermis is much thicker than the epidermis and contains a much wider range of structures.
- Sweat glands in the dermis produce sweat, which is released most actively when the temperature rises. It cools the skin by absorbing energy to evaporate.
- Hair follicles are embedded in the dermis. Sebaceous glands, found where the hair exits the skin, produce a fatty secretion called sebum. Bacteria living on the skin surface digest this to create acids that inhibit the growth of certain pathogenic organisms.
- The dermis also contains a wide range of sensory nerve endings.
- Blood vessels in the dermis can expand and contract to regulate heat loss from the skin.

Subcutaneous fat
- Subcutaneous fat gives the skin a plump, padded look.

Excretion: skin structure

Skin
Vertical section

Coordination: nervous system

© Diagram Visual Information Ltd.

Nervous system

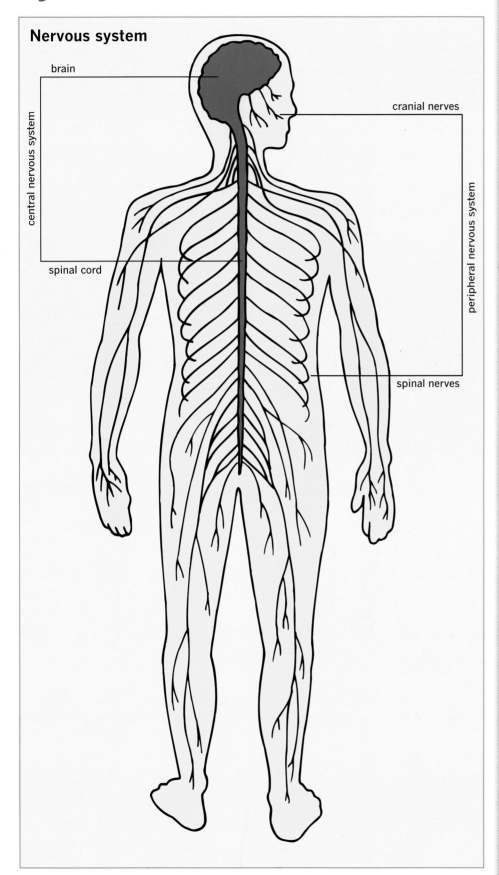

brain

cranial nerves

central nervous system

spinal cord

peripheral nervous system

spinal nerves

CNS and PNS

- The human nervous system divides into two main parts: the *central nervous system* (CNS) and the *peripheral nervous system* (PNS).
- The CNS includes the brain and spinal cord. The PNS includes everything else and consists of paired nerves that arise from the *spinal cord*. A single nerve is a bundle of elongated cells called *neurons*.

Neurons

- Neurons are the cells of the nervous system that carry nerve impulses. There are three basic types:
- *Sensory neurons* convey messages from the sense organs into the CNS.
- *Motor neurons* carry messages from the CNS out to muscles or glands.
- *Association neurons* carry messages around inside the CNS. They are different from sensory and motor neurons in that they do not possess myelin sheaths, the insulating envelopes that surround the core of a nerve fiber and facilitate the transmission of nerve impulses.
- Neurons pass messages between themselves across synapses. A *synapse* forms where two nerve cells are in close contact. Messages pass across the small gap as secretions of chemicals called *neurotransmitters*.
- Impulses passing along neurons are waves of electrical activity created by the movement of sodium ions into and out of the nerve fiber.

© Diagram Visual Information Ltd.

Electrical balance

- A nerve fiber is long and tubular in shape. It is normally *impermeable* to sodium ions, and these are pumped to the outside of the cell so that an electrical potential exists across the cell membrane.
- This means that the outside is more positive, with a higher concentration of sodium ions than the inside.

Depolarization

- When a *neuron* is stimulated, the membrane is changed to allow ions to pass, and sodium ions rush in to equalize the potential difference. This is called depolarization. A number of other ions inside also move, particularly potassium ions, which flow out of the neuron.
- The inside of the neuron is now neutral or slightly negative. This lasts for a very short time, and soon the active pumping of sodium ions and reversion of the membrane back to impermeability reasserts the positive charge outside the cell.

A wave of depolarization

- A nerve impulse is a wave of depolarization that moves along the neuron.
- Depolarization in one part stimulates the next part of the neuron to depolarize. This moves the impulse forward. Behind the depolarization, the cell is repolarizing the membrane again to leave it ready to receive the next *stimulus*.

Coordination: nerve impulse

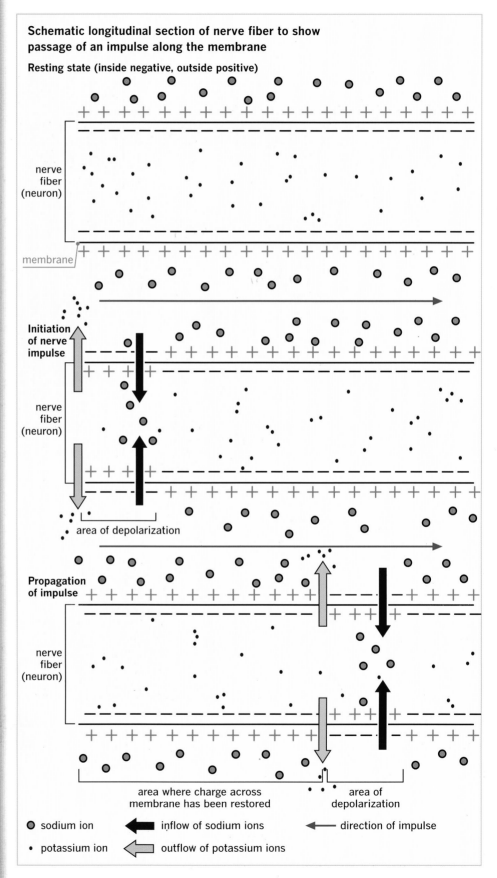

Schematic longitudinal section of nerve fiber to show passage of an impulse along the membrane

Resting state (inside negative, outside positive)

nerve fiber (neuron)

membrane

Initiation of nerve impulse

nerve fiber (neuron)

area of depolarization

Propagation of impulse

nerve fiber (neuron)

area where charge across membrane has been restored

area of depolarization

- ● sodium ion
- · potassium ion
- ⬅ inflow of sodium ions
- ⬅ outflow of potassium ions
- ⬅ direction of impulse

Coordination: synapse

Connections between association neuron and motor neuron

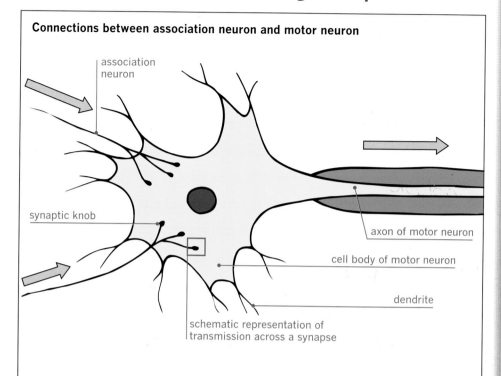

association neuron

synaptic knob

axon of motor neuron

cell body of motor neuron

dendrite

schematic representation of transmission across a synapse

Transmission across a synapse: schematic representation

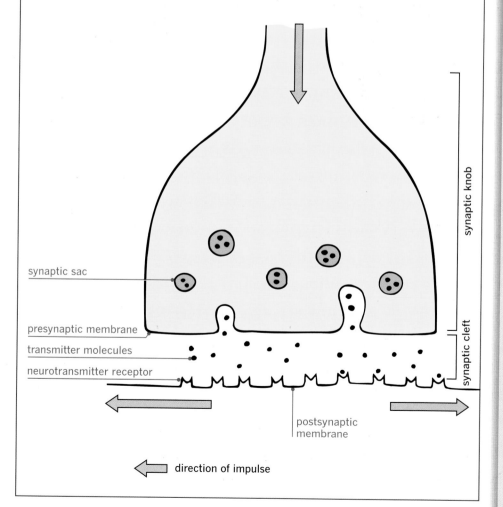

synaptic knob

synaptic sac

presynaptic membrane

transmitter molecules

neurotransmitter receptor

synaptic cleft

postsynaptic membrane

direction of impulse

Key words

axon
dendrite
neuron
neurotransmitter
synapse

vesicle

Links between cells

- Nerve cells do not exist in isolation. They must pass messages between themselves in order to function.
- The point at which *neurons* meet is called a *synapse*. The cells do not actually join; there is always a small gap between them.
- The ends of neurons are often specialized to encourage the passing of messages; for example, they can have an increased surface area, or have a number of shorter processes called *dendrites* that link into the cells around them.

Chemical messengers

- Each impulse travels down the *axon* of the neuron to its end, which is swollen to form a synaptic knob.
- The synaptic knob (see bottom diagram) is filled with *vesicles* called synaptic sacs, which contain chemicals called *neurotransmitters*.
- When an impulse arrives at the synaptic knob, chemicals trigger the ejection of neurotransmitters from some of the vesicles, and their neurotransmitter is released into the synaptic cleft.
- The neurotransmitter molecules bind to receptors on the postsynaptic membrane.
- Some neurotransmitters stimulate an impulse in the next neuron. Some inhibit the neuron, stopping the impulse or blocking a pathway.
- Neurotransmitter molecules are broken down after a short time, so that the synapse becomes open for new impulses again.
- Certain types of poisons (e.g., curare) affect these chemicals and the enzymes that regulate them. These poisons kill the body by effectively destroying the functionality of the nervous system.

Key words

adrenalin
autonomic
  nervous system
parasympathetic
  nervous system
spinal cord
sympathetic
  nervous system

No conscious control

- The *autonomic nervous system* consists of two systems that control many of the automatic responses in the body.
- They are not normally under conscious control and mainly deal with the control of glands and the internal body condition.

Sympathetic system

- The *sympathetic nervous system* prepares the body for activity and has effects that are similar to the effects of the hormone *adrenalin*. This is the fight or flight response.
- The sympathetic system arises from the *spinal cord* but with a ganglion (lump) of nervous tissue found near the root of the nerves.

Parasympathetic system

- The *parasympathetic nervous system* relaxes the body. Its effects are antagonistic to the sympathetic system.
- Parasympathetic nerves arise directly from the spinal cord without any ganglia. The most important parasympathetic nerve in the body is the vagus nerve, which connects to a wide range of organs in the chest and abdominal areas.

Coordination: autonomic nervous system

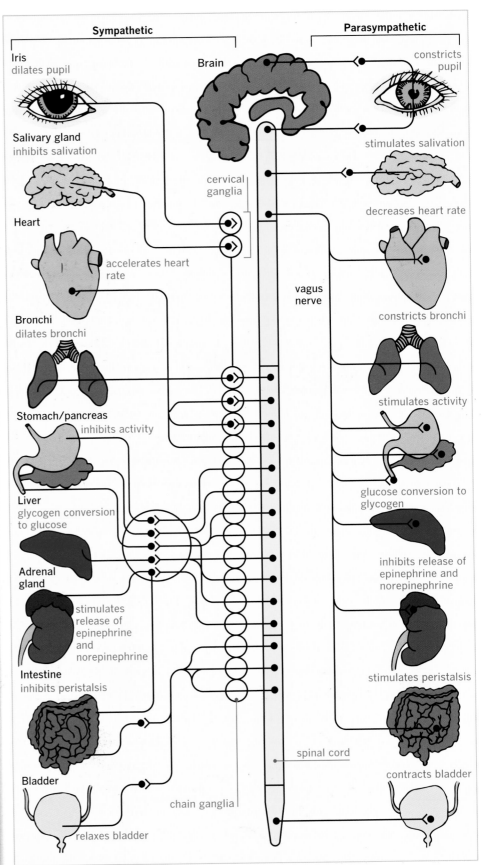

Coordination: brain structure

Key words

cerebellum	spinal cord
cerebral hemispheres	
medulla oblongata	

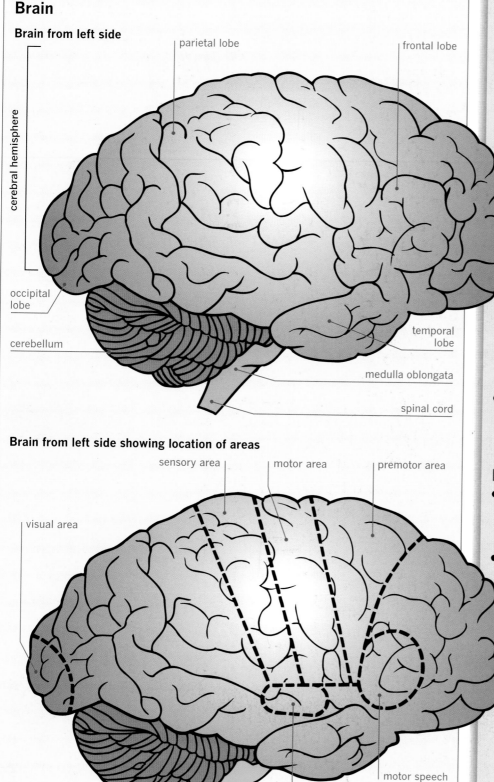

Brain

Brain from left side

cerebral hemisphere

parietal lobe

frontal lobe

occipital lobe

cerebellum

temporal lobe

medulla oblongata

spinal cord

Brain from left side showing location of areas

sensory area

motor area

premotor area

visual area

motor speech area

auditory area

Brain structure

- The brain is actually a tubular structure that can be interpreted as a swelling of the end of the spinal cord. The central canal of the spinal cord is continuous with spaces at the center of the brain. However, because the tube is folded and expanded, this structure can be obscured.
  - Starting from the top of the *spinal cord*, the first swelling is the *medulla oblongata*. Growing out from this toward the back of the head is the *cerebellum*.
  - Further along the structure are the two largest swellings—the *cerebral hemispheres*. The cord has also bent through a right angle so that the hemispheres seem to sit on top of the cord.
- Neurologists normally subdivide the cerebral cortex into four lobes: the frontal lobe, the parietal lobe, the occipital lobe, and the temporal lobe.

Key areas

- Different parts of the brain have different functions. Broadly speaking, the further down the tube, the more unconscious or automatic the activity.
- The medulla oblongata coordinates involuntary activities. The cerebellum coordinates complex muscle movements and is involved in maintaining balance.
  - Thinking and voluntary action seem to be coordinated by the cerebral hemispheres.
  - The cerebral hemispheres have been extensively mapped to identify areas concerned with senses and movement (see bottom diagram). Locating the area that is concerned with conscious thought has been much more difficult.

Key words	
cerebellum	thalamus
cerebral hemisphere	
hypothalamus	
spinal cord	

Brain stem

- This is really an extension of the *spinal cord* and is a swollen area that deals with many automatic and maintenance functions.
- Control of breathing, heartbeat, dilation of pupils, vomiting, and coughing are organized in this region. Lack of activity of the brain stem is taken as a conclusive sign of death—without these automatic functions, the body cannot survive.

Cerebellum

- The *cerebellum* consists of two paired hemispheres growing out of the back of the brain stem.
- The decision to move a muscle is taken in the higher centers of the cerebral hemispheres, but the cerebellum coordinates the firing of the thousands of nerve cells and contraction of individual muscle fibers to achieve this movement.

Thalamus

- The *thalamus* (not visible in the diagram) is located in the center of the brain beneath the central hemispheres. It connects the midbrain to the higher centers in the cerebral hemispheres. It has a more active role in emotions, arousal, and some reflexes than the automatic systems of the brain stem.

Hypothalamus

- The *hypothalamus* (not visible in the diagram) lies beneath the thalamus and coordinates links between the hormone and nervous systems.

Coordination: brain function

Brain functions

- Certain brain functions can be mapped to particular areas of the cerebral cortex.
- For example, a fold of the cortex immediately behind the frontal lobe, called the primary motor area, controls muscle activity in various parts of the body. Hence, muscle activity in, say, the hand or tongue, can be pinpointed to a specific location in this area of cortex.
- Similarly, the primary sensory area, lying just behind the motor area, receives sensory information from specific parts of the body responsible for the sensations of touch, pressure, temperature, and body position.
- Hearing, sight, taste, and smell, which involve more complex signaling, are mapped to separate areas of the cortex.
- The cerebral cortex is also responsible for consciousness and emotions, and for mental activities such as language, learning, and memory—functions that require the integration of signals from various parts of the brain.
- Several areas of the cortex have been mapped as speech centers. These are confined to the left hemisphere in about 9 out of 10 persons.

Brain from left side showing functions of areas

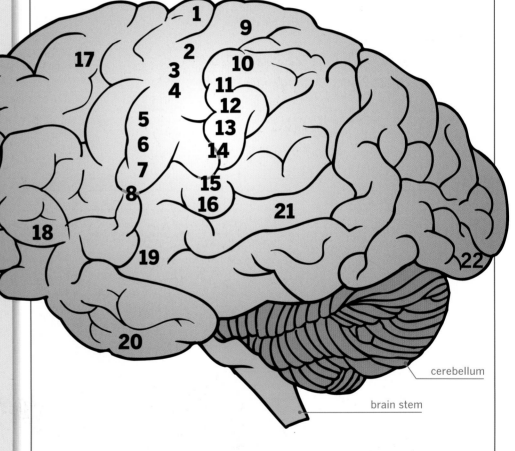

1–8	Motor area functions	9–16	Sensory area functions		
1	Abdomen	9	Abdomen	17	Limb movements
2	Thorax	10	Thorax	18	Speech control
3	Arm	11	Arm	19	Hearing
4	Hand	12	Hand	20	Taste and smell
5	Finger	13	Finger	21	Speech understanding
6	Thumb	14	Thumb	22	Vision
7	Neck	15	Neck		
8	Tongue	16	Tongue		

Coordination: taste

Tongue

Taste areas

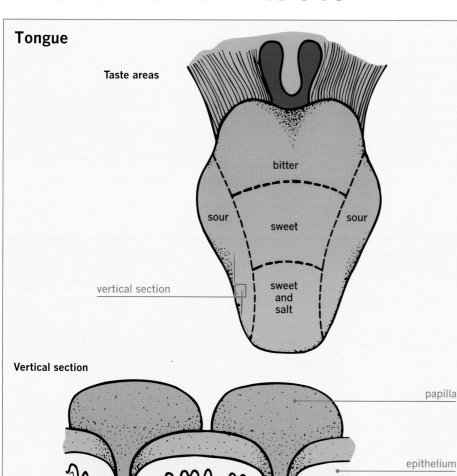

Vertical section

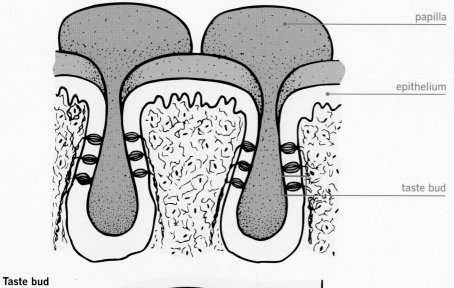

- papilla
- epithelium
- taste bud

Taste bud

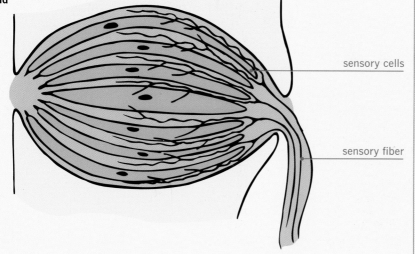

- sensory cells
- sensory fiber

Key words

epithelium
papilla

Tongue structure

- The tongue is a muscular organ that helps to mix the food and saliva in the mouth. The top surface is covered with specialized epithelial cells, called *papillae*, which hold the taste buds.
- The taste buds are collections of nerve cells that respond to a range of chemicals. They line the papillae in the gaps between them.

The four tastes

- The tongue responds to four basic tastes: bitter, sweet, sour, and salty.
- The different areas of the tongue respond particularly well to one of these tastes. The tip can detect both sweet and salty flavors.
- There appears to be limited structural differences between the taste buds in these different areas of the tongue, although the sensory nerves that arise from them run to slightly different areas of the spinal cord.
- Sweet tastes are the most difficult to detect, with bitter tastes a thousand times more dilute easily detected.

© Diagram Visual Information Ltd.

Key words

olfactory neuron

Site of detection

- The sensory cells responsible for smell are found in the cavities behind the nose.
- Smell is a chemical sense, and the relevant chemicals must dissolve in the layer of mucus lining the nasal cavities before they can be detected.
- If the nose is blocked, for example by mucus secreted during colds and flu, the sense of smell is degraded. Since smell has a strong influence on taste, the sense of taste is also compromised.

Sensory cells

- Chemicals that have dissolved in the mucus lining the nasal cavities react with *olfactory neurons*. These send impulses along to the olfactory bulb near the base of the brain.
- Smells have never been sorted into four categories as tastes have been, and all olfactory neurons seem to be structurally identical.
- Olfactory neurons have a short life span (typically 1–2 months) and, uniquely for nerve cells, can be regenerated throughout life.
- Smells appear to be able to evoke associations much more readily than tastes. A number of reflexive actions are also mediated by smells, from sneezing to feeling hungry when food is smelled.

Coordination: smell

Nose
Section through head to show nasal cavity

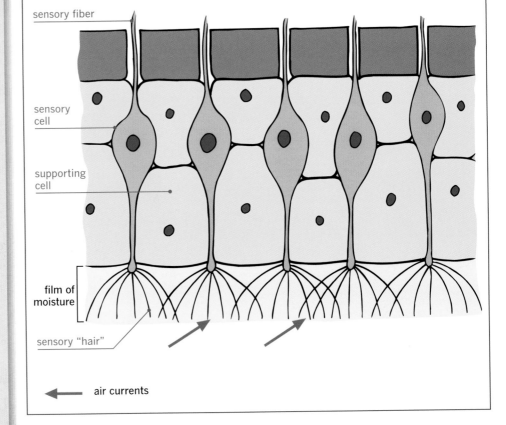

sensory fiber

smell sensory cells

nasal cavity

Smell sensory cells

sensory fiber

sensory cell

supporting cell

film of moisture

sensory "hair"

← air currents

Coordination: ear structure

Key words

auditory ossicle
cochlea
eardrum
eustachian tube
semi-circular
  canal

Ear

Section of the head to show internal structure of the ear

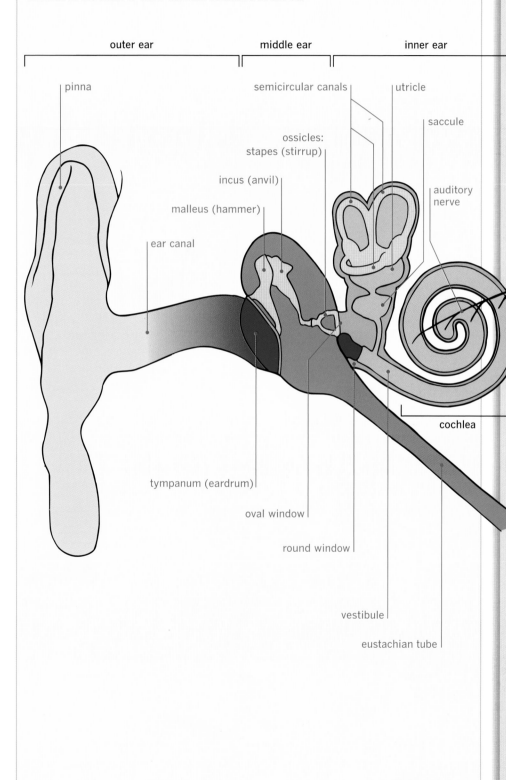

outer ear

middle ear

inner ear

pinna

semicircular canals

utricle

saccule

ossicles:
stapes (stirrup)

incus (anvil)

malleus (hammer)

auditory
nerve

ear canal

cochlea

tympanum (eardrum)

oval window

round window

vestibule

eustachian tube

The outer ear

- The outer ear consists of the pinna, which projects beyond the bone of the skull. It gathers sound waves and funnels them toward the ear canal, which ends in the *eardrum*.
- Sounds make the thin membrane of the eardrum vibrate.

The middle ear

- The middle ear consists of an air-filled cavity inside the eardrum. It links to the back of the throat through the *eustachian tube*, which allows air pressure to be balanced on both sides of the drum.
- Crossing the space of the middle ear are the *auditory ossicles*: the hammer, anvil, and stirrup. These pass vibrations across the middle ear and into the inner ear via the oval window. The auditory ossicles act as a mechanical amplifier and increase the amplitude of the sound waves as they pass.

The inner ear

- The inner ear is completely encased in the bone of the skull and is a fluid-filled cavity containing the *cochlea* and the *semicircular canals*.
- Vibrations enter the inner ear through the oval window and are converted into pressure waves that pass along the coiled tube of the cochlea and leave through the round window. The cochlea can interpret these pressure waves as sounds.
- The vestibular apparatus—consisting of the semicircular canals, utrile, saccule, and vestibule—is the organ of balance.

© Diagram Visual Information Ltd.

Key words

auditory ossicle
cochlea
otolith
semicircular
  canal

Path of vibrations

- Sound entering the outer ear passes along the ear canal to the eardrum. Here it is converted to movement and passes along the *auditory ossicles*.
- The stapes passes these movements into the *cochlea*, where fluids call perilymph and endolymph create pressure waves. The frequency of the pressure waves matches the frequency of the original sound entering the ear.

Hearing

- The pressure waves stimulate the hair cells of the organ of Corti, a membrane lying between the basilar and tectorial membranes. It is the movement of these hair cells that converts the vibrations into nerve impulses.
- The auditory cortex in the brain receives these impulses and interprets them as sounds.

Balance

- The *semicircular canals* are concerned with balance.
- When the head moves, endolymph in the canals moves due to momentum. The movement of the fluid disturbs the *otoliths*, which are suspended on sensory hair cells.
- The brain can use information from these sensory cells to detect body movements, even when other sources of information (e.g., visual) are unavailable.
- Normally, balance is assessed using information from both eyes and ears.

Coordination: hearing and balance

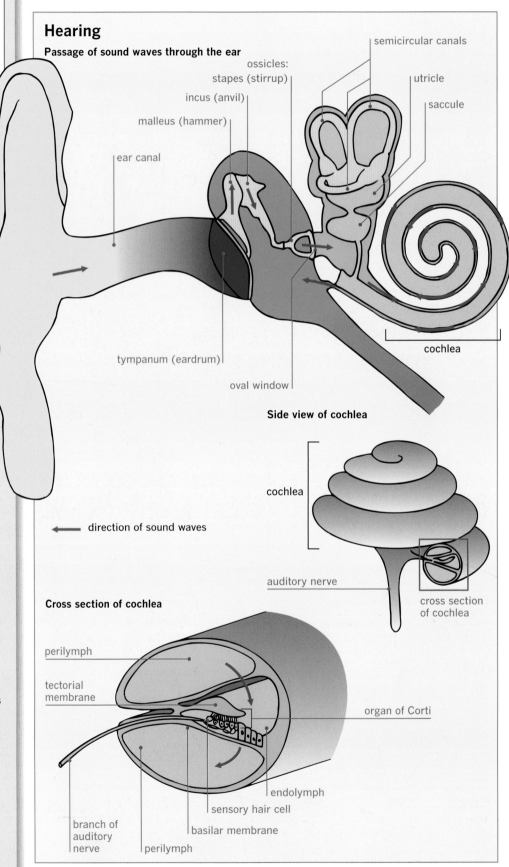

Hearing

Passage of sound waves through the ear

semicircular canals

ossicles:
stapes (stirrup)
incus (anvil)
malleus (hammer)
ear canal
tympanum (eardrum)
oval window
utricle
saccule
cochlea

Side view of cochlea

cochlea
auditory nerve
cross section of cochlea

← direction of sound waves

Cross section of cochlea

perilymph
tectorial membrane
organ of Corti
endolymph
sensory hair cell
basilar membrane
branch of auditory nerve
perilymph

Coordination: eye structure

Key words

optic cortex
optic nerve
vitreous humor

Sight

Partial section of eye to show orbit and extrinsic muscles

optic nerve   extrinsic muscle   tear gland   eyelid

pupil

iris

eyeball

eyelid

bone of orbit   conjunctiva

Vertical section

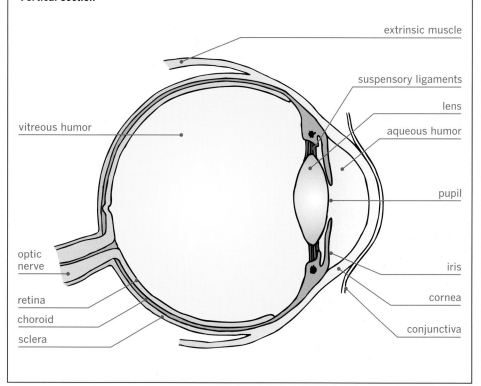

extrinsic muscle

suspensory ligaments

lens

aqueous humor

pupil

iris

cornea

conjunctiva

vitreous humor

optic nerve

retina

choroid

sclera

External structure

- The eye is a light-proof ball filled with a clear jelly-like substance. The tough outer layer is called the sclera (see bottom diagram) and is transparent at the front to let light in.
- Muscles are attached to the sclera to turn the eye in its socket. A single *optic nerve* comes out of the back of the eye and connects directly to the *optic cortex* at the back of the brain.

Internal structure

- The eyeball is filled with a clear, jelly-like substance called the *vitreous humor*. This keeps the eyeball fully inflated—if it were to deflate it would not be able to focus correctly.
- The choroid is a layer found inside the sclera. It is black in color to help reduce internal reflections.
- Blood vessels in the choroid supply the retina with food and oxygen, and take away waste products.
- Light entering the eye passes through the cornea, the transparent layer at the front of the eye covered by the conjunctiva. It refracts light to aid focusing.
- The iris, behind the cornea, is a colored ring of muscular tissue. By altering the size of the pupil, its central opening, it controls the amount of light entering the eye.
- The aqueous humor connects the cornea with the lens and helps maintain the convex shape of the cornea necessary for the convergence of light at the lens.
- The transparent lens focuses light on to the retina.
- The retina contains the light-sensitive cells called rods and cones. Rods respond to light level alone and enable black and white vision in dim light. The brain combines information from these three cell types to produce a full color image. Cones need a higher light intensity to function than rods do.

© Diagram Visual Information Ltd.

Key words

neuron

Retina

- There are two types of light-sensitive cells in the retina: rods, which are most numerous and provide vision in dim light; and cones, which work in bright light and provide color vision. Cones exist in three different forms, with each one responding to a slightly different color of light (broadly red, green, and blue).

- The cells contain visual pigments. When light strikes the cell, it is temporarily bleached, producing an electrical signal. These signals are conveyed to the brain as nerve impulses via connecting *neurons* and sensory nerve fibers.

Coordination: light sensitivity

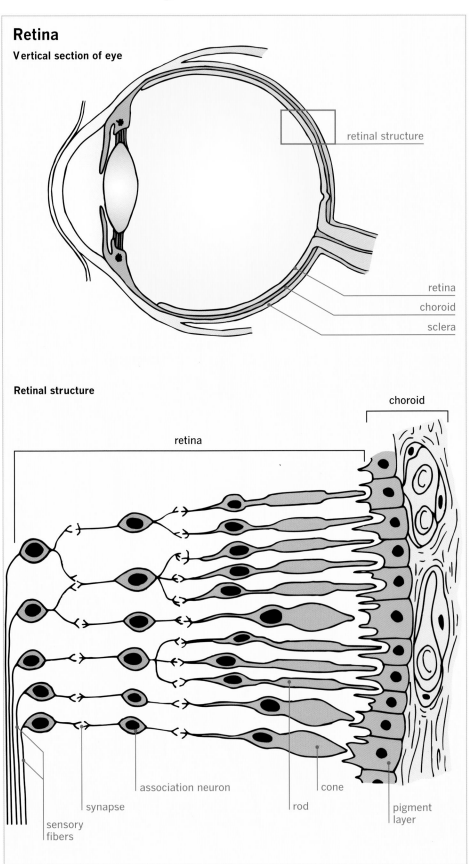

Retina
Vertical section of eye

retinal structure

retina

choroid

sclera

Retinal structure

choroid

retina

association neuron

cone

rod

pigment layer

synapse

sensory fibers

Coordination: endocrine system

Key words

adrenalin
basal metabolic
  rate
endocrine gland
hormone

insulin
pituitary gland

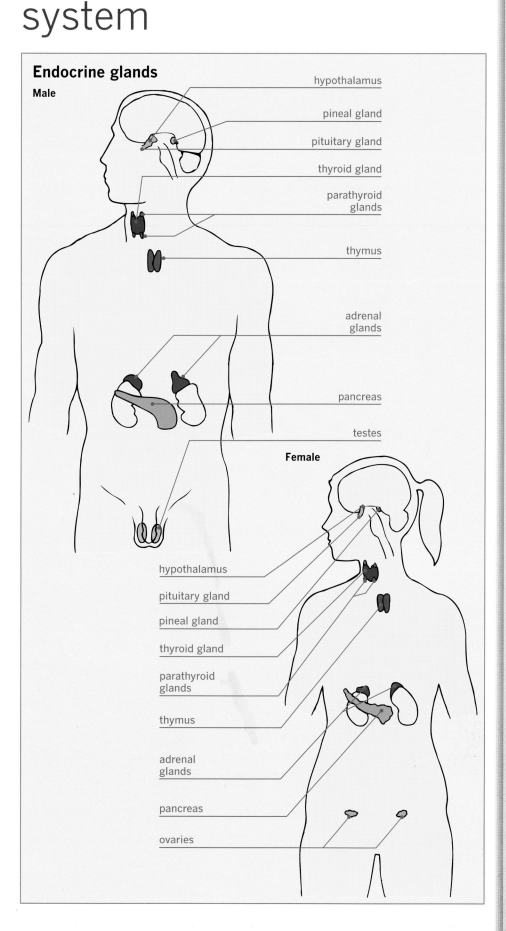

Endocrine glands

Male

- hypothalamus
- pineal gland
- pituitary gland
- thyroid gland
- parathyroid glands
- thymus
- adrenal glands
- pancreas
- testes

Female

- hypothalamus
- pituitary gland
- pineal gland
- thyroid gland
- parathyroid glands
- thymus
- adrenal glands
- pancreas
- ovaries

Endocrine glands

- *Endocrine glands*, sometimes called ductless glands, produce secretions that pass directly into the blood.
- Endocrine secretions are called *hormones* and change the functioning of a distant organ in the body. So, the hormone *adrenalin*, produced by the adrenal gland, increases the heart rate.
- The organ affected by a particular hormone is called the target organ.

Hormonal coordination

- Hormonal coordination is used by the body to control many long-term changes, e.g., growth and development.
- The most important endocrine gland in the body is the *pituitary gland*, which secretes hormones that regulate other endocrine glands.

Key endocrine glands

- The adrenal glands secrete adrenalin, which stimulates the body to produce a "fight or flight" response to stress.
- Testes and ovaries secrete a range of hormones to control sexual development.
- The thyroid gland secretes a hormone that controls the *basal metabolic rate*.
- The pancreas contains cells that secrete *insulin*, which reduces the level of sugar in the blood.
- Parathyroid glands produce hormones that regulate the amount of calcium and phosphorus in the body.
- The pineal gland secretes melatonin, which plays a role in sleep, aging, and reproduction.
- The thymus and the pituitary and hypothalamus in the brain also have endocrine functions.
- The thymus gland is also involved in the production of T-lymphocytes, essential components of the immune system.

Key words

endocrine gland
hormone
hypothalamus
pituitary gland

The "master gland"

- The *pituitary gland* is called the "master gland" because it secretes *hormones* that control the activity of a range of other *endocrine glands*.
- The pituitary gland consists of two types of tissue: endocrine at the anterior, and nervous at the posterior. Development in the embryo clearly shows the two sources of tissues that make up this hybrid organ.
- The posterior lobe is connected to the brain through the *hypothalamus*. These connections link the two coordination systems in the body: the nervous system and the endocrine system.

The anterior lobe

- The anterior lobe secretes hormones that influence the activity of glands like the adrenal, thyroid, and gonads.
- Growth hormone regulates the growth of long bones.
- Prolactin stimulates the mammary glands to secrete milk.

The posterior lobe

- Hormones secreted by the posterior lobe tend to produce more rapid short-lived responses than hormones from the anterior lobe.
- Vasopressin (an anti-diuretic hormone) increases water reabsorption by the kidney to produce more concentrated urine.
- Oxytocin stimulates the contraction of uterine muscles during childbirth.

Coordination: pituitary gland

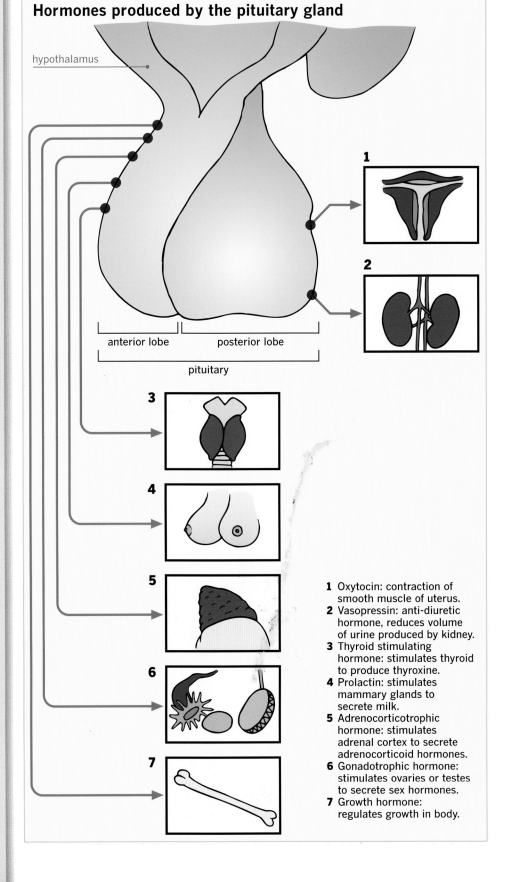

Hormones produced by the pituitary gland

hypothalamus

anterior lobe   posterior lobe

pituitary

1 Oxytocin: contraction of smooth muscle of uterus.
2 Vasopressin: anti-diuretic hormone, reduces volume of urine produced by kidney.
3 Thyroid stimulating hormone: stimulates thyroid to produce thyroxine.
4 Prolactin: stimulates mammary glands to secrete milk.
5 Adrenocorticotrophic hormone: stimulates adrenal cortex to secrete adrenocorticoid hormones.
6 Gonadotrophic hormone: stimulates ovaries or testes to secrete sex hormones.
7 Growth hormone: regulates growth in body.

Locomotion: skeleton

Skeleton

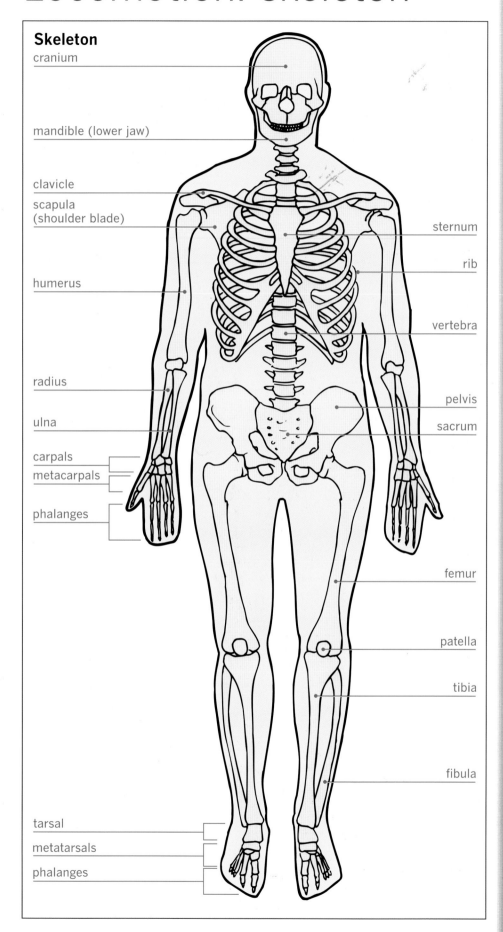

cranium

mandible (lower jaw)

clavicle

scapula (shoulder blade)

humerus

radius

ulna

carpals

metacarpals

phalanges

sternum

rib

vertebra

pelvis

sacrum

femur

patella

tibia

fibula

tarsal

metatarsals

phalanges

Key words

axial skeleton
pentadactyl limb

Bones

● The adult human skeleton contains 206 bones, though some are so closely fused together (e.g., the plates of the skull) that they effectively form a single bone.
● The largest bones in the body are the femurs of the legs. The smallest are the auditory ossicles in the middle ear.
● The skeleton provides places to attach muscles, acts as a mineral store, protects key body organs, and manufacturers certain types of blood cells.

The axial skeleton

● The *axial skeleton* consists of the head, spine, and associated structures like the ribs and shoulder blades.
● The axial skeleton protects key body organs (the brain, spinal cord, heart, and lungs).

The pentadactyl limbs

● The limbs in humans follow the standard pentadactyl pattern.
● A single bone at the top of the limb links to two bones below.
● A set of five bones form the next section leading in turn to five digits terminating in five phalanges.
● The presence of the *pentadactyl limb* in many animals is evidence for descent from a common ancestor— a key feature of evolutionary theory.

Key words

cartilaginous
  joint
synovial joint

Types of joint

- A joint is formed where two or more bones link together. There are three basic types of joint.
- Fixed joints in the cranium of the skull allow no movement at all. The bones are fused together.
- *Cartilaginous joints* have a cartilage connection between bones and allow some movement. The joint between the two halves of the pelvis is a cartilaginous joint. In pregnancy this cartilage is softened by hormone action so that during childbirth the pelvis has enough flexibility to facilitate passage of the baby's head.
- *Synovial joints* allow a much wider range of movement and can be further classified into ball and socket joints, hinge joints, and others based on their arc of movement.

Synovial joints

- Ball and socket joints allow movement in two planes.
- The hip joint is a ball and socket joint. The ball at the head of the femur fits into a boney socket in the pelvis. Ligaments hold the bones together. A synovial membrane lines the inside of the joint and secretes a lubricating fluid called synovial fluid. The parts of the bone that move against each other are covered with a smooth tough form of cartilage. The loose fibrous capsule permits the hip joint to have a large range of movement.
- The knee joint is an example of a hinge joint. The bones are shaped to allow movement in only one plane.
- The knee is made up of the lower end of the femur, which rotates on the upper end of the tibia, and the patella, which slides in a groove on the end of the femur. The joint is bathed in a viscous fluid that is contained inside the synovial membrane. Cartilage serves to cushion the knee and helps it absorb shock during motion.

Locomotion: joints

Joints

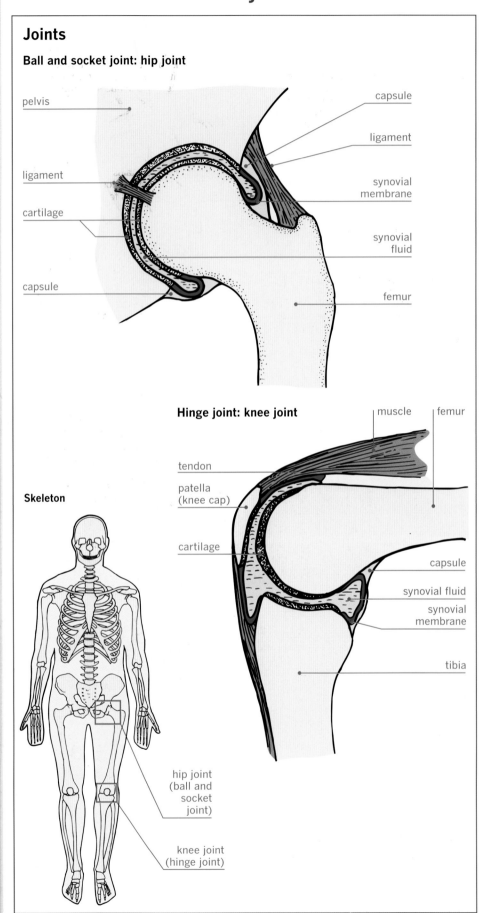

Ball and socket joint: hip joint

pelvis

capsule

ligament

ligament

synovial membrane

cartilage

synovial fluid

capsule

femur

Hinge joint: knee joint

muscle

femur

tendon

patella (knee cap)

cartilage

capsule

synovial fluid

synovial membrane

tibia

Skeleton

hip joint (ball and socket joint)

knee joint (hinge joint)

Terrestrial biomes

Biomes

Rain forest
This biome is found in tropical regions with high rainfall close to the equator. It consists chiefly of tall trees that form a dense canopy high above the ground. Shrubs and smaller plants live on trunks and branches in the canopy, while the forest floor supports mainly fungi and invertebrates that live off decomposing vegetation.

Desert
Desert is found in regions where rainfall is below 10 inches (25 cm) per year. Perennial plants such as cacti, yuccas, and agaves are resistant to drought, while quick-growing annuals appear and disappear with the rains.

Grassland
This biome is typical of continental interiors and is dominated by grasses, which survive the dry season by means of underground stems (rhizomes). Herbivorous animals, such as antelope, zebra, and cattle, are common here.

Deciduous forest
Deciduous forest is found in temperate regions with evenly distributed rainfall, and is dominated by deciduous hardwood trees such as oak, beech, and maple. The forest floor often supports shrubs and ground plants.

Taiga
Taiga is typical of cool regions in high latitudes and mountains with a short growing season. It consists almost entirely of evergreen coniferous forest, with sparse herbs and shrubs.

Tundra
Tundra is found especially encircling the North Pole, and also on high mountains (alpine tundra), where temperatures are low and the growing season is short. In Arctic regions the ground is permanently frozen (permafrost) below the surface layer. Hardy plants such as mosses, sedges, and lichens form the sparse vegetation.

Key words

biome

Biomes
- A *biome* is a large community of living organisms that are adapted to a particular climate and soil conditions. Biomes are characterized by their dominant vegetation, for example, grasses or tropical trees. Biomes may stretch across entire continents and gradually merge with adjoining biomes.
- The dominant factor controlling establishment of a biome type appears to be incoming sunlight, as biomes are broadly parallel bands aligned with the equator.

Biome types
- Rainforest depends on high solar radiation and rainfall. It is a complex system with many species.
- Desert has similar sunlight input but has very low rainfall: below 10 inches (25 cm) per year. This leads to a very impoverished vegetation cover.
- Grasslands predominate further away from the equator.
- Still further away are forests, initially the deciduous forest, with trees that lose their leaves in the winter. Nearer the poles are coniferous forests, with trees that can survive in ground that is frozen solid for at least part of the year. These forests form the taiga. The most extreme biome is tundra. This has very limited vegetation cover, no trees, and is sometimes referred to as a "cold desert."

Distribution of biomes

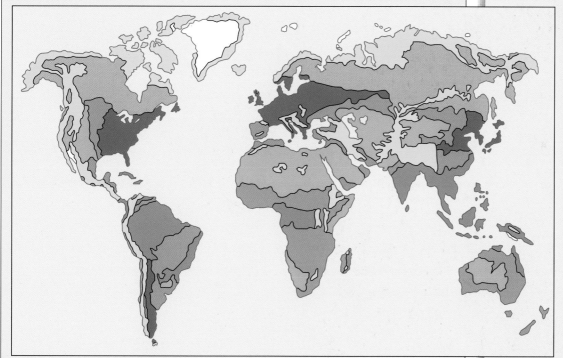

Key

▨	rain forest	▨	deciduous forest
▨	desert	▨	taiga
▨	grassland	▨	tundra

Key words

carbon cycle
photosynthesis
respiration

Carbon cycle

- Carbon, the fourth most abundant element in the Universe, is the building block of life. It is the element central to all organic substances, from fossil fuels to DNA.
- The total amount of carbon on planet Earth is fixed. The same carbon atoms in the atmosphere and in your body have been used in countless other molecules since the Earth began. The *Carbon cycle* is the complex set of processes through which all carbon atoms rotate.
- Carbon exists in Earth's atmosphere primarily as the gas carbon dioxide (1). Through *photosynthesis* plants fix carbon dioxide from the atmosphere into sugars, which they need to grow (2).
- Animals eat the plants and use the carbon for their own maintenance and growth (3). Animals return carbon dioxide into the air through *respiration* (4) and when they die (7), since carbon is returned to the soil during decomposition.
- Plants and animals decay and, over the course of millions of years, create fossil fuels—coal, oil, natural gas (5).
- Burning fossil fuels returns the carbon in these fuels to the atmosphere (6).

Carbon cycle

Global warming

- In recent times, humans have been burning large quantities of fossil fuels, which has led to a rising concentration of carbon dioxide in the atmosphere.
- This is intensifying the "greenhouse effect," whereby carbon dioxide and other gases in the Earth's atmosphere act like the glass in a greenhouse, trapping heat near the Earth's surface.
- Consequently the average temperature at the Earth's surface is gradually rising—the phenomenon called global warming—with potentially disastrous consequences. These may include rising sea levels, disrupted weather patterns, devastation of farming and natural ecosystems, and mass extinction of organisms.

Carbon cycle

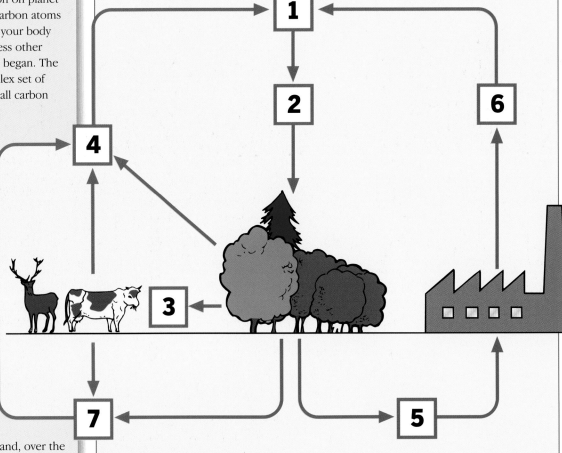

1 Atmospheric pool of carbon dioxide	5 Fossil fuels
2 Plants take up carbon dioxide for photosynthesis	6 Carbon dioxide released by combustion
3 Animals eat plants	7 Death of organisms and decay by bacteria
4 Carbon dioxide released by respiration	

Nitrogen cycle

Key words

decomposer
nitrogen cycle

Nitrogen cycle

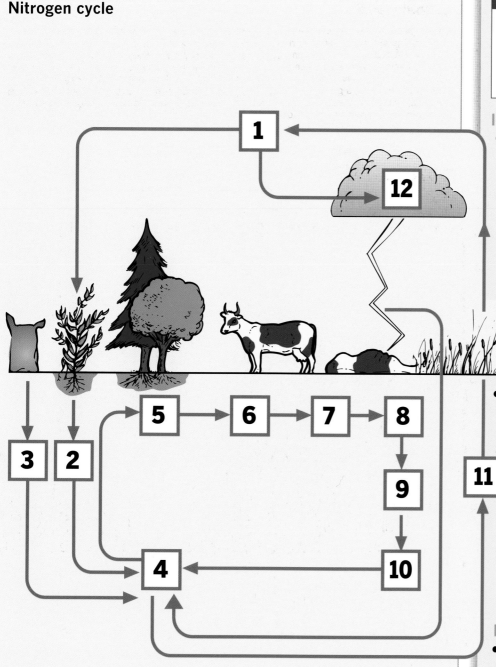

1 Atmospheric pool of nitrogen
2 Nitrogen-fixing bacteria in root nodules of legumes
3 Fertilizers
4 Soil nitrate
5 Nitrate taken up by plant roots
6 Plant and animal proteins
7 Dead organisms
8 Decomposers
9 Nitrite bacteria
10 Nitrate bacteria
11 Denitrifying bacteria
12 Lightning

Importance of nitrogen

- All living things need nitrogen to build protein. However, most organisms cannot use nitrogen gas and nitrates (the dominant form of the element in the soil) are poisonous to animals.
- Four processes cycle nitrogen through the biosphere: nitrogen fixation, decay, nitrification, and denitrification.

Nitrogen fixation

- Plants must secure their nitrogen in "fixed" form, as soluble nitrates. Nitrogen can be fixed in three ways.
- Lightening helps oxygen and nitrogen to react to form nitrogen oxides, which dissolve in rainwater to become nitrates in the soil (1, 12)
- Nitrogen fixing bacteria in the root nodules of legumes and in the soil can convert nitrogen into usable compounds (2, 4).
- Fertilizers can contribute useable nitrogen compounds to the soil (3).
- Plants take in soluable nitrates through their roots and use them to build proteins that can be taken in by animals (5, 6).

Decay

- Nitrogen leaves plants and animals when they rot, and *decomposers* break down dead organic matter (7, 8).

Nitrification

- Nitrifying bacteria convert the ammonia produced by decay into nitrates (9, 10) used by plants.

Denitrification

- Bacteria that use nitrates as an alternative to oxygen in respiration reduce nitrates to nitrogen gas, thus replenishing the atmosphere (11).

Key words

respiration	water cycle
transpiration	

One cycle—two components

- Earth's water is always moving in a cycle called the hydrologic or *water cycle*.
- The water cycle is of paramount importance to living things, but most of the cycle actually takes place outside living organisms.

Non-living cycle

- The cycle begins when water evaporates from the surface of the oceans (1).
- As the moist air rises, it cools and condenses into water vapor, which forms clouds (2).
- Water then falls to the Earth as precipitation (3). Once on the ground, some of this water is absorbed into the soil (4).
- Plants and animals take up this ground water and discharge it into the atmosphere during *transpiration* and *respiration* (5–7)
- Some of the precipitation does not penetrate Earth's surface. Instead, this runoff empties into lakes, rivers, and streams and is carried back to the oceans, where the cycle begins again.
- Some precipitation evaporates directly back into the atmosphere.

Living cycle

- This is globally insignificant but can be locally important. Trees and vegetation give out water by transpiration. This affects the areas adjacent to the vegetation, creating pockets of humidity that affect the growth of a range of organisms. Animals have minimal effect on the water cycle.

Water cycle

Water cycle

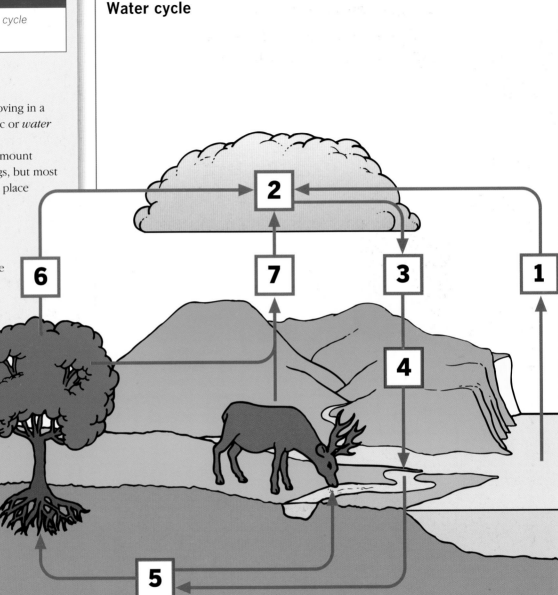

1	Evaporation	**5**	Water taken up by plants and animals
2	Water in clouds	**6**	Water loss by transpiration
3	Rain and snow	**7**	Water loss by respiration
4	Water drains into river and soil		

Energy flow

Key words

carnivore
feces
herbivore
photosynthesis
organic matter

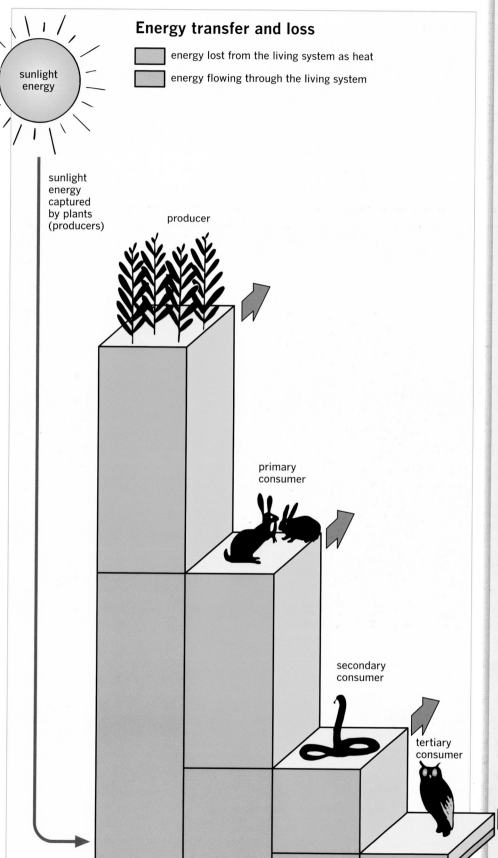

Energy transfer and loss

☐ energy lost from the living system as heat

☐ energy flowing through the living system

sunlight energy

sunlight energy captured by plants (producers)

producer

primary consumer

secondary consumer

tertiary consumer

Incoming

- All energy in living systems is ultimately derived from sunlight.
- Photosynthetic plants capture energy in sunlight and use it to make sugar. This sugar provides energy for all other processes in the organism and results in the creation of organic matter.

Transfer

- Animals cannot carry out *photosynthesis* and so get their energy from the *organic matter* stored by plants.
- *Herbivores* eat the plants directly. *Carnivores* eat herbivores or other carnivores that will—ultimately in this food chain—have eaten herbivores.

Energy loss

- Some energy is lost during transfer between organisms. Roughly 25 percent of the food input for an animal is wasted as *feces*. Another 25 percent is used to keep the animal alive, which leaves only about 50 percent that contributes to the production of new organic material.
- These losses are repeated at every transfer. This explains why food chains can only be about four links long—if they were any longer, too much energy would be lost in each transfer to make the chain sustainable.
- The energy is given out as heat and is radiated from Earth into space.

Key words

photosynthesis
trophic level

Energy input

- All energy in living systems is ultimately derived from sunlight.
- Energy absorbed by green plants in *photosynthesis* is used to build new cells. These cells increase the size of the plants. The mass of material is called the biomass, and it is the biomass that provides the energy input for the next *trophic level*.

Trophic levels

- Photosynthetic plants are called Trophic level 1. The animals that eat them exist at Trophic level 2, and so on.
- The biomass of all organisms at each trophic level is significantly lower than the biomass of the organisms in the level below. When plotted on a graph, this shows itself as a pyramid— a pyramid of biomass.

Pyramid of biomass

Biomass

- The mass of organisms (biomass) that can exist at any given stage in a food chain is much smaller than that in the preceding stage.
- This can be shown as a pyramid of biomass, in which different levels of the pyramid represent the biomass in successive stages of the food chain.
- The base of the pyramid is the biomass of primary producers, and the peak depicts the biomass of the top consumer.
- The base represents the algae and the peak is the amount of human biomass contributed by fish (i.e., bass) harvested and fed to humans.
- In this case, 10,000 kg of algae are required to produce 1 kg of human biomass, a huge difference that reflects the large energy losses at each stage of the food chain.

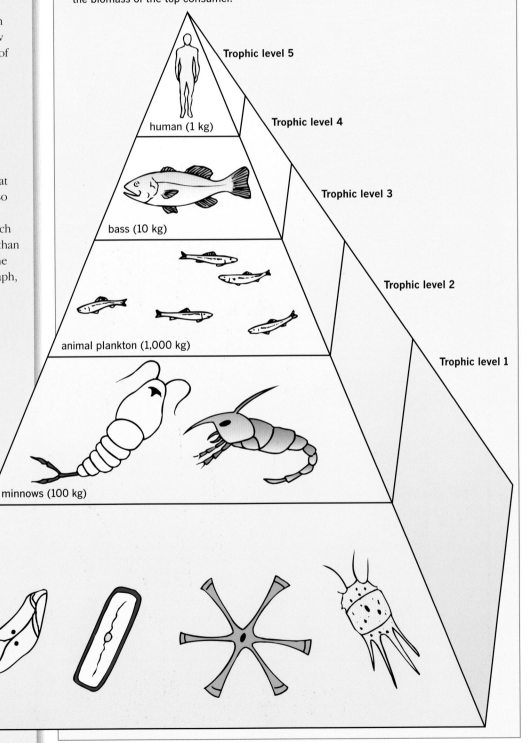

Trophic level 5

human (1 kg)

Trophic level 4

bass (10 kg)

Trophic level 3

animal plankton (1,000 kg)

Trophic level 2

minnows (100 kg)

Trophic level 1

algae (10,000 kg)

Food web

Key words

consumer
decomposer
food chain
food web
producer

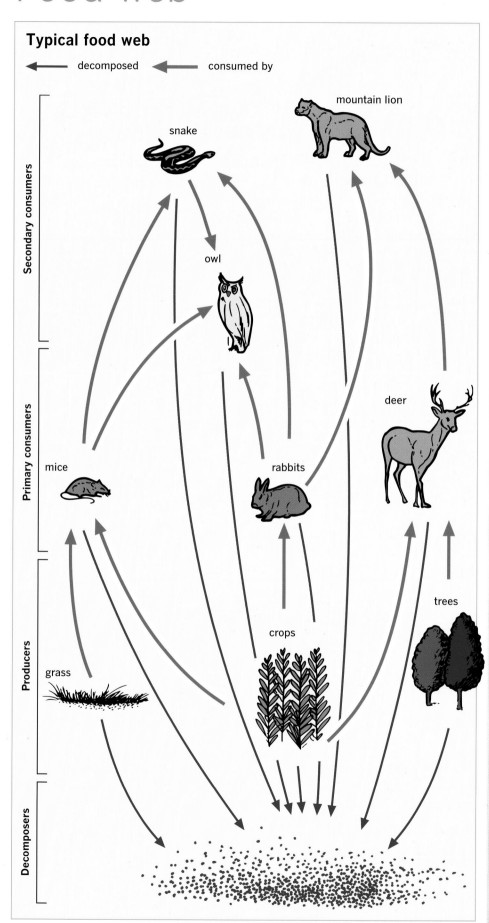

Typical food web

← decomposed ← consumed by

secondary consumers
Primary consumers
Producers
Decomposers

mountain lion
snake
owl
deer
mice
rabbits
trees
crops
grass

Feeding relationships

- The relationship between an animal and its prey can be shown with an arrow. The arrow always points to the consumer.

Food chains

- Starting with a single plant, it is possible to plot a chain of relationships showing an animal eating the plant, the *producer*, and then the same animal, the primary *consumer*, being eaten by another animal, the secondary consumer, and so on.
- *Food chains* typically have about four or five links.

Food webs

- The feeding relationships in an area are typically much more complex than a simple food chain.
- A *food web* shows the ways that the food chains in an area interact. Many organisms will exist in more than one chain.

Decomposers

- *Decomposers* are not usually shown in food webs, but all living organisms eventually die and are broken down by decomposer organisms.
- Since all organisms in the web would be connected to this decomposer level, it would make a very complex diagram that would be difficult to interpret. For this reason, these links are often omitted from more complex food webs.

Key words

abdomen (1) The area below the rib cage and above the legs. (2) In arthropods, the hind region of the body.

absorption The taking of dissolved substances into cells.

active process A process that requires an energy input from the organism.

active site The part of the enzyme to which the substrate binds. It is where catalysis occurs.

active transport The use of energy to transport substances across cell membranes against a concentration gradient.

adenosine triphosphate (ATP) A chemical in cells that produces the energy that drives biological processes. ATP becomes adenosine diphosphate (ADP) when it releases its energy.

adrenaline A hormone the body releases in situations of stress.

aerobic respiration Respiration requiring oxygen.

allele Variants of the same gene.

alveolus The sac-like end of an airway in the lungs.

amino acid An organic compound that forms the basic structural unit of proteins and peptides.

amnion The fluid-filled sac that encloses the embryo.

anaphase The stage of mitosis or meiosis in which the chromatids move to opposite poles of the cell.

anaphase II The second anaphase stage in meiosis.

antagonistic pair A pair of muscles that pull in opposite directions.

anther In flowers, the part of the stamen that produces pollen.

antibody A chemical produced by B lymphocytes that attacks invading microorganisms.

anticodon Set of three tRNA nucleotides that binds with its complementary codon in an mRNA molecule.

antigen A chemical found in cell membranes and cell walls that triggers the production of antibodies.

aorta The artery that carries high-pressure blood away from the left ventricle of the heart.

artery A blood vessel carrying blood away from the heart under high pressure.

asexual reproduction Reproduction in which offspring arise from a single parent. It does not involve the union of gametes. The offspring are identical to the parent.

assimilation The use of absorbed materials to produce new cells in an organism.

association neuron A neuron in the brain or spinal column that forms the connecting link between sensory and motor neurons.

ATP See adenosine triphosphate

auditory ossicle A bone in the middle ear that transmits acoustic vibrations from the eardrum to the inner ear.

autonomic nervous system The collection of nerves that regulate the unconscious or automatic processes in the body.

auxin Hormones that regulate plant growth.

axial skeleton The skull, spine, rib cage, and pelvis.

axon A long extension from the body of a nerve cell along which impulses are conducted away from the cell.

bacteriophage A virus that attacks bacteria.

bacterium A microscopic single-celled organism that has no nucleus.

basal metabolic rate The energy expended by the body at rest to maintain vital functions.

bilateral symmetry The property of being symmetrical on a vertical plane.

bile Secretions made in the liver from the breakdown of red blood corpuscles.

biome A major ecological region with characteristic climate and organisms.

bond The chemical connection between atoms in a molecule.

Bowman's capsule A cup-shaped structure in the kidney where blood is first filtered.

bronchiole One of two tubes in the lungs connecting the bronchi to the alveoli.

buccal cavity The cavity at the anterior end of the alimentary canal.

calcification The deposition calcium in cartilage.

cambium A layer of actively dividing cells between the phloem and xylem in flowering plants.

canine tooth A long, pointed tooth used to tear food.

capillary The smallest blood vessel in the body.

carbon cycle The cycling of carbon through the living world by photosynthesis and respiration.

carnivore A flesh eating animal.

carpel The female reproductive organ of flowering plants, consisting of the stigma, style, and ovary.

cartilaginous joint A joint in which bones are attached by cartilage, e.g., the joint between the two halves of the pelvis. The joint allows only slight movement.

cell The basic structural and functional unit of an organism.

cellulose A polysaccharide molecule used to strengthen cell walls in plants.

central nervous system The brain and spinal cord.

centriole The organelle in animal cells that controls the formation of the spindle during mitosis.

centromere The center of a chromosome, where the chromatids are attached. It has no genes.

cerebellum A part of the brain at the back of the head that coordinates voluntary movement and balance.

cerebral hemisphere One of two parts of the brain at the top of the skull. The cerebral hemispheres are the seat of conscious thought and voluntary movements.

cervix The entrance to the uterus.

chiasma The point at which nonsister chromatids of homologous chromosomes cross-over each other.

chlorophyll A green pigment found in most plants that absorbs light energy during photosynthesis.

chloroplast In green plants, an organelle in which photosynthesis takes place.

chromatid One of the two chromosome strands that become visible during cell division. The strands are joined at the centromere.

chromosome A threadlike structure in cells that contains genetic material.

chyme The partially digested contents of the stomach before it passes into the duodenum.

cilium A tiny hair found on the surface of cells and some microorganisms.

cloaca An opening through which the intestinal, urinary, and reproductive tracts empty in birds, reptiles, amphibians, and many fish.

clone A genetically identical organism.

cochlea The organ in the inner ear that converts sound into nerve impulses.

codon The triplet of bases held on the DNA that codes for a particular amino acid.

coenzyme Chemicals that are required by enzymes to complete a reaction.

collagen The structural protein in connective tissue.

colonial polyp A coelenterate that is attached to a substrate and lives in giant colonies.

concentration gradient A difference in the concentration of a substance from one area to another.

condensation reaction A reaction that binds two chemicals together and releases water.

consumer An organism that consumes organic matter.

continental drift The movement of large plates of the Earth's crust.

continuous variation Variation that shows a complete spectrum of values, e.g., height or weight.

contractile vacuole An organelle in many single-celled organisms that expands and contracts to expel water from the cell.

cotyledon The leaf-like part of the plant embryo that is the food reservoir.

crista A fold of membrane projecting into the matrix of mitochondrion.

cyst A reproductive structure often strengthened by external walls to survive periods in inhospitable or dangerous conditions.

cytoplasm The material that maintains a cell's shape and consistency. It stores chemical substances needed for life and is the site of important metabolic reactions.

decomposer An organism that breaks down dead organic material.

dehiscence The process of splitting open to release reproductive structures.

dendrite The branched filament of a nerve cell that receives impulses from other nerve cells and passes them on to the cell body.

dentine The calcified tissue that makes up the bulk of a tooth.

deoxyribosenucleic acid (DNA) The molecule that holds the genetic code.

diaphragm A sheet of muscle lying over the liver and stomach and under the lungs.

diastole The phase of the heartbeat when the heart muscle relaxes and the heart fills with blood.

dicotyledons Plants with two seed leaves (cotyledons) in the embryo.

diffusion The spreading of gases or liquids caused by random movement of their molecules.

digestion The mechanical and chemical breakdown of foods into nutrients an animal can absorb.

diploid The number of chromosomes of a normal cell.

discontinuous variation Variation that does not have a spectrum of types, e.g., being able to roll your tongue or not.

DNA See deoxyribosenucleic acid.

dominant In genetics, the allele that masks another allele.

double circulation A circulatory system where the blood passes through the heart twice—once for the body and once for the lungs.

Down syndrome A genetic condition in which an extra chromosome causes a number of significant mental and physical problems. It is caused by an extra copy of all or part of chromosome 21.

eardrum The thin membrane at the junction of the middle and outer ear.

ectoplasm The gel-like outer cytoplasm of the cell found close to the plasma membrane.

egg The female gamete.

electron transfer chain A series of enzymes that can transfer energy from excited electrons into ATP.

embryo The early stages that develop from the fertilized egg.

embryo sac The structure in the ovule of a flowering plant containing the female nuclei that will fuse with nuclei from the pollen grain to form the zygote.

endocrine gland A gland that secretes hormones directly into the blood.

endocytosis The engulfing of materials by a cell.

endodermis In plants, the innermost layer of cells that separates the cortex of the root from the pericycle.

endoplasmic reticulum The network of plasma membranes running throughout the cytoplasm. It is involved in the synthesis, storage, and transport of cell products.

endosperm The food storage tissue found in the seeds of flowering plants.

enzyme A protein found in living organisms that speeds up the rate of a chemical reaction.

enzyme-coenzyme complex The giant molecule formed by an enzyme and coenzyme.

epidermis The outer, protective layer of cells in animals and plants.

epididymis The part of the testis that stores sperm.

epithelium A sheet of tissue that covers the internal surfaces of the body.

eustachian tube A tube connecting the middle ear and the back of the throat to equalize pressure on both sides of the eardrum.

KEY WORDS

exocytosis The release of intracellular materials to the outside of the cell via vacuoles or vesicles.

exoskeleton The hard skeleton on the outside of the body.

factor VIII A blood protein required for clotting that is missing in people suffering from hemophilia.

fallopian tube The tube leading from the ovaries to the uterus.

fatty acid An acid with long hydrocarbon chain (roughly 30–40 carbon atoms) that is the major component of natural fats and oils.

feces The waste and indigestible food that passes out of the gut through the anus.

fertilization The fusion of gametes from two sexes to produce the zygote.

fetus The developing young in the uterus before birth.

fission Splitting of a cell or organism into two or more daughters.

food chain A simple diagram showing feeding relationships between some plants and animals.

food web A diagram showing how all of the food chains in an area link together.

fossil record The evidence from studies of the fossils for a particular line of evolution.

fruit A structure developed from the swollen wall of the ovary that helps the dispersal and survival of seeds.

gamete A mature male or female reproductive cell. It contains half the number of chromosomes of normal body cells. At fertilization, male and female gametes fuse to form a zygote.

gametophyte In plants, the generation that produces gametes.

gaseous exchange The movement of gases—usually carbon dioxide and oxygen—across an exchange membrane.

gastrodermis The inner body layer in Cnidaria.

gene A length of DNA that determines inherited characteristics.

generative nucleus The nucleus in the pollen grain that eventually fuses with the egg nucleus in the ovule.

genotype The genetic composition of an organism.

germ cell A cell involved in sexual reproduction. Also called a gamete.

germination In plants, the first stages of growth of a seed or spore.

gill The respiratory organ of most aquatic animals that breathe water to obtain oxygen.

glomerulus A mass of capillaries at the entry of a kidney tubule. Blood plasma is filtered out of the blood in the glomerulus into the tubule.

glucose The most widely distributed six-carbon sugar in animals and plants. It is the energy source in respiration.

glycerol A small alcohol with three OH groups. It combines with fatty acids to form fats and oils.

glycogen A polysaccharide used in animals to store energy.

glycolysis The breakdown of six-carbon sugars to three-carbon sugars in the cytoplasm.

glycosidic bond A bond formed between monosaccharides by a condensation reaction.

Golgi body An organelle involved in assembling and storing metabolic substances.

granum A chlorophyll-rich membrane structure present in chloroplasts.

guard cell A cell that changes shape to open or close a stoma in a leaf.

gut The long tube that starts at the mouth and leads to the anus. It includes the large and small intestine and is sometimes called the digestive tract.

haploid Having half the number of chromosomes normally found in the cells of an organism.

hemoglobin A protein found in red blood cells in mammals. It reacts reversibly with oxygen.

hepatic portal vein The vein carrying blood from the gut to the liver.

herbivore An animal that only eats plants.

hermaphrodite An organism with both male and female sexual organs.

heterozygous An organism having two different alleles for an inherited trait.

homologous chromosome Chromosomes that pair up during meiosis. They have the same genes but may have different alleles so are not identical.

homozygous An organism having two identical alleles for an inherited trait.

host The organism that supports the parasite.

hypothalamus A small organ at the base of the brain that coordinates visceral functions.

impermeable Material that it is not easily penetrated.

incisor A chisel-shaped tooth at the front of the mouth used for cutting and biting.

inhibitor A chemical that slows down the speed of a chemical reaction.

insertion In genetics, the process by which a base is added to a sequence of DNA.

insulin The hormone secreted by the pancreas that controls the blood glucose level.

intercostal muscle A muscle between the ribs.

interphase The period between cell divisions.

intestine The region of the alimentary canal between the stomach and anus or cloaca where nutrients are digested and absorbed and feces produced.

invertebrate An animal without a backbone.

karyotype The number and types of chromosomes characteristic of a species.

keratin A structural protein found in hair and nails.

kidney The organ responsible for filtering and excreting liquid wastes and maintaining the composition of the blood.

Krebs cycle Sometimes called the tricarboxylic acid cycle, it occurs in the matrix of mitochondria and involves the break down of three-carbon sugars into carbon dioxide and hydrogen ions.

larva An immature form of an animal that has a different structure and way of life from the adult.

lateral line A pressure-sensitive sense organ running along the sides of a fish or larval amphibian.

lenticel A small raised pore in the epidermis of the stem or bark of a plant with gaps between cells that permit gaseous exchange.

life cycle The successive stages organisms go through from birth to death.

light-dependent reaction The first stage in photosynthesis that converts light energy into chemical energy.

light-independent reaction The reduction of carbon dioxide to glucose in photosynthesis using energy captured during the light-dependent reaction.

lignin A complex polymer in the cell wall of plants that gives them strength and rigidity.

lipid An organic molecule, insoluble in water, that is formed by the reaction of a fatty acid with glycerol. It is the chief component of fats, oils, and phospholipids in the body.

liver The large gland opening into the gut that has multiple functions and plays an important role in metabolism.

lung The respiratory organ of air-breathing vertebrates across which carbon dioxide and oxygen diffuse.

lymph vessel A vessel that transports lymph fluid.

lymphatic system The complete system of lymph vessels and nodes that conduct lymph from tissues to the circulatory system.

lysosome A membrane-bound organelle containing a mixture of powerful enzymes that are capable of breaking down many substances.

Malpighian layer The layer of cells at the base of the epidermis. The epidermal cells all originate from cell division in the Malpighian layer.

mammary gland A milk producing gland in female mammals.

matrix (1) The material in which another substance is embedded. (2) The central space of the mitochondrion.

maxilliped One of a pair of appendages in crustaceans and centipedes that manipulate food prior to ingestion.

medulla oblongata The part of the brain near the junction with the spinal cord that controls involuntary body functions such as breathing.

meiosis A specialized form of cell division that produces cells carrying half the usual number of chromosomes. These cells, called gametes, are used in sexual reproduction.

mesoglea The layer between the outer and inner layer in cnidarian bodies.

mesosome The infolding of the plasma membrane into the main body of the cell in some bacteria.

messenger RNA (mRNA) The RNA molecule that transfers the genetic code for a protein from the DNA in the nucleus to a ribosome in the cytoplasm, where it serves as the template for the synthesis of that protein.

metabolism The range of living processes within an organism that provides for its needs.

metamorphosis A large change in the shape of the body during growth.

metaphase A stage in mitosis when the nuclear membrane breaks down and the spindle begins to form.

metaphase II The second metaphase in meiosis.

micropyle In plants, the pore in the ovule through which the pollen tube enters before fertilization.

mitochondrion A membrane organelle, sometimes called the powerhouse of the cell, that produces the cell's energy in the form of ATP.

mitosis The process of cell division that gives rise to cells genetically identical to the parent cells.

molar A large tooth at the back of the mouth used to crush food.

molecule The smallest naturally occurring unit of an element.

molting The loss of the outer body surface (feathers, fur, skin, exoskeleton) and its replacement by a new one.

monocotyledon A plant with a single seed leaf (cotyledon).

monosaccharide A simple sugar with only one ring unit in its molecule, e.g., glucose. It cannot be further decomposed by hydrolysis.

motor neuron A neuron that carries impulses from the central nervous system to muscles or glands.

muscle Tissue the contraction of which causes movement.

mutation A variation caused by a change to an organism's genetic material.

mycelium The body of a fungus made up of many thousands of branching connected hyphae.

NAD See nicotinamide adenine dinucleotide

NADH See nicotinamide adenine dinucleotide phosphate.

NADP See nicotinamide adenine dinucleotide phosphate.

nematode Any of a group of mainly parasitic worms.

nephron The functional unit of the kidney. Nephrons are long microscopic tubules that produce urine from blood.

neuron A nerve cell.

neurotransmitter A chemical that carries information across the small gap at a synapse.

nicotinamide adenine dinucleotide A coenzyme that functions as a hydrogen carrier in a wide range of redox reactions.

nicotinamide adenine dinucleotide phosphate A coenzyme, functioning as a hydrogen carrier, important in the creation of ATP. NADH is the reduced form.

nitrogen cycle The cycling of nitrogen through living systems as proteins, nitrates, and nitrites, etc.

nucleic acid An organic substance found in cells that is involved in the storage of inherited information. It is the collective name for DNA and RNA.

KEY WORDS

nucleotide A molecule formed from a sugar, a phosphate group, and a nitrogenous base. It is the basic building block of DNA and RNA.

nucleus The control center of a cell. It contains the genetic material.

objective lens The lens near the specimen in a light microscope.

ocular lens The eyepiece lens in a light microscope.

olfactory neuron A nerve cell that detects chemicals in the nasal cavity and so provides the sense of smell.

oogonium A cell that divides by mitosis to produce primary oocytes.

operon The collection of structural genes that work together with associated repressor and operator genes to control the production of a particular characteristic.

optic cortex The part of the brain concerned with the interpretation of nerve impulses from the eyes.

optic nerve The nerve taking information from the eyes to the optic cortex in the brain.

organelle A specialized structure in the cell that carries out a particular function, e.g., the nucleus, mitochondria, or chloroplasts.

organic matter Material produced by living organisms.

osculum In Porifera, a large pore that lets water out of the body.

osmoregulation Regulation of salt and water balance.

osmosis The passage of a solvent (usually water) through a semipermeable membrane. The movement is from a higher concentrated solution to a lower concentrated solution until the concentrations of both solutions reach equilibrium.

otolith A particle of calcium carbonate in the inner ear that when displaced signals position and movement of the head.

ovary The female organ that produces the egg.

ovule The structure in plants in which the female gamete is fertilized. It will develop into a seed.

ovum The mature female gamete or egg cell prior to fertilization.

papilla A small lump or knob arising from a surface, such as that on the surface of the tongue.

parasite An organism that gets its food from a host but does not kill the host in the process.

parasympathetic nervous system Part of the autonomic nervous system that regulates the routine functions of the body such as digestion, elimination, and heartbeat.

passive transport Movement of chemicals down a concentration gradient. Passive transport does not require an energy input from an organism.

pathogen A microorganism that causes disease.

pedipalp A pair of specialized legs at the front of a spider used to manipulate food and clean the body.

pentadactyl limb A limb based on a pattern of one bone leading to two bones and on to hands or feet ending in five digits.

peptide Two or more amino acids linked by a peptide bond.

peptide bond A link between two peptides in a protein molecule. It is formed between the carboxyl group of one amino acid and the amino group of another.

peripheral nervous system The nerves outside the brain and spinal cord.

permeability The ability of a compound to diffuse across a membrane.

phagocytosis The engulfing and ingestion of materials by a cell.

phenotype The external features of an organism. The phenotype depends on the genotype of the organism and the action of the environment.

phloem In plants, specialized transporting cells that form tubules to carry sugars and organic materials from the leaves to all other parts of the organism.

photosynthesis In green plants, the production of sugar and oxygen from carbon dioxide and water using light as an external energy source.

pistil (1) Another name for carpel, the female reproductive organ of flowering plants consisting of the stigma, style, and ovary. (2) The part of the flower made up of one or more carpels.

pituitary gland A small pea-sized gland hanging from the base of the brain that produces a range of hormones to control other endocrine glands.

placenta The vascular organ that allows materials to be exchanged between a mother and a fetus in the uterus.

plasma The clear, fluid portion of the blood in which platelets and blood cells are suspended.

plasma membrane The membrane surrounding all living cells that is composed of lipid and protein molecules.

plasmid A circular molecule of DNA found in some bacteria.

platelet A small, sub-cellular component in the blood concerned with clotting.

pollen In flowering plants, the microspores containing the male gamete.

polypeptide A molecule formed by a long string of amino acids joined by peptide bonds. Proteins are composed of polypeptides.

polypeptide chain A chain of amino acids joined by peptide bonds.

polyribosomes A series of ribosomes arranged along a piece of endoplasmic reticulum to form a chain of ribosomes.

polysaccharide An insoluble, long-chained carbohydrate usually used for storage or cell structure, e.g., cellulose, starch, and glycogen.

predator An animal that hunts and kills other animals.

premolar A crushing tooth located in front of the molars and behind each cuspid.

primary oocyte A cell formed while the female was an embryo that divides by meiosis to produce ova.

producer An organism that makes organic material.

prophase The first stage of cell division in which the chromosomes become visible in the nucleus.

protein An organic molecule composed of one or more chains of amino acids. Proteins have fundamental structural and metabolic roles in cells and tissues.

pseudopodium An extension of the cell in an ameba.

pupa In insects, a phase between larva and adult in which the organism undergoes major tissue reorganization.

pyrenoid Small structures in the chloroplast concerned with the formation of starch.

radial symmetry A body that can be divided along the same axis through several planes to form two halves that are near mirror images of each other.

recessive In genetics, the feature that does not appear when a gene contains two different alleles.

red blood corpuscle A disc-shaped cell without a nucleus, filled with hemoglobin, and found only in the blood.

respiration The chemical process by which organisms make energy from food.

restriction enzyme An enzyme that recognizes specific, short nucleotide sequences and can cut DNA molecules into shorter portions.

ribosome An organelle involved in the manufacture of protein.

root hair In plants, an extension of a cell in the root epidermis. Root hairs massively increase the surface area of the root available for the uptake of water and mineral salts.

rough endoplasmic reticulum A complex network of sacs and tubes in cells. It contains ribosomes involved in the synthesis of proteins.

secondary thickening Extra strengthening in stems laid down as they age to allow taller stems.

secondary oocyte On oocyte after first meiotic division. It eventually matures into an ovum and a polar body.

seed In plants, the structure formed from a fertilized ovule. The seed is the dormant phase of the plant life cycle and is used to spread new plants.

segment One of several or many similar body compartments. Insects show segmented bodies.

selective reabsorption Reabsorption of particular substances, and not others, by cells lining the nephrons in the kidney.

semen The fluid, manufactured in the male urinogenital system, that contains sperm.

semicircular canal One of the three fluid-filled canals in the inner ear that are concerned with the sense of balance and movement detection.

seminiferous tubule A tube in the testis that produces spermatozoa.

semipermeable membrane A membrane that allows the passage of small but not large molecules.

sensory neuron A neuron that carries impulses from sense organs to the central nervous system.

sexual reproduction Reproduction that involves two sexes producing gametes that join together to produce the next generation.

sinoatrial node An area of the left atrium of the heart that is the source of the signal that controls contraction of muscles in the walls of the heart.

smooth endoplasmic reticulum A complex network of sacs and tubes in cells involved in lipid synthesis.

smooth muscle Muscle, such as that found in the blood vessels or intestine, that performs automatic tasks via contraction.

solute A substance that is dissolved in another substance.

species A taxonomic group whose members can interbreed.

specimen (1) An individual used as a representative to study the properties of a whole. (2) The sample studied under a microscope.

spermatids A cell produced by meiosis that matures into a spermatozoon.

spermatogonium A cell that divides repeatedly to produce a line of spermatids and hence spermatozoa.

spermatozoon The male gamete in many higher animals, including humans.

spinal cord The collection of nerve tissue in the spinal canal. It is part of the central nervous system.

spiracle In insects and some arachnids, the external opening of the tracheal system.

spleen An organ in the abdominal cavity concerned with destruction of old red blood corpuscles.

spore In primitive plants, a reproductive cell, formed without the union of sexual cells, that gives rise to a new organism.

sporophyte The generation that produces spores without sexual reproduction.

stamen In flowering plants, the male reproductive organ that produces pollen. It is composed of an anther and a filament.

starch A large carbohydrate molecule made up of small sugar molecules joined together in a chain.

stigma In flowering plants, the sticky part of the carpel that receives pollen.

stimulus That which produces a response in an organism.

stoma In plants, an opening in the epidermis of a leaf that allows for the exchange of gases.

stroma The chlorophyll-free matrix between the grana in chlorplasts. It is involved in the light independent reaction.

style The narrow elongated part of the carpel between the ovary and the stigma.

suberin A waxy substance used to waterproof certain cell walls in the endodermis.

substitution In genetics, a mutation in which a single base is changed for another one.

substrate (1) The surface on which a plant or animal grows or is attached. (2) The chemical an enzyme works on to produce the product.

sugar A soluble carbohydrate composed of one or a few monosaccharide units.

sympathetic nervous system Part of the autonomic nervous system that prepares the body for dealing with demanding or dangerous situations.

synapse The place where two nerve cells meet. The cells do not touch, but the gap between them is very small.

synovial joint A joint between two bones that allows considerable movement.

systole The phase of the heartbeat when the muscle is contracting.

telophase The final phase of cell division in which the two daughter cells separate.

telophase II The second telophase in meiosis during which the visible chromosomes disappear and the nuclear membrane reappears.

tentacle In invertebrates, a long slender extension of the body, often containing sense organs, used for feeding, grasping, and swimming.

testis The male sex organ that produces sperm.

thalamus The portion of the brain that transmits sensory information to the cerebrum.

thorax (1) The chest region between the head and the abdomen. (2) In insects, the segment of the body that bears the legs.

thylakoid A flattened photosynthetic membrane present in chloroplasts.

tracheole A thin tube carrying air throughout the body of an insect.

transcription The manufacture of an RNA molecule from information contained in DNA.

transformation The genetic alteration of a cell or organism by the incorporation of exogeneous DNA.

transfer RNA (tRNA) A type of RNA with an amino acid at one end of a molecule and three exposed bases at the other.

translation The manufacture of a protein based on information contained in an RNA molecule.

translocation A mutation in which a part of one chromosome is transferred to, or exchanged for, another part of a different chromosome.

transpiration Evaporation of water from a plant.

trophic level The level at which an organism gets its food. Primary producers are level one, primary consumers are level two, etc.

tropism A directional growth in a plant in response to an outside stimulus.

tuber A swollen underground stem or root used for storage.

ultrafiltration Filtration of the blood in the Bowman's capsule of the nephrons.

umbilical cord The cord that connects the fetus to the placenta.

urea A white soluble crystalline substance made in the liver from waste amino acids and passed out of the body in solution as urine.

ureter The tube leading from the kidney to the bladder.

uterus The organ in female mammals in which the fetus develops during pregnancy.

vacuole A membrane-bound sac in a cell usually containing nutrients and water.

vascular bundle A strand of vascular tissue composed of xylem and phloem that conducts fluids in higher plants.

vas deferens The tube that carries sperm from the testes.

vein (1) In animals, a blood vessel carrying low-pressure blood toward the heart. (2) In plants, the vascular bundle and supporting tissue in a leaf.

ventricle The chamber of the heart that receives blood from the atrium and pumps it into the arteries.

vertebrate An animal that has a bony or cartilaginous backbone, skeleton, and skull containing a brain.

villus A small projection on the inner surface of the gut that increases the surface area and so speeds up absorption.

virus An infectious agent composed of nucleic acid wrapped in protein that replicates only within a living host cell. Some viruses cause very serious diseases.

vitreous humor The clear, jelly-like material between the lens and the retina of the eye.

water cycle The continuous process of recycling water between Earth and the atmosphere.

white blood cell A blood cell, made in lymph nodes and the bone marrow, that fights infection.

xylem The tissue that carries water and dissolved mineral salts in plants.

zygote The cell produced by the fusion of gametes. The fertilized ovum before cell division.

Internet resources

There is a lot of useful information on the internet. Information on a particular topic may be available through a search engine such as Google (http://www.google.com). Some of the sites that are found in this way may be very useful, others not. Below is a selection of Web sites related to the material covered by this book.

The publisher takes no responsibility for the information contained within these Web sites. All the sites were accessible in March 2006.

Access Excellence
A resource for teachers and students of health and bioscience provided by the National Health Museum.
http://www.accessexcellence.org

American Association for the Advancement of Science
Information on scientific developments and education programs for all ages.
http://www.aaas.org

Anatomy of the Human Body
Online version of Gray's Anatomy—over 13,000 entries and 1,200 images.
http://www.bartleby.com/107

Animal Diversity Web
Database of natural history, distribution, classification, and conservation biology.
http://animaldiversity.ummz.umich.edu

Animal Physiology
Clear, concise presentation of animal classification and physiology.
http://www.teachnet.ie/farmnet/Animal_physiology.htm

Arkive
Film, photographs, and audio of endangered species.
http://www.arkive.org

Ask a Biologist
An educational resource for students K–12, their teachers and parents.
http://askabiologist.asu.edu

BBC Nature-Wildfacts
Facts about and images of thousands of species.
http://www.bbc.co.uk

The Biology Project
Resources in biochemistry, cell biology, human biology, genetics, and molecular biology.
http://www.biology.arizona.edu

BioNews
The latest news and discoveries from the worldwide biology community.
http://www.bionews.in/biologynews.htm

Biotech Life Science Dictionary
Over 8,000 terms dealing with biochemistry, biotechnology, botany, cell biology, and genetics.
http://biotech.icmb.utexas.edu

Brains Rule!
Information, interactive games, and lesson plans on the human brain; includes "Ask the Brain Expert" and "Meet a Neuroscientist" features.
http://www.brainsrule.com

Cells Alive
Animations, movie clips, and interactive diagrams of cells and cell processes.
http://www.cellsalive.com

Curriculum Center: Discoveryschool.com
Classroom activities supporting core curriculum topics.
http://school.discovery.com/curriculumcenter

DNA-Interactive
A comprehensive overview of the science of DNA.
http://www.dnai.org

Dr. Saul's Biology in Motion
Interactive biology learning featuring animations of basic biological processes.
http://biologyinmotion.com

The Electronic Naturalist
Features catagorized units with illustrations, experiments, and other activities aimed at the young naturalist.
http://www.enaturalist.org

EverythingBio
The "all encompassing biology resource." Includes a vast links section.
http://www.everythingbio.com

INTERNET RESOURCES

Exploratorium
Experiments, exhibits, and sound and video files exploring hundreds of different topics.
http://www.exploratorium.edu

The Franklin Institute Online: BioPoint Hotlist
Links to hundreds of excellent sites on a wide variety of biology topics.
http://sln.fi.edu/qa97/biology/biolist.html

Froguts.com
Virtual frog dissection using photos of frogs recycled from schools.
http://www.froguts.com

The Geee! In Genome
An overview of the science of genetics from the Canadian Museum of Nature.
http://nature.ca

Genetic Science Learning Center
Activities and information on topics in genetics, genetic disorders, and genetics in society.
http://gslc.genetics.utah.edu

HHMI's Biointeractive
Virtual labs, activities, and interactive demonstrations on many subjects related to the human body and health.
http://www.biointeractive.org

Human Anatomy On Line
Over 100 descriptions, animations, and anatomy images detailing body systems and organs.
http://www.innerbody.com

Kimball's Biology Pages
Online biology encyclopedia.
http://users.rcn.com/jkimball.ma.ultranet/BiologyPages

MicrobeWorld
Provides information about all aspects of microbiology and includes a dedicated section for kids and educators.
http://www.microbeworld.org

NASA Astrobiology Institute
The study of the origin, evolution, distribution, and future of life in the universe.
http://nai.arc.nasa.gov

National Biological Information Infrastructure: Botany
A large resource of links to all areas of botany including extensive kids' and teachers' sections.
http://www.nbii.gov

National Wildlife Federation
Web site of the organization dedicated to the preservation of America's wildlife since 1936.
http://www.nwf.org

Red Gold: The Epic Story of Blood
Describes blood production and function; discusses facts and myths about blood and its impact on everything from religion to commerce and popular culture.
http://www.pbs.org/wnet/redgold/about/index.html

The Tree of Life
Presents an overview of the "evolutionary tree that unites all organisms on Earth."
http://tolweb.org

The Virtual Cell Web Page
Interactive, animated exploration of the cell with virtual textbook.
http://www.ibiblio.org/virtualcell

The Virtual Library of Biochemistry and Cell Biology
Advanced papers and articles on all aspects of biochemistry and cell biology.
http://www.biochemweb.org

World Biodiversity Database
Taxonomic database and information system documenting and disseminating information on all known species.
http://www.eti.uva.nl/tools/wbd-php

Index

Index of subject headings.